The Crime of Crimes

Demonology and Politics in France
1560-1620

The Crime of Crimes

Demonology and Politics in France
1560-1620

Jonathan L. Pearl

Wilfrid Laurier University Press

This book has been published with the help of a grant from the Humanities and Social Sciences Federation of Canada, using funds provided by the Social Sciences and Humanities Research Council of Canada.

We acknowledge the financial support of the Government of Canada through the Book Publishing Industry Development Program for our publishing activities.

Canadian Cataloguing in Publication Data

Pearl, Jonathan L.
  The crime of crimes : demonology and politics in France, 1560-1620

Includes bibliographical references and index.
ISBN 0-88920-296-6

1. Demonology – France – History – 16th century.
2. Demonology – France – History – 17th century.
3. Demonology – France – History – 16th century – Sources.
4. Demonology – France – History – 17th century – Sources.
5. France – Politics and government – 16th century.
6. France – Politics and government – 17th century.
7. Witchcraft – France – History – 16th century.
I. Title.

BF1517.F5P42 1999   133.4'0944'09031   C98-930430-2

© 1999
WILFRID LAURIER UNIVERSITY PRESS
Waterloo, Ontario, Canada N2L 3C5

Cover design by Leslie Macredie.
Cover illustration: *Justicia* engraved by Phillip Gall, 1559,
after Peter Breugel the Elder, Bibliotheque Nationale, Paris.
Permission courtesy of Armand Colin Publishers, Paris.

Printed in Canada

All rights reserved. No part of this work covered by the copyrights hereon may be reproduced or used in any form or by any means— graphic, electronic, or mechanical—without the prior written permission of the publisher. Any request for photocopying, recording, taping, or reproducing in information storage and retrieval systems of any part of this book shall be directed in writing to the Canadian Reprography Collective, 214 King Street West, Suite 312, Toronto, Ontario M5H 3S6.

Contents

Chronology	vii
Introduction	1
One **Early Modern Demonologists and Modern Historians**	7
Two **Witchcraft, Politics and Law**	23
Three **Politics and Demonic Possession**	41
Four **The Jesuits, Maldonat and the Development of French Demonology**	59
Five **Politics, Morality and Demonology**	77
Six **Three Adversaries of Political Demonology**	101
Seven **Pierre de Lancre**	127
Conclusion	149
Notes	153
Bibliography	169
Index	179

Chronology

1559 Death of Henry II, accession of Francis II. Ascendancy of Guise at royal court.
1560 Growing unrest and violence. Death of Francis II, Catherine de Medici regent. Jesuits begin founding colleges in France.
1561 Colloquy of Poissy approves Jesuits' right to found a college in Paris.
1562 Toleration of Protestants. Massacre at Vassy, war breaks out.
1563 Guise killed. Peace returns. End of the Council of Trent.
1564 Classes begin at the College of Clermont, lawsuit against it before the *Parlement* of Paris.
1565 Maldonat becomes professor of theology at Clermont. Exorcism of Nicole Aubrey begins.
1566 Nicole freed of her demons—the "Miracle of Laon."
1567 War breaks out again.
1569 Coligny, head of Protestant forces, defeated in the Poitou. Maldonat and other missionaries go there.
1570 Peace of St. Germain restores many Protestant places. Maldonat returns to Paris, begins new lecture series, concentrating on connections between heresy and demons.

1572   Marriage of Marguerite de Valois and Henry of Navarre. Massacre of St. Bartholomew's Day. Civil war starts again.
1574   Charles IX dies, Henry III becomes king.
1576   First formation of the Catholic League.
1577   Peace of Bergerac stops fighting.
1580   War starts again. Navarre leads Protestant forces.
1584   Duke of Anjou, younger brother of Henry III dies. Catholic League revived to prevent Navarre from succeeding to the throne.
1588   Guise and the Sixteen control Paris after Henry III forced from the city. Later in the year, Henry III orders the assassination of Henry of Guise and his brother, the Cardinal of Guise.
1589   Widespread revolt of the League. Catherine de Medici dies. Henry III assassinated, Henry of Navarre now Henry IV.
1593   Henry IV converts to Catholicism. Opposition declines.
1594   Henry IV occupies Paris.
1598   Edict of Nantes establishes toleration of Huguenots in France.
1599   Registration of the Edict of Nantes. Exorcism of Marthe Brossier in Paris.
1609   Pierre de Lancre's inquiry in the Pays de Labourd.
1610   Death of Henry IV.
1611   Trial of Louis Gaufridi in Aix.

Introduction

One of the most intriguing—and disturbing—aspects of the history of European culture in the sixteenth and seventeenth centuries is that most people believed in witchcraft. It was widely held that, through the aid of the Devil, witches could seriously harm other people, livestock and crops. A complex of ideas came together to form an elaborate and full account of humans voluntarily renouncing God, Christianity and society in order to join forces with the Devil. All over Europe, witchcraft was regarded as a serious crime. The established court systems, both ecclesiastical and secular, tried thousands of people accused of crimes of witchcraft. The death penalty was universally considered to be the appropriate punishment.

While the views of the masses of ordinary people were shaped by their semi-pagan magical worldview, the elites' views on this subject evolved through a long process of intellectual development. Many dozens of books and hundreds of pamphlets on the subject of witchcraft were written and published in this era by learned theologians, physicians and legalists. These works of demonology developed and explained the role of the Devil in the world, his relationship to witches,

---

Notes to the Introduction are on p. 153.

the crimes perpetrated by witches and the measures that should be taken against them. These works were designed to create alarm about witchcraft, so that political and legal officials would take the problem seriously and act strongly to suppress witchcraft and to punish anyone involved with it. The demonologists cited many cases of contemporary witchcraft and referred to many trials and executions.

For a long time, these demonology books and pamphlets served as the primary record of the whole witchcraft episode in European history. Generations of historians, philosophers and critics, appalled at the bigotry, superstition, ignorance and violence contained in demonological texts, have condemned this genre of literature and have looked at the witchcraft crisis in Europe with horror and disdain. The belief in witchcraft, and the resultant accusations, trials and executions for this crime have served as a prime example of human folly caused by religious hatred and obscurantism. Witchcraft was probably the first area of "social" history to interest historians, who otherwise were concerned with the development of more "rational" aspects of society such as politics and political institutions.[1]

Witchcraft has attracted broad interest. Visual, literary and dramatic artists as well as filmmakers have explored the witchcraft phenomenon in various ways. Most laypersons know that witches were burned at the stake in this period. For academics, witchcraft has crossed over many disciplinary boundaries. Literary scholars, anthropologists, sociologists and religious specialists have all studied aspects of this complex problem.

While rejecting the content of demonological works, scholars who worked with this material often regarded the accounts of accusations, investigations, trials and punishments of witches as accurate historical reports. This led to a significant qualitative and quantitative misunderstanding of the witchcraft episode in early modern Europe. Because of the severity of most of these texts, many historians assumed that any person accused of witchcraft was helpless before a court, and virtually assured of being brutally tortured, forced to confess to horrific imaginary crimes and hustled off to be burnt alive at the stake. If this were the case, and the demonologists' "statistics" on the number of witches that existed and the numbers of executions that were carried out were at all accurate, then hundreds of thousands, or perhaps even millions of innocent people were destroyed in this legal juggernaut.

The historical picture of witchcraft in Europe has been refined in the last generation. Since the mid-1960s, many scholars have published books and articles that examine the complex and fascinating phenomenon of witchcraft in early modern Europe. The nature of popular religious culture and the possible function of witchcraft beliefs have been examined. Social and statistical studies have revealed much about the patterns of accusations of witchcraft and the number of trials that actually took place in specific areas. The scale of the "witch craze" has been, through this research, reduced considerably. In many jurisdictions, not very many people were tried or punished for witchcraft, and many of those accused of the crime were punished with lesser penalties than death or released with no punishment at all.

Furthermore, witchcraft and the whole area of the occult, including astrology, alchemy, hermetic magic and pagan folklore have been integrated into the complex world of social, political and intellectual change in this period. Views on the Renaissance and Reformation have had to change considerably, at least partly in response to findings in this area of study. Witchcraft has been portrayed as an important aspect of Reformation culture, and part of the confrontation between popular and elite culture that is held to be a central ingredient of the intellectual dynamic of the period.

But scholarly approaches to the demonologists have not changed very much at all. The study of demonology has not been in vogue, as scholars have prefered to examine aspects of popular society and religious culture. Demonology works are generally read unsympathetically by modern readers, when examined at all. An air of contemputous scorn is common when discussing their distasteful content. Furthermore, most scholars still confine themselves to a well-trod demonological road, starting with the *Malleus Maleficarum*, and jumping to Bodin's *De la démonomanie des sorciers*, James I's *Daemonologie*, de Lancre's *L'incredulité et mescreance du sortilege*, and so on.

Most historians have regarded the demonologists as spokesperson for widely held elite views. Another important aspect of most works in this field, both older and more recent, is that the historians of this phenomenon have regarded the demonologists who wrote the tracts on the subject of witchcraft and the judges who heard the cases as close partners in the persecution of witches. Most studies hardly distinguish between the two, seeing them as part of the same force.

Over a period of years, I have been examining the writings of the French demonologists in an attempt to discover who they were and what they were really writing about. My approach to this subject is quite different from that taken by others who work in this peculiar field. In this study, French demonology is examined as a genre of religio-political literature, the product of an identifiable group of writers who had a strong party attachment in a violent and troubled period. I have attempted to look at a large number of these writers rather than only the few who are best known among them. The confusion of demonology with the history of witchcraft trials and popular beliefs has obscured the content and influence of this literature. I have made every effort to keep the categories separate and to differentiate clearly between the writings of demonological authors and what courts actually did when accused witches came before them.

I have restricted myself to France, and make no attempt to generalize my findings to other parts of Europe. Indeed, I believe that the situation in France was significantly different from anywhere else, and that these books were about its complicated politico-religious situation. I have not regarded these writers as spokespersons for a worldview or as mere names on a title page, but have tried to determine who they were, and to discover the aspects of their careers that may have influenced their writing. This was possible for a substantial group of demonologists, many of whom were fairly well known. For others, the texts themselves often revealed important clues for determining the writers' political and religious sympathies. Through this approach, I have been able to describe a network of connections and allegiances that shaped French demonology for over sixty years.

I also make no attempt to offer a general theory to explain withcraft accusations, trials or beliefs. This study is a discussion of one aspect of a very complex issue.

There is no doubt that this literature is often distasteful and offensive to modern sensibilities. Long periods of concentrating on these texts can be more than a bit depressing. However, I have tried to read these texts in an unbiased way in order to understand what their authors actually wrote, and what they saw as their mission.

After surveying French demonological literature during two research trips to France, it became clear that politics were a very significant aspect of these works. Some of these writers were well known in their own day and their political connections are clear. Others identified themselves as advocates of a party platform. Most scholars who have worked in this field have not examined this issue at all, or have merely mentioned politics in passing in connection with demonology. Politics is

certainly not the only theme of this literatu[...]
to the connections, motivations and goals o[...]
Through politics we can see the demonologists as something other than members of the social, religious and intellectual elites reacting to irrational fears of a dangerous and uncertain world. It also provides a key to a more accurate understanding of the degree of power and authority of demonology in France in the late sixteenth and early seventeenth centuries.

In speaking of politics, I do not intend to exclude or minimize the religious issues involved. I subscribe to the views recently expressed by John Bossy, criticizing the tendency of many historians to reduce the bitter religious conflicts of this age to national political struggles or sociological changes. And certainly, one cannot read the tremendous work of Denis Crouzet without being convinced that, in order to understand the militancy and violence of the bitter struggles in late-sixteenth-century France, we must look at the "religious heart" of the conflict and not concentrate only on social, economic and political factors.[2] A pair of recent histories of this period make strong efforts in this direction. The works of Mack Holt and R.J. Knecht take the religious beliefs of the day very seriously,[3] as did the most zealous members of the various groups who were willing to die for them. They were also willing to kill others for failing to share their beliefs. But the fact is that the religious groups in the French religious wars organized themselves into parties. They fought their wars and conducted their propaganda campaigns as organized forces, each looking to their great nobles to lead them.

A primary goal of this study, then, is to place French demonology in the political, religious and intellectual context of the Wars of Religion that devastated France for thirty-five years. This task has been made possible by the many excellent historical works that have appeared in the last two or three decades, studying conditions of life, and responses to them in the early modern period. There has also been an explosion of specific historical work that has centred on many aspects of life in France during the religious wars. The legal and judicial aspects of early modern societies have been the subject of many works as well. Oddly, though, most historians interested in witchcraft have not much delved into these areas. Recent historical approaches to witchcraft have concentrated on other matters, more often related to broad social and intellectual questions than to matters of law and politics.

The history of witchcraft trials in the whole of France remains to be written. The picture that has been emerging from the work of Alfred

Soman on the judicial practices of the *Parlement* (high court) of Paris, which had jurisdiction over about one-half the kingdom, is one of consistent moderation in the area of witchcraft. Evidence given by the demonologists themselves supports Soman's statistical findings. The advice and exhortations of the demonologists seemed to have remarkably little direct effect on the legal handling of people accused of witchcraft in France. The demonologists were certainly not able to cause a "witchcraze" in France.

Demonology in France was an intensely political genre of religious writing. With the important exceptions of Jean Bodin, who was in his own intellectual and religious world, and Lambert Daneau, France's only Protestant demonologist, these writers were virtually all zealous Catholics, men who adhered to the Holy League when it flourished in the 1580s and 1590s. Their point of view was not just a worldview or religious inclination, but a party allegiance in a time of bitter sectarian violence. French demonology was, to a large extent, propaganda in the conflicts of the era, designed to convert or neutralize the enemies of the cause of Tridentine Catholicism. "Pure demonology," so to speak, hardly existed in France.

Many of these zealot demonologists were Jesuits. As discussed in this study, there was an important network of Jesuit demonologists in France in the 1570s and beyond. The role of the Jesuits in the development of demonology and in the European witchhunt is an area of considerable controversy.[4] I have no axe to grind on this subject. I do not "blame" anyone for their actions or beliefs. The role of Father Maldonat and his students is clear, though, and provides the necessary connections for this study. It also helps us to understand the very limited effect that demonology seemed to have in France.

Demonology can be seen as a part of the propaganda effort on the part of zealot Catholic forces. As described by Jacques Ellul, propaganda, while usually addressed to large groups in society, often really only reaches the already convinced or like-minded group. It serves to reinforce the allegiance of those of the propagandizing group and often does not even reach its nominal target groups. As Ellul states, "the more propaganda there is, the more partitioning there is . . . the main opponent is no longer an interlocutor, but an enemy . . . the more one talks, the more one isolates oneself, because the more one accuses others and justifies oneself."[5] This is an important insight and a clue to the limited ability of the French demonologists to convert others to their view of things. The strident and violent nature of their polemic is thus a sign of their weakness and isolation in the larger French society, rather than of their strength and influence.

One

Early Modern Demonologists and Modern Historians

Historians have been interested in the problem of witchcraft in early Modern Europe for a long time. It is an extraordinarily complex issue which crosses many disciplinary boundaries involving politics, religion, cultural anthropology, law, gender, psychology and intellectual life. One can sense, in this literature, a certain frustration as researchers try to establish facts rather than continually dealing in hypotheses. While a degree of consensus has emerged as to what happened in early modern Europe relating to beliefs and trials for witchcraft, this consensus rests on a high degree of imaginative reconstruction, and sometimes even guesswork.[1] Significant issues remain unresolved.

The focus for most recent historical work on witchcraft has been on the social, sexual and psychological dynamics of witchcraft accusations and trials. Scholars have concentrated on the issues of class and gender to analyze a situation in which large numbers of lower class men and women were accused (usually by their neighbours), and often tried and punished for a crime that we hold to be imaginary.

Notes to Chapter One are on pp. 153-55.

Most recent historians have not been much interested in the area of demonology. Often, demonological works are used by historians because they contain invaluable information about cases of witchcraft, but most modern readers tend to be scornful and dismissive about the beliefs espoused by the authors of these works. After all, with the exception of Bodin (who is not a typical French demonologist) most of these writers were second-rate at best. Their attitudes seem to exemplify a world we reject: a world of superstition, paranoia, violent repression of dissent and extermination of perceived threats to society.

The few current historians who have specialized in demonology have concentrated on its intellectual and linguistic aspects.[2] The most interesting specialist in this area is Stuart Clark, who has published several stimulating atricles over a twenty-year period that deal with intellectual aspects of demonology. He has argued that demonology was not a "bizarre incongruity in an otherwise normal world" or a sign of some collective psychosis. He places demonology at the centre of the literature of religious reform, a key part of the effort to help priests and ministers convince their flocks to turn from traditional magic and spell-casting to appropriate orthodox religious practices. It was an integral part of what Clark calls an "intended cultural revolution."[3] His work is illuminating and has helped place demonology in its intellectual context.

While Clark has worked to place demonology in the context of Renaissance and Reformation controversy, most historians who deal with witchcraft have not examined the tensions and deep divisions that splintered society in early modern Europe. In fact, several of them have explicitly rejected the idea of a direct relationship between the brutal conflicts of the wars of religion and concern about demons and witches.[4] Generally, modern historians have preferred to examine the broad, underlying social causes for the growth of witchcraft beliefs, accusations and trials, rather than the area of politics and the politics of ideas.

An integral aspect of the process of analyzing patterns of witchcraft ideas and accusations has been the view, stated or implied by most historians of this phenomenon, that the educated upper classes, or elites, were unified in their views on witchcraft. According to this historical interpretation, it was the social-intellectual-political elites that defined witchcraft, made it a serious crime and used their power to impose their views on the entire populace. The elites preached demonology, conducted trials and punished people for witchcraft beliefs and practices, largely as a means to establish tighter control over the unruly masses during a disordered transitional age.

In a well-known and frequently reprinted essay, Hugh Trevor-Roper discussed mass trials for witchcraft in early modern Europe. Trevor-Roper exemplified the modern liberal response to witchcraft, which he regarded as a delusion on the part of the learned religious elite. This essay lays great stress on the religious and intellectual aspect of the fight against witches in Europe. Most of Trevor-Roper's discussion was a sweeping overview of the subject, in which he painted a picture of almost universal commitment to witchcraft beliefs on the part of the elites. He stated, "Throughout the sixteenth and seventeenth centuries, men believed in the reality of this struggle [between God and the Devil].... For two centuries the clergy preached against witches and the lawyers sentenced them." It was only in the 1650s, he said, that skepticism broke through, and witchcraft and demonology, "the rubbish of the human mind," dissolved.[5]

His essay was very influential for a decade or more, but many of the central ideas he presented have since been revised or rejected by subsequent scholarly approaches. However, while Trevor-Roper was in error on several important matters of fact, and may have overstated several of his arguments, he made some interesting and valuable observations. For example, he pointed out the importance of the Catholic religious orders, particularly the Jesuits, in the formulation of demonological thought. He also alluded, though not in any detail, to divisions of opinion on matters relating to witchcraft among the elites, and even to a degree of skepticism about this issue.

Partly in reaction to Trevor-Roper's work, and shaped by the development of the field of social history, the scholarship of the last twenty-five years or so has concentrated on the underlying social causes for the rise and spread of witchcraft ideas. Peasant society and mentalities have been examined, as has the pattern and dynamics of witchcraft accusations. Valuable statistical work has been done on trials for witchcraft as well.

Robert Mandrou published his *Magistrats et sorciers en France* in 1968, and it was reissued in 1980.[6] Mandrou's book was a significant advance on Trevor-Roper's approach. It was an attempt to avoid broad generalization, and to examine an important aspect of the witchcraft phenomenon in one country. This work is still probably the fullest discussion of the legal and intellectual aspects of witchcraft in France. Together with Robert Muchembled, whose works began to appear in the late 1970s, Mandrou set the tone for the study of witchcraft in France.[7]

Mandrou's book still has value for the historian, but over time several problems have become apparent. For one thing, Mandrou defined France as including several regions that were French-speaking but were outside of the political boundaries of France for most of the period in which witchcraft was a concern. These areas, including Flanders, Franche Comté and Lorraine, happened to be regions of very high incidence of witchcraft trials and executions so this inclusion seriously distorted Mandrou's arguments for France itself. These regions, while culturally and linguistically French, were not part of the French state or the French legal system.

Only about one-quarter of Mandrou's book dealt with the sixteenth century, which we now know was the period of most intense persecution of witches in France. The period from around 1560 to 1610 was, for Mandrou, dominated by a "traditional mentality" in which virtually all the powerful elites, including theologians and judges, believed in the reality and danger of witches and worked diligently to extirpate them. Mandrou was convinced that it was in only in the late 1630s and 1640s that intellectuals and judges began to question traditional approaches to witchcraft and the *Parlement* of Paris reduced and gradually ended prosecutions for that crime. Most of the work concentrates on this period and the later seventeenth century, when the government of Louis XIV formally ordered the end of trials for witchcraft in France.

Mandrou could provide no statistical basis to support his central argument, but he described witchcraft prosecutions as very numerous. He used terms like "innumerable" and "waves of persecution" to describe trial rates. His assumption was that, in the early period at least, witchcraft prosecutions followed the same course as in the bordering regions, where historians have long known that executions were indeed very numerous.

According to Mandrou, the judges followed the advice of the theologian-demonologists and they formed a unified front in the fight against witches. The demonologists provided an intellectual and religious framework for the judges, and shaped their legal approaches to this crime. With very few exceptions, the magistrature was devoted to the cause of wiping out witches, pursuing them energetically.

When people were accused of witchcraft and associated crimes, they were handled in such a way that most of them were convicted and accused, according to Mandrou. Hostile leading questioning, intimidation, false evidence like diabolical marks and especially torture were frequently used in order to squeeze confessions from the accused. These extorted confessions then guaranteed that they could not avoid a gruesome death in the flames.[8]

Similar views are put forward by Jean Delumeau in his study *La peur en occident*. He stressed the profound difficulties of the sixteenth century, an age of rapid population growth, galloping inflation, shortage of land, high unemployment, poverty and continual warfare. He also pointed out the great intellectual gulf that had opened between classically educated Renaissance elites and the popular classes, deeply immersed in an ancient primitive magical world.[9]

Delumeau was convinced that the witchhunt was intense in France, that it was driven by the torture of the accused, and that theologians and judges were close partners in the process. He argued that it was impossible to distinguish judges from theologians, because they shared a common mental formation. He called them the "two pillars of Christianity" who presented a united front in the war against Satan.[10] Witches were one of the scapegoated groups that suffered because of the extreme difficulties of the period.[11]

This general line of argumentation was continued by the prolific French scholar, Robert Muchembled. The bulk of Muchembled's research on witchcraft accusations and trials has been concentrated in the far north of France, which was part of the Spanish empire in the sixteenth and seventeenth centuries. In this region, the political and legal structure—and the nature of religious conflict—were completely separate and significantly different from the situation within the borders of the kingdom of France. Furthermore, and perhaps even more importantly, the legal system was different, as *Parlements* or their equivalents did not exist in the region he studies. Thus, village judges often had full and final authority in cases of accusations of witchcraft. However, these important differences did not prevent Muchembled from generalizing his findings to include France in his earlier works.

In Muchembled's works of the 1970s and early 1980s, one of the keys to understanding witchcraft in early modern Europe, France included, is the process he described as the acculturation of the masses by the elites. He developed an interesting psychologically based hypothesis to describe the process, in which sexual, social and religious anxieties came together that caused women to be targeted as witch scapegoats. Witchcraft was a tool in this process, one that enabled the elites to label popular culture as evil and diabolical, and to attempt to stamp it out through preaching and legal repression. Theologians, parish priests and lay judges of lower and higher courts were described as part of a solidly unified elite, intent on the reformation of popular culture, and the creation of an orthodox and obedient peasantry. Muchembled stated this argument in several books, articles and conference papers, and repeatedly and explicitly insisted that the elites were unified in this process. He stated, for example, "It [witchcraft] was essentially a construction of theologians and judges confronted with rural paganism, with the magical thought of the peasants. That the cultural elites totally adhered to this vision of things is not to be doubted."[12]

In working out his concept of the acculturation of the masses, Robert Muchembled stated strongly that the lay judges played a crucial role in close cooperation with theologians and parish priests. In his essay, "Lay Judges and the Acculturation of the Masses," he argued,

> Sixteenth and seventeenth century magistrates considered themselves invested with a quasi-divine mission and applied to human society a dualistic vision of the battle of good and evil, which had been forcefully reaffirmed by the Counter-Reformation. Their acculturising functions with regard to the masses proceeded from their social role and ideology.... All magistrates, even the most humble, took part in the battle against the paganism of the masses.... The judges therefore played an important role in the application of Tridentine ideology to society and in particular to the masses.... Though invented and systematised by churchmen at the end of the middle ages, demonology was put to work by lay judges, from the most humble to the most prestigious, fuelling an intense witch hunt from the middle of the sixteenth century onwards.... As bearers of the ideology of the Counter-Reformation and of absolutism, lay judges played a leading role in the acculturation of the rural and urban masses in the sixteenth and seventeenth centuries. Their discourses and their attitudes to criminals indicate a social ideal which recalls the monastic model and still more that offered by the Society of Jesus.... The judges of the sixteenth and seventeenth centuries were laymen only in appearance. Their person, their ideology and their actions linked them with the missionaries of the Catholic Counter-Reformation. They belonged to the shock troops charged with inculcating a new definition of the sacred to the polytheist and animist masses, a new definition of authority and obedience. They took an active part in the vast offensive led by the elites against popular culture.[13]

Muchembled also stressed that the judges acted with a mixture of fear and contempt for the common people with whom they dealt in their courts.

This view on acculturation and on the unity of the elites in carrying it out has become widely accepted, and is incorporated into most recent studies of witchcraft.

In his solid and interesting work *Servants of Satan* Joseph Klaits states,

> Nearly everyone—from intellectuals to peasants—believed in the reality of invisible spirits, both angelic and demonic. Hardly anyone challenged the universal opinion that supernatural forces constantly intervened in everyday life.... The educated were at the forefront of the witch hunts. It was learned men who gave to the Western concept of witchcraft its most distinctive and most disturbing characteristic, the relationship with Satan.

He constantly pictures a unified elite, imposing its views on the popular culture.[14]

Brian Levack states similar views. He writes, "Most educated Europeans believed in all the aspects of witchcraft; the demonic pact, sabbats, etc." Further, "for the intensive hunting of witches to take place, it was necessary for the ruling class to believe that the crime was of the greatest magnitude and that it was being practiced on a large scale and in a conspiratorial manner." He states quite definitely that, "Taken together, the witchcraft treatises of the early modern period succeeded in making the literate members of European society aware of witchcraft and convinced of its reality."[15]

Criticism of these views has developed in recent years. In a paper critical of the acculturation thesis of Muchembled, Delumeau and others, Jean Wirth examined several aspects of religious practice in early modern Europe that, for him, showed the weakness of this approach. He pointed out that it was generally held to be true that, in spite of its shortcomings, the acculturation thesis "is on the way of becoming a commonplace."[16] Peter Burke also questioned the value of the concept of acculturation in a 1980 conference paper. Burke proposed a refinement of the term and the concept, suggesting that "negotiation" between cultures might be more subtle and thus more useful than acculturation, a process in which the dominant learned culture imposes its views on the subordinate popular culture.[17] However, neither Burke nor Wirth suggest the possibility that the upper classes were not as united in their views and their approach to issues like witchcraft as the proponents of acculturation insist that they were.

Robin Briggs has criticized Muchembled strongly in two major works. In his *Communities of Belief* (1989) he took Muchembled to task over the acculturation thesis, stating that it "appears basically Marxian in inspiration" and "runs way ahead of the evidence." He goes on to state that Muchembled wrote "as if all the products of urban literate society were somehow united by a common class interest, a frequent fallacy in Marxist interpretations. . . . The social groups concerned were far from having a common view on everything. . . . The whole conception of the elite as a single identifiable group is a highly dangerous one."[18] His *Witches and Neighbours* (1996) addresses many theories of the witchcraft issue, including Muchembled's more recent formulations. After looking at political, social, sexual and psychological models presented by various historians, he states that the issue is too complex and too dependent on local situations to lend itself to any "broad-brush theory."[19] Briggs' work is about witchcraft on the village level, and he does not concern himself much with learned demonology. He does point out though, that there were divisions among the elites on this issue and that the demonologists' arguments were evidence of these divisions.[20]

While Mandrou's and Muchembled's picture of witchcraft trials in France has been very influential for all the historians of the early modern period, important findings in the archives of the *Parlement* of Paris have thrown a shadow over their scenario. Over the last twenty years, Alfred Soman has produced close to twenty articles on this subject. Recently, fifteen of these have been collected and published by Variorum Press.[21] This valuable collection makes these studies much more available to scholars and students.

The *Parlement* of Paris was a unique court in Europe at this time. Its area of jurisdiction was enormous, comprising at least half of France, with a population of between eight and ten million people.[22] The justices of this high court were a particularly interesting elite group (this is the case for the provincial *Parlements* as well). They were wealthy, highly educated and politically influential. The high magistracy was the centre of French intellectual life in this age. The justices owned their offices, which guaranteed them a considerable degree of autonomy in their application of the law. In the sixteenth century, this group was in a process of claiming nobility through their offices, and the high magistrature became an important part of the French nobility throughout the old regime.

There is a major error in seeing the entire judicate in early modern France as one great unified institution, with common training and outlook. There was an enormous social and intellectual gap between the *parlementaires* and local judges in the villages and towns of France. The local judges were village dignitaries, the *coqs de village*. They were well-off peasants who served as mayors and other officials of their local areas. They lacked legal training and were often illiterate.[23] These men, who took turns serving as judges of their neighbours, were often very severe and even abusive to many of those accused of witchcraft.

Over many decades, the *Parlement* worked to improve this situation. They endeavoured to supervise the local courts more closely and end abusive illegalities in prosecutions. In some instances, this involved bringing criminal charges against local officials. For example, in 1601, the executioner-torturer of Rocroi, Jean Minard, a self-proclaimed expert on finding the infamous witches' mark who claimed to have executed 274 witches (only eight of these were in France), was arrested and tried by the *Parlement* of Paris. He was sentenced to a life of servitude in the Mediterranean galley fleet.[24]

The *Parlement* also strove to correct abuses of the lower courts through the imposition of proper rules of procedure. In 1588 the *Parlement* ordered a halt to the traditional water trial, used in all over Europe, in which suspected witches were thrown into water to see whether they sank or floated. This folkloric trial, a remnant of the medieval trial by ordeal, resulted in many deaths and was formally forbidden by the *Parlement* of Paris in 1601.[25]

The most important means of judicial oversight by the *Parlements* was the appeal. The *Parlements* of France heard some cases on first instance, but in criminal procedure, they dealt with most cases as appeals. The *Parlement* of Paris took this responsibility seriously. The most important aspect of Soman's research deals with the *Parlement*'s role as an appeal court in witchcraft cases. Contrary to many statements, witches were not all sentenced to death. A range of penalties, including whipping, galley service, fines and banishment were used as well as the death penalty. Many people found guilty of witchcraft and sentenced to serious punishments in local courts appealed to the *Parlement*. It worked, over many decades, to guarantee that all people found guilty in witchcraft trials in lower jurisdictions would automatically appeal to Paris. By 1624, the *Parlement* of Paris ruled that lower courts could not carry out the death penalty in witchcraft cases and that all such cases would be transferred to Paris, confirming practices already well established.[26]

Appeals were not easy for the local jurisdictions. In France, unlike other places in Europe, the appellant had to be physically brought to Paris and lodged in the Conciergerie at the expense of the local court. Soman points out that, "Typically it cost the equivalent of fifty to one hundred cows to send an appellant in person to the capital."[27] The *Parlement*'s growing insistence that witchcraft cases be appealed, together with the way they disposed of such cases, came to serve as a disincentive for the local courts to undertake witchcraft prosecutions.

Before the *Parlement*, the case was treated as a new case. Soman's findings on what actually happened to the people brought to Paris to be tried for witchcraft are astonishing for those who are familiar with most older conventional discussions of witchcraft in Europe. Of 1,272 cases of witchcraft referred to the *Parlement* of Paris between 1540 and 1670, with the vast majority occurring between 1580 and 1610, only 103 were condemned to death. This was a death rate of 8.2 percent, probably the lowest in any jurisdiction in Europe.

The accused were roughly evenly divided between men and women; of the condemned, 57 were women and 46 were men.[28] The usual stereotype that witchcraft was overwhelmingly identified as a woman's crime does not seem to have applied in this large jurisdiction.

Another surprising finding concerns the *Parlement* of Paris' use of torture. Historians have been virtually unanimous in seeing torture as a central factor in the generation of accusations and confessions in witchcraft cases. Soman states, "Research on torture imposes a radical revision of all our suppositions in this domain." In fact, the *Parlement* applied torture or threats of torture to only 185 of the appellants, or 14.8 percent. Torture in witchcraft cases virtually disappeared in the *Parlement* of Paris, especially for women, by 1610. The means of torture most commonly used was the forcing of quantities of water down the victim's throat. This was doubtlessly painful, but not sufficiently so to produce confessions. Of the group tortured in their Paris trials, only *one* confessed. The last use of torture in a witchcraft trial in Paris was in 1593. In the seventeenth century, the court tortured very rarely in any of its criminal procedures. Since the *Parlement* in the late sixteenth century had a monopoly on the legal application of torture, it practically ended for witchcraft proceedings.[29]

The implications of this research are very significant. Throughout most of his work, Soman concentrated on the legal practice of the high court, insisting that its extraordinary moderation in the area of witchcraft was the result of the *Parlement*'s legal conservatism, their close attention to proper legal procedure. But there is a strong implication that these high court justices were not convinced that witchcraft was a grave danger to French society. They did not share the apocalyptic sense of urgency of the demonologists. Soman points out that many demonological texts "turn out to have been written *against* the jurisprudence of the *Parlement*, which was always reluctant to condemn accused witches to death." He also criticizes widely accepted social class interpretations:

> Almost all historians today conceive of witch hunting as an activity imposed upon the peasantry by the "elite." The trouble with this formulation is that it ignores both the multiplicity of elites and the diversity of their interests. In France the zealous faction within the magistracy turns out to have been a rabble of parvenu village judges, many of whom were illiterate.[30]

This account shows that demonologists' complaints of judicial lack of zeal in the matter of witchcraft were founded on fact. The zealot demonologists were clearly frustrated and infuriated by the refusal of the high courts to set aside its traditional ponderous care and scrupulousness for people accused of witchcraft. Interestingly, when the notorious Sixteen ran Paris between 1588 and 1594, and the *Parlement* was, through intimidation or sympathy, the closest to the Catholic League than at any point in this whole period, the *Parlement*'s toughness on lower court abuses was relaxed, and its percentage of death penalties rose to 27 percent of the cases heard.[31]

Jonathan Dewald's brief examination of the involvement of the *Parlement* of Rouen with witchcraft has turned up results not unlike Soman's. Dewald looked at the sample years of 1585-88 and 1604-1606. In these years, which are during the height of witchcraft prosecutions in France, the court dealt with only twenty cases of witchcraft. The Rouen *Parlement* was relatively more severe than its Paris counterpart, executing seven of the twenty (28.5 percent), and reduced at least ten sentences imposed by lower courts.[32] If these years were typical, the *Parlement* of Rouen might have executed perhaps sixty or seventy for witchcraft in total, a much higher rate than in Paris, but still not a huge number. When this body discussed royal attempts to control witchcraft prosecutions in 1670, its brief stated that the court had handed down judgments in over two hundred witchcraft cases in its history.[33] If the 28.5 percent execution rate in Dewald's sample years is applied to this figure, the estimate of sixty or seventy executions seems reasonable. It is also clear from Dewald's account, that the *Parlement* of Rouen was also in the process of strengthening its overview of local courts in its region, was hearing more appeals from rural regions, curtailing the frequency of overly severe sentencing by these courts.

In the last few years, as his earlier views have become generally accepted and incorporated into major syntheses, Robert Muchembled has shifted his approach to the functioning of early modern European societies. He has dropped the theory of acculturation of the masses as oversimplified, one-dimensional and no longer fitting the evidence. In a 1988 work, for example, he drops the "top-down" notion of social interaction implied in acculturation in favour of a more complex notion of social interaction which was considerable in the sixteenth century. Over time, the interaction between elites and masses changed, as upper class culture evolved in different ways and at different rates from popular culture. In *Le roi et la sorcière* (1994), Muchembled calls the acculturation theory "a too vague theory that I formulated at the beginning of my studies."[34]

Recent studies have shown that the level of persecution for witchcraft varied widely accross Europe. Spain, Italy, England, the northern Netherlands and France had very low levels of executions for witchcraft, while the southern Netherlands, Scotland, Lorraine, Luxembourg and parts of Switzerland and Germany had much higher rates of trials and executions. The sharply different ways that neighbouring states dealt with witchcraft has become one of the issues that Muchembled has been dealing with.

He states, "In total, the kingdom of France was not a zone of an active witch hunt at the time of the paroxysms of pursuits in Europe between 1580 and 1630. The psychic economy of the governors, especially the judges of the *Parlement* of Paris were not really inclined to burning witches at the stake."[35] In France, a highly centralized state with a long-standing tradition of central legal institutions, witchcraft was never really a major problem of criminal law.[36]

In Europe as a whole, Muchembled states, witchcraft was very actively pursued in the areas on France's northern and eastern borders, that formed the "Spanish Road" in the sixteenth and seventeenth centuries. This group of states was the scene of an extraordinary combination of situations. These regions were ruled by a far-off foreign ruler, the King of Spain. They formed the major political and religious battleground of Europe for at least two centuries. According to Muchembled's penetrating and challenging work, it was the peculiar stresses in these regions that led to age group and gender conflict that underlay the particularly high level of witchcraft trials and executions in an atmosphere of religious and political warfare.

Muchembled, citing Soman, repeatedly emphasizes the important role played by the *Parlement* of Paris in controlling local courts and imposing its conservative jurisprudence on a very large jurisdiction.

In this book, as in his earlier work, Muchembled's main goal is to understand the dynamics of small communities in troubled political, economic and social situations in order to understand how accusations for witchcraft came to be made. The role of the demonologists, and their relationship with legal officials and with ordinary people is not really the subject of his work, and is not examined in any depth. In general, Muchembled continues to hold that demonologists and judges worked together to eliminate witches from the community. When he looks at demonologists, he does not go beyond the well-known writers, and certainly does not examine the works of several dozen French writers who addressed the issue. In a work published in 1990 and reissued in 1994, Muchembled states,

> Profoundly impregnated by the combative Catholicism of the Counter Reformation, lay governments, like the ecclesiastics, see on earth an inexpiable war between Good and Evil. . . . Judges, or more generally, the social elites, are in effect so intimately convinced of the reality of satanic action in the world that they were persuaded of the obligation to oppose it with all their power. Lacking a 'sense of the impossible' before the development of rationalist ideas in the second half of the seventeenth century, the greatest thinkers shared these convictions. All supported in conscience the efforts made by state and church to purify the City of God on earth.[37]

While it seems clear that demonology was an elite construction, spread by printed books and then by preachers, trials for witchcraft cannot also be identified as an elite program. Theories of acculturation, or the more recent notion of confessionalization, depict pressure for trials as coming from the religious and legal elites, imposing trials as a way to educate and discipline the popular classes. This view is widely held.

But several recent studies have pointed out that, in reality, pressure for trials often came from the people themselves. Courts responded to accusations of witchcraft by neighbours and demands that the authorities deal with them. How the courts responded is a complex business.[38]

Muchembled's implication in this statement is that judges and demonologists worked together as agents of the evolving modern state and churches in imposing central authority on the masses. Those who sided with Satan were depicted as religious and political rebels. Echoing his earlier statements, he writes that "secular judges were impregnated with religion" in their work against witches.[39]

In France the higher court magistrates turn out to have been the most important restraining factor on witchcraft proceedings. Even the lower courts, while more severe that the *Parlements*, do not seem to have been as active in this area as those in many other parts of Europe.[40] Yet, there were at least several dozen works published in France, many by reputable writers, between 1570 and 1620, that declared that witchcraft was real, that it was a serious crime against God and human society, and that it had to be sought out, tried and punished by the secular authorities. These authors were mainly churchmen, but several were part of the legal world. What is striking about these works, when read seriously, is the powerful sense that not only did the writers seem to be at odds with the judges who were responsible for trying cases, but that they often expressed frustration and even hostility toward the high magistrates. It is clear that demonologists did not direct the justices in their deliberations.

This is the heart of the issue. Through repetition, the opinion of some scholars that the upper classes were, as a whole, united in their views on witchcraft, and that they used their control of the courts to impose those views on the rest of society has come to be regarded as fact. But, can it really be considered a fact?

The work of social historians has in many ways advanced and enriched our understanding of the effect of ideas in the age of the reformation and of their role in society. We know far more about the lives of Europeans and the function of witchcraft beliefs, accusations and prosecutions than we did twenty-five years ago. But there is danger in picturing the social-intellectual-political elites as a monolithic bloc in the area of witchcraft beliefs. The divisions among religious party lines, and between people of similar underlying worldviews and social positions were very real in this period, and were life and death matters. Arguments for the unity of elite views do not sufficiently take into account the wide variety of intellectual options available in this extraordinarily complex period of history.

In a rare work that examines divisions of opinion in the elites' views on witchcraft, Bernadette Paton looks at fifteenth-century Italy. At this time, demonological views were spreading among European theologians. But they seem to have been held and preached only by a particular group of preachers. Her study examines the attempt of Bernardino of Siena to engender a witch hunt. Other churchmen and civic officials opposed him though and a large scale trial did not occur.[41]

One very important distinction that is rarely made by scholars is the tremendous gulf that separated the militant religious zealots who were very important in this age, but who always seem to be a minority in society, from the less dedicated. There is a broad spectrum of religious commitment, for both Protestants and Catholics, from the zealot stance, through less intense, lukewarm and indifferent all the way to covert and overt hostility to the established churches. We must also keep in mind that, even in a narrowly defined entity like "pro-League zealot Catholics between 1560 and 1590," there were individuals whose approaches were not the same as everyone else's. And people changed their views over time, as circumstances changed. According to A. Lynn Martin, for example, the Jesuit Father Emond Auger, who was a fire-breathing radical Catholic zealot in the early years of the religious wars, settled into an almost *politique* position in the 1580s.[42] In the late 1580s, Jean Bodin, the most distinguished intellectual *politique*, actually joined the Catholic League, apparently through a sense of disgust at the conduct of Henry III.[43] The cardinal of Lorraine, brother of Duke François of Guise worked diligently in the early 1560s for an accommodation with the Protestants. He became their bitter enemy after the assassination of his brother in 1563.[44]

There is little doubt that the demonologists were sometimes obsessed with their topic, that they had an essentially repressive attitude to law, and that they were in part motivated by contempt for and fear of the ignorant, superstitious and unruly peasantry. But the thesis that the demonologist authors were spokespersons for a unified elite reacting against peasant folkloric religion that was discovered in the missionary effort of the Reformation rests on very shaky ground.

The science of demons, in France at least, was developed and disseminated in order to tie the Protestant heresy to the machinations of the Devil, and to convince the learned classes, especially indifferent or incredulous clergy and judges that witchcraft should be taken seriously as a pressing danger that had to be addressed energetically.

Two

Witchcraft, Politics and Law

It seems clear that something very profound happened to European civilization between the fourteenth and sixteenth centuries. The change from "late medieval" to "early modern" is real and significant. Dramatic changes occurred in political organization, the concept of the state and the obligations of subjects to monarchs, the introduction and spread of Roman law, the diffusion of humanist scholarship, the invention and dissemination of printing, developments in capitalism, increased standardization and usage of vernacular languages. Of course, the great upheaval of the Reformation was part of this transformation of European societies along with new attitudes to moral and social control, and sexuality and the body. When we add to this explosive population growth, agricultural crises brought on by unfavourable climatic conditions, waves of disease epidemics and never-ending warfare, the period is one of enormous complexity.

As one aspect of this era of massive change, the image and role of the Devil as the personification of evil altered as well. The Devil was well known throughout the Middle Ages. While his role became magni-

---

Notes to Chapter Two are on pp. 156-57.

fied by theologians as time went on, for the common people he was seen as a relatively benign, sometimes even humorous character. Robert Scribner points out that ordinary people were accustomed to thinking of God, the saints and demons as part of a feudal system of mutual obligations. He states "the demonic was not regarded by the laity with the same abhorrence as it was by the clergy or theologians. Rather, it was an alternate means of access to efficacious sacred power. Thus, one turned to the professional magician or sorcerer, folk who knew how to deal with spirits or demons and their power."[1] But by the early sixteenth century, the Devil had come to assume tremendous powers, at least in the minds of leading religious thinkers. John Bossy has discussed the magnification of the Devil's role in a compelling article called "Moral Arithmetic: Seven Sins into Ten Commandments"[2] He argues that, for most of the Middle Ages, Christian morality was based on the Seven Deadly Sins. From the late thirteenth to the early sixteenth century, the Ten Commandments gradually came to replace the Seven Sins as the touchstones of individual morality. The crucial difference in these models is that while the Seven Sins emphasized community ethics, the Ten Commandments emphasized humans' obligations to God and explicitly condemned idolatry and heresy. The Seven Sins offered a model of behaviour to avoid, while the Commandments were the law of God. Bossy goes on to point out, "Under the old moral regime the Devil had been the anti-type of Christ, teaching universal hatred where Christ taught love: he was the Fiend. Under the new regime, he became the anti-type of the Father, the source and object of idolatry and false worship." Witchcraft thus shifted from being a crime against neighbours to a crime against God.[3]

In the later Middle Ages and the early modern period, people of all social classes, from peasants to the elites, shared views of the reality of spells and magical manipulations of the natural world. Many historians have discussed the process through which these views were distilled by theologians into a theology of evil in the later Middle Ages. The centre of this elaborate new theology was the Devil and his army of demons, intent on causing chaos in the created world and the fall of mankind.[4] In this scenario, the Devil, working with God's permission, sought to use a wide range of illusions, false promises and tricks in order to trap humans into worshipping him, in order to bring them to damnation. Propogated by preachers, this new Christian demonology spread first among the learned upper classes, and then to the common people, who were already imbued with a mixture of Christian and pagan magical worldviews. When, in the course of the seventeenth century, the elites lost interest or rejected the late medieval demonology, the common folk's magical outlook persisted, but the role of the Devil as the personification of evil diminished and trials for witchcraft ceased.

During the fifteenth century, learned discussions of the Devil's role in the world and of the evils perpetrated by human witches began to appear. With the perfection of print in mid-century, demonology books spread widely across Europe. Most historians agree that the proliferation of demonology books had much to do with the development of witchcraft trials in the closing days of the Middle Ages. The best-known demonology works of the fifteenth century—the *Formicarius* of Johann Nider (c. 1435) and the *Malleus Maleficarum* of Heinrich Sprenger (Kramer) and Jacob Kramer (1486)—were German, reflecting conditions peculiar to their regions. Without doubt, though, they helped interested clerical and lay readers across Europe to become familiar with the theology of evil that had developed by that period.

Demonological literature was not produced by French writers until significantly later. In fact, it was not until after the 1560s that French authors began to publish works in this field. From that point, demonology books were published with some frequency for around sixty years, though one cannot claim that they were anything but a tiny minority of the output of French presses.

French demonological works were not general theoretical legal or theological studies. Rather, they were written in response to specific situations and discussed specific cases of perceived demonic involvement in the world. While they probably reflected general perceptions held by most people of the age, they can only partly be understood as expressions of a worldview. They emerged from and reflected a very specific context. The first French Catholic demonological works dealt with a single dramatic case of demonic possession that occurred in 1566, in the midst of a bitter period of religious rivalry and violence.

The outbreak of the Wars of Religion in 1562 in France was the culmination of several decades of complex developments.[5] The wars of Francis I in the early sixteenth century caused a sharp rise in taxation which in turn helped cause a sharp increase in social and political tension in France. From the 1520s on, hundreds of incidents of local violence involving peasants, urban workers, local officials and royal armies occurred in almost every part of the kingdom. This rising tension and violence contributed to the decline of royal prestige late in the reign of Francis I, which became extremely grave in the reigns of his grandsons, Francis II, Charles IX and Henry III. The breakdown of social and political consensus was an important ingredient in the growth of Calvinist Protestantism and of militant reformed Catholicism.[6]

Calvinist Protestantism grew illegally as an underground movement, beginning in the 1540s and gathering momentum in the 1550s, arousing deep hatred and resentment among devoted Catholics. While the Protestants probably never attracted over two million adherents out of a total population of sixteen or seventeen million, their power was disproportionate to their numbers because of the active involvement of some very powerful nobles and scholars, because of their concentration in certain geographical regions, and because of the Protestants' deep personal commitment to their religion.

The participation of great nobles in religious controversies was central to the development of the Reformation in France. The Bourbons of Navarre, the Condés and the Colignys joined the Protestant movement and became devoted practitioners and promoters of the new religion. Their hated rivals, the Guises, who had recently risen into the ranks of the highest nobility, assumed the role of protectors of the Catholic faith. As time went on, their Catholicism, always militant, became increasingly ultramontane, pro-papal and allied with Spain. At times, the religious conflict took on the character of clan warfare.

Conceivably, the growth of Protestantism and the division of the nobility along religious lines could have been held in check by a strong king like Francis I or Henry II. But Henry II died in an accident in 1559, leaving four young sons and an unpopular widow, Catherine de Medici at the head of the French state. The first of her sons, Francis II, was married to Mary, Queen of Scots, a niece of the duke of Guise. Under Francis II, Guise practically ruled France and maintained the same pressure on the Protestants that Henry II had. But Francis died in 1560 at seventeen years old. At that point, Catherine, acting in the name of her nine-year-old second son, Charles IX, took control of the situation in alliance with Guise's enemies, many of whom were Protestants.

Violence between the religious and political factions grew in frequency and intensity from 1560. The regent attempted to keep the peace, or to arrange truces in the fighting, by not letting any group become too strong for too long. Inevitably, this meant the recognition and legalization of the Protestant heresy by a royal edict in January

1562.[7] Through astute shifting and encouragement of compromise, Catherine was able to limit the power of the Guises as well as that of the Protestants without destroying either. But as time went on, the Protestant minority, protected by this complex political situation, became well established, confident and militarily powerful, causing many devout Catholics great pain and anger. Organized armed conflict broke out following a massacre of a Protestant congregation at Vassy by troops of the duke of Guise in March of 1562.

Denis Crouzet describes a widespread eschatological panic among Catholics, who saw the growth of Protestantism and the discord it caused as proof of God's anger toward France. The appropriate response for these people was to strike out violently at the Protestants in order to destroy their heresy, and to assuage the wrath of God.[8] Indeed, Crouzet catalogues many horrific acts of extreme violence that occurred at this time.

But French Catholics were not united. Many Catholics in France did not support the Guise/zealot version of Catholicism. France had a long tradition of a national Catholic church, called Gallicanism. This style of Catholicism was the result of centuries of sometimes very bitter relations between the kings of France and the papacy. By 1550, the king of France practiced a "monarchical Gallicanism," in which he governed the church as an institution autonomous of Rome.[9] The monarchs insisted that the Catholic church in France was a national church, not to be meddled with by foreigners, including the pope. In this view, the monarchs were supported strongly by most of the elites, and especially the influential *Parlements*, or high courts.

The *Parlements* also saw themselves as protectors of France's traditional "Gallican liberties." In this, they competed with the monarchs of the sixteenth century. The ideas of Gallicanism and French nationalism were tied closely together. Many *parlementaire* intellectuals, like Estienne Pasquier, were nationalists and students of history, which they used to support their particular views of France's history and destiny.[10]

A crucial episode in the history of the Catholic church in the sixteenth century was the Council of Trent. In three sittings, between 1545 and 1563, this council confirmed its traditional theology and organization and militantly opposed the existence of the Protestant heresy. Trent enacted many important reforms aimed at correcting the abuses that had helped stimulate the Protestant Reformation. It was the beginning of a long process of reform and rebuilding of the Catholic church. The institution that eventually emerged became, in time, very different from that which existed earlier.[11]

Kings Francis I and Henry II, for political reasons, opposed the convocation of the Council of Trent and refused to take active roles in it.[12] Very few French bishops attended its meetings.[13] Much of the power to enact the decisions of the council was left to the pope. The *Parlement* of Paris also opposed the imposition of Trent's decrees in France. They saw them as a violation of the customary tradition of Gallican liberties and refused to register the the edicts of the Council of Trent. This was a sore point among Catholic zealots for generations.

Very deep hostility developed between the zealots and the Gallicans. For the Gallicans, the zealots were tools of the pope who wanted to destroy the whole Catholic tradition of France. For the zealots, the Gallicans were the allies of the heretics, and were perhaps even worse that heretics. The *Parlements'* Gallican position was essentially conservative, based on a tradition of a close relationship between state and church. They mistrusted what they saw as excesses in the reformed Catholic practices of the Tridentine church and especially to the resurgent power of the papacy.

In their conservative, nationalistic Catholicism, most Gallican Catholics were fierce opponents of Protestantism throughout the religious wars. For some though, it seemed better to arrive at a temporary *modus vivendi* with the Protestants rather than destroy the country in civil war. From the beginning of the armed struggle, those who expressed these views were called *politiques*. While there was no organized *politique* faction or party until very late in the wars, the *politique* attitude was important throughout the conflict.[14] The conversion of Henry IV to Catholicism in 1593 and his eventual triumph represented the victory of the *politique* approach.

Generally, the French Catholic zealots get pretty short shrift from the historical community, which has concentrated on the political aspects of the crisis or on the development of Protestantism. When they are discussed at all, they are generally dismissed as bigots and fanatics, dancing to the tune of the pope and the king of Spain. In an historical tradition dominated by anti-clerical liberal sentiment, these intense Catholics of the French religious wars are seen as backward looking, obscurantist self-serving fanatics.

In fact, many of these people were among the intellectual elite of their day. Highly educated and dedicated to their religion, the Catholic zealots were on the leading edge of the Catholic Reformation, intent on implanting the Tridentine reform program in France. They were papalist in their religious politics, and many of them were Italian or Spanish. Many of them, clergy and laypersons alike, were shining examples of the new knowledgeable, devoted and activist Catholic, dedicated to reforming religious belief and practice among a mass of uneducated and indifferent laity. They lived in a violent age, and were not alone in counselling the use of force against their enemies. They saw their church as the one true church and those who opposed it as the enemies of God, traitors and rebels who deserved death. That political machinations had resulted in the toleration and survival of heresy in France was bitterly resented by these people. Without an appreciation of the intensity and durability of these sentiments, the actions and arguments of this faction cannot properly be appreciated.

As has already been mentioned, the primary noble leaders of this group, known in the later phases of the civil wars as the Holy League, came from the Guise dynasty. For thirty years, dukes of Guise led the Catholic forces. After the murder of King Henry III in 1589, there was even an attempt to crown a Guise king. Many other important nobles and laypersons supported the League. While many *parlementaires* were *politiques*, there was, on most *Parlements*, a pro-Guise faction that was violently anti-Protestant. In many cities, including Paris, popular sentiment was, for a time at least, overwhelmingly in favour of the zealot Catholic cause and its leaders as well.

Bishops, priests and the religious orders were never solidly in one Catholic political camp or the other. Substantial numbers of clergymen adhered to the Gallican approach, while others were intense zealots, calling for the slaughter of the heretics and applauding when it actually happened, as in the St. Bartholomew's Day Massacre in 1572.

While this zealot group was quite powerful between 1560 and 1595, it was never able to impose its view of religion and politics on the large, decentralised French nation. In France the religious issues were never black and white, as they may have seemed for committed Catholics to be elsewhere. Geneva, England and much of Germany were in the heretic Protestant camp. There, a devoted Catholic had to practice and propagate his religion in secret, and if detected, could die a martyr's death. In Spain or Italy, the reformed Catholic church was triumphant, protected by princes and the pope, with powerful Inquisitions as their judicial weapons in the fight against heresy, blasphemy and irreligion.

But France was more complex. It was legally Catholic, with a monarch who, for a thousand years, was a quasi-religious figure. France had been one of the principal centres of medieval Catholicism and scholastic studies. But in that country, Catholics who were enthusiastically committed to the reformation as it was shaped by Trent were a minority, despised or ignored by huge numbers of their ostensible co-religionists. From this peculiar situation came their frustration, and their demonology.

One other important area needs at least to be mentioned in this discussion. The French legal system was, by 1560, almost entirely independent of direct royal or ecclesiastical control. There was no Inquisition in France. In Italy, Spain or the Spanish Netherlands matters relating to faith would fall under the jurisdiction of an Inquisition, staffed by legally trained clerics.[15] But in France, these problems could only be dealt with in the lay criminal courts. In the late 1550s Henry II, alarmed at the growth of Protestantism, negotiated with the pope for the establishment of an Inquisition in France. A royal ordinance for this was handed down in July of 1557 but was rescinded a year later, as the king apparently yielded to opposition to this move.[16] The *Parlements* generally showed themselves loath to deal with matters of belief after 1561 or 1562. At that time, as part of her accommodation with the rival factions, Catherine de Medici ordered the end of trials of Protestants who were merely observing their religion. The legal existence of Protestantism was recognized by the Crown.[17]

As criminal courts, the *Parlements* were interested in criminal behaviour, not in how people thought or prayed. They tended to prosecute cases of gross blasphemy and immorality as well as witchcraft, but stayed away from many of the kinds of cases with which the Inquisitions dealt, relating to purity of the faith. What is more, on the political level, the *Parlements* were often explicitly hostile to the zealot Catholic position. They refused to establish the edicts of the Council of Trent (concluded in 1563) in France, and were very hostile to new reformed religious orders, especially the Jesuits.

For the committed French Catholics, the Protestant minority was at least a clear and obvious enemy. But the mass of Catholics, including many who were among the elites of society who were not of the same intensity as the zealots, were in their own way as big a problem. The zealot demonologists worked to define Protestantism as demonic heresy and to destroy it. In order to do this, they had to convert the less committed majority to their position. Failing that, they sought to advance their cause by discrediting lukewarm Catholic officials by accusing them of passive support for heresy, atheism and the Devil.

A crucial clue that helps to give an insight into this aspect of French demonology during and immediately following the religious wars is the widely stated view among the writers of these works that scepticism and incredulity about demons and witches was widespread and that it was a very serious problem. Complaints of unbelief were spun out at great length.

In their discussion of the prevalence and dangers of unbelief in witchcraft, the demonologists made several basic points. Many writers identified scepticism and unbelief in demons and witches with an attack on the doctrine of the immortality of the soul. They all considered unbelief in demons to equal unbelief in God—atheism. These frequently stated complaints of judicial incredulity and leniency form an important clue in understanding what actually went on in the courts in witchcraft cases. As discussed above, a long historical tradition has seen the magistrates of France as key players in the application of witchcraft beliefs, as developed by the theologians, to the sphere of everyday life. The judges have been portrayed as active participants of the witch hunt in France, and as committed agents of the Counter-Reformation's suppression of popular culture. The works of the demonologists are seen to have been taken seriously by the judges and were used as guides to the legal prosecution of witches. The work of judges like le Loyer and de Lancre is cited as proof that the legal community was totally committed to the violent eradication of witchcraft.

But a different picture emerges when the demonologists are consulted. These writers, mainly clerics and others of Tridentine pro-League sympathies, complained at length about the beliefs and actions of the judges, who have been portrayed as their allies. The demonologists, shaped by the Jesuits and Leaguers during the religious wars, had sharp political differences with many *parlementaires* who tended to be Gallicans in their Catholic sensibilities, and were generally supporters of the *politique* approach to the problems of the day. The arguments of the demonologists against judicial unbelief and the resultant leniency it caused might indicate that the French magistrates were not, as a whole, their allies in the fight against heresy and witchcraft and did not let themselves be instructed by demonology books in their legal work. But instruction of sympathetic judges was not necessarily the real purpose of demonology books in any case. While the demonologists might have hoped to convince the judges to adopt their views, the real point of the appeals to the judges and the attacks on their record in witchcraft matters was to demonstrate that the *politique* judges were part of the widespread satanic conspiracy that prevented the rule of godly reformed Tridentine Catholicism in France. The courts were to be exposed as active participants in the betrayal of France by the overly tolerant and indifferent ruling elites. That sense of betrayal had grown since 1560, and was an important ingredient of the Leaguer/dévot mentality.

Several historians have written at length about the role of the justice system in fostering witchcraft trials. They have described a process where the "Inquisitorial system" replaced traditional modes of conflict resolution. The new system supposedly stripped defendants of the ability to defend themselves and exposed them to gruesome torture. Torture has been depicted as an essential element in fuelling the chains of accusations that are seen as necessary in the creation of witch panics.[18]

A brief review of legal procedure in early modern France might be helpful in understanding how the system really worked in France. This will help to show how French courts acted as they did, and why the demonologists were so frustrated with the magistrates.

In old regime France, as elsewhere in continental Europe, Roman law prevailed, as revived and adapted in the later Middle Ages. France had a legal ordinance—the Ordinance of Villers-Cotterêts was in effect from 1539 to 1670—but not a detailed code that specified what constituted crime, what procedures were to be followed, and the penalties for those crimes.[19] High court judges in France were highly educated professionals, who had enormous latitude in determining what cases they would hear and take seriously, how to proceed in the investigation and trial, and in assigning punishments to the guilty.[20]

Cases could come to the attention of the courts in two ways. An individual could charge another with an offence. In such cases, the plaintiff had to bear the costs of the legal proceedings that ensued. This could be an expensive proposition as cases could drag on for years, and was a strong disincentive to making a formal accusation. The expenses involved and a traditional dislike of dealing with the authorities meant that very few accusations were forwarded by peasants—the people most involved in witchcraft matters. The other way for cases to develop was for the regional crown attorney—the *procureur du roi*—to lodge the complaint in the king's name, in which case the expenses were borne by the crown. But the funds available to the *procureurs* were limited, as was their time. They had to be selective in their decisions as to which complaints and reports they would investigate and in which cases they would lay charges. Generally, civil suits or private quarrels were of little interest to the *procureurs* who concentrated on serious crimes like murder or threats to the public order.[21]

The rules of proof in Roman law were explicit and very difficult to satisfy. In capital cases, where the death penalty was the normal punishment, two unimpeachable eyewitnesses had to testify against the accused or the accused had to confess in order for a guilty verdict to be handed down. One of the results of these standards, which seem generally to have been adhered to, was that old regime courts had very low conviction rates. The judges seem to have been careful in their evaluation of evidence and many cases either never came to judgment or resulted in the release of the accused.[22]

The other result of the two eyewitness rule was that confessions became all-important in getting to the bottom of serious cases. For the legal theorists from the thirteenth century on, confession came to rank as the most important proof of guilt and as necessary for condemnation—"The queen of proofs."[23]

From ancient Greek times on, torture was used upon certain categories of accused in order to facilitate confessions. In the revival of Roman law in medieval Europe, the use of torture was broadened, and it became an integral part of the legal system, as a means to confessions. An elaborate code of torture was developed, both to make it effective and to limit excesses in its application. John Langbein states, "Torture was part of ordinary criminal procedure, regularly employed to investigate and prosecute crime before the ordinary courts."[24]

Most of the demonologists who discussed legal proceedings against witches, and especially Jean Bodin, considered witchcraft an exceptional crime, or *crimen exceptum*. Christina Larner stated, "The idea of *crimen exceptum*, while a commonplace, was given prominence by Jean Bodin."[25] It would probably be more accurate to restate this to say, "The idea of *crimen exceptum* was a commonplace, known to any student of law in Bodin's time. The prominence he gives it in his famous work has led many historians to treat it as a notion that Bodin invented." *Crimen exceptum* was a category of crime, made up of grave offences like heresy, treason, counterfeiting and murder, in which witnesses were difficult to find. To apply the rules of exceptional crime to a case was not to throw out all the rules, but to introduce broader rules of procedure. Basically, it permitted a judge to move along a prosecution on strong suspicion, even if the proofs necessary in ordinary cases were not present.

The *Parlements* were important provincial institutions, often numbering hundreds of officials, including judges, lawyers, secretaries, clerks, and guards. The judges heard cases in panels, not alone. Overall, the magistrates of the *Parlements* were well educated and conscious of their dignity. In the early seventeenth century, Bernard de la Roche Flavin, a long-time member of the *Parlement* of Toulouse, compared the *Parlements* to the Roman Senate, "the soul, the reason, the intelligence of the Republic." He stated, "The *Parlements* are the firm columns and flying buttresses of the State."[26] Judicially and politically, they were quite independent of the monarchy and cannot be seen as agents of centralization. They were also at the heart of the intellectual elite of France. Most of the leading intellectuals of the time had origins in the *parlementaire* families of Paris or the provinces. It was in *parlementaire* circles that the scientific revolution was established in France in the early seventeenth century. Descartes, Montaigne, the Dupuy brothers, Fermat, and Peiresc were all part of this milieu.

What we cannot fully know is upon what the relative moderation of the high courts was based. Were the judges sceptics on the subject of witchcraft? Did they believe, following Montaigne's opinion, that the stories of supernatural characters and powers central to witchcraft theory was just old women's fantasies? Or was the key rather legal conservatism and attention to form and rules of procedure, which meant that judges were not easily convinced to dispense with these rules and forms, even if exhorted to do so by irreproachable theological authorities?

La Roche Flavin argued that the courts had an obligation to honour and safeguard the principles of justice. He wrote, in his elevated prose, "Since the magistrates are the living mirrors of the peoples and the nations it is to them to show them the virtues and above all justice, which is the queen and the soul of all virtues, the virtue of souls and the treasure of the universe." He stressed the need for careful procedure and avoidance of "impassioned opinion." He stated, "Judges in all their actions should be free of all animosity and desire for vengeance.... Gentleness and moderation [must] dominate their humours and be the most powerful in all their actions."[27]

La Roche Flavin was a firm Catholic and enemy of Protestantism, and a believer in the reality and dangers of witchcraft. But he constantly counselled moderation in all criminal proceedings, and care in the use of torture and the death penalty. He wrote, "The rarer the extreme punishments, the more effective they are as examples.... Too great rigour renders the punishment contemptible and increases the number of miscreants." He wrote that torture was "a dangerous invention... that seems to be more a trial of endurance than of truth. For he who can suffer it can hide the truth. To tell the truth, it is a means full of incertitude and danger. What would people not say or do to avoid such great pain?"[28]

This caution on the part of high court magistrates is an important aspect of the story of witchcraft prosecution in France. Robin Briggs points out that the structure of the French legal system "gave the senior judges in the *parlements* a power and prestige unequalled elsewhere in Europe." Furthermore, "the attitude of many *parlementaires*, in the provinces, as in Paris, was evidently one of practical scepticism, not denying the possibility of witchcraft, while fearing that persecution led only to miscarriages of justice and social disruption."[29]

The tendency of the high courts to reduce the often brutal sentences of the lower courts was well known in the period. This is demonstrated by the record of the involvement of two *Parlements* in the witchcraft-related area of lycanthropy—the diabolical transformation of a human into a werewolf. Several cases of lycanthropy are very well documented for our period, and make fascinating reading.

Lycanthropy seems to have been widely believed in, especially among the common people. It was a question of some controversy in the demonological literature. In his famous but highly unorthodox *Démonomanie*, Jean Bodin had maintained that the transformation of man into beast was real, and had to be taken literally. But the majority of orthodox writers rejected this stand, arguing that the transformation was only an illusion that was caused by the Devil. There was some lack of clarity as to whether the supposed werewolf was an ally and agent of Satan in the transformation, a mentally disturbed melancholic, or an innocent victim, like a demoniac. One French physician wrote in 1615, for example, that there were no real werewolves, but merely melancholic or otherwise disturbed people who were misled by the Devil or by vapours in their brains.[30] This diversity of opinion left the courts in a difficult position when confronted with charges of lycanthropy.

In 1599, a crazed young man confessed to being a servant of Satan, who had transformed him into a wolf. He said that as a werewolf, he had eaten men and women, and even a windmill. The case was first heard by the court of Angers, hardly a poor rural village. The judges there found him guilty of diabolical doings, though they rejected his confession of eating the windmill and other large objects as a satanically inspired ploy to be seen as insane. He was sentenced to death. As was usual in witchcraft cases by this date, the case was appealed to Paris. There the outcome was radically different. "Messieurs of the *Parlement* of Paris who ordinarily, through their clemency and mildness, are accustomed to overruling the rigour of [lower] judges, having more regard for equity that the rigour of the law, moderated the Angers judgment and only relegated him for two years to the Hospital of St. Germain."[31]

The author of the pamphlet reporting this case was an Angevin gentlemen who supported the Paris judgment. He saw lycanthropy as a problem of the imagination, not of reality. But he certainly believed in the Devil and the reality of witchcraft. He stated that the strange cases of the day "serve as a key to open the eyes of understanding of those who are persuaded that there are no witches, which puts all into doubt, seeming to deny flatly that there are demons or Devils and who are, as a result, good Atheists."[32]

Pierre de L'Estoile commented on this case as well, stating that the *Parlement* of Paris had found him "alienated from his mind" and ordered him confined, overturning the Angers judgment.[33]

A case just a few years later, in Bordeaux, has left a fascinating record. An extraordinary full account of this proceeding, with the reasoning and deliberation of the *Parlement* exists, and has been published by Robert Mandrou. This long document gives the modern reader a remarkable insight into the legal thinking involved in a case of this kind that is rarely seen.

In this case, a fourteen-year-old peasant boy named Jean Grenier was arrested on charges of having attacked several children. He confessed that he had transformed himself into a wolf, and in this guise had attacked and devoured several children. He stated that he had been helped to become a werewolf by a "large Monsieur dressed in black, mounted on a black horse, who after they greeted him, kissed him with a very cold mouth, made him promise to come to him whenever he demanded, and that he marked him with a sharp object high on his left thigh." He also said that his father had helped him dress in a wolf's skin and had helped in greasing him before his transformation. The boy's father was then arrested as well.[34]

Jean Grenier and his father were sent to the prison in Coutras and the court there undertook a painstaking investigation of the case. The Father stated that his son, who had run away several months earlier, was an idiot who would say anything. He denied that he or his son were involved with any "Monsieur of the forest."[35]

On interviewing local peasants, Jean Grenier's testimony seemed to be corroborated by accounts of children being attacked by savage animals. After a lengthy investigation and trial, the Coutras court found the boy guilty and sentenced him to be burnt at the stake after being strangled. The judge also, at the prosecuter's request, ordered that the boy's father be tortured in order to "pull the truth from his mouth." All through the proceedings, Jean Grenier maintained his guilt and his father his innocence. The elder Grenier appealed to the *Parlement* of Bordeaux.[36]

The *Parlement* had two physicians examine the accused, but their opinions did not help to advance the case. They were able to agree that the boy was full of melancholic humours, and was not really a werewolf. But they differed as to his guilt, one saying that he had commited crimes with the aid of the Devil who had truly marked him, while the other stated that the whole thing was a fable, emanating from the boy's fantasies.[37]

The criminal chamber of the *Parlement* found this case strange and novel, but was also sharply divided. One group of judges believed the confession and held for execution, but others accepted none of it. So the court decided to conduct a research exercise in order to determine whether lycanthropy was real and possible, and to help determine what to do in this strange situation. Jean Filesac, a local priest and theologian,[38] produced a long treatise on the subject. He found that the ancient authorities were divided on the subject, many holding that these transformations were all illusion, having no objective reality. The problem for Filesac was that this viewpoint "has often caused impunity for such people and has marvellously multiplied the number of witches who have spread today to all places, to the ruin of Christianity." Even though St. Augustine had written that such things were illusions, times had changed, "The Inquisitors and Judges who have worked for the last hundred years have shed more light on these matters than any others. For witches have come by the dozens to the courts, speaking the same language through their confessions and proclaiming the works of their master Satan." Incredulity on the part of judges was an impediment to the determination of the true guilt of these witches, according to the writer. "And certainly the difficulties of proof often came from the incredulity of judges who could not believe in such changes and effects. In these matters, there is no less vice in believing nothing than in believing everything." So this writer was certainly not a sceptic. He disapproved of too much judicial incredulity and argued a conventional orthodox demonological view for this time. He was convinced that witchcraft was a pervasive and dangerous reality.[39]

There follows a long and quite learned treatise on transformations of plants, animals and humans, based on a broad selection of ancient sources. Filesac mentioned the condemnation of werewolves by several *Parlements* (Dole in 1583, Rennes in 1598, Grenoble in 1603), but not the Paris case discussed above.

The point is strongly argued in this discussion that no real transformation of created beings can take place in the world, except by God, who is the only one with the power of creation. This repeated the orthodox opinion. But simulated transformations were possible and were still very dangerous. Those who, through diabolically inspired illusion, took on the appearance of wolves, actually could commit the "ravages and cruelties of wolves, strangling dogs, cutting the throats of young children, [and] tasting human flesh like [real] wolves.... This should not be found unbelievable or impossible, for the effects of the evil demon helps them."[40]

After all this, though, there still remained the problem of determining whether Jean Grenier was capable of the crimes he had confessed to, and what to do with him if he was guilty. This necessitated a hard look at the accused.

> The stupidity of this miserable boy is quite apparent, reported not only by the physicians, but witnessed throughout the trial procedures and represented by the boy himself. He is a badly instructed child or truly, one not instructed at all in the knowledge and fear of God, and even less in the means to defend himself from the subtleties of Satan.... How can one accuse a poor young boy of not having discerned the evil spirit, of not having fought against it, of having been seduced by it? The means of protecting himself from Demons were unknown to him.... The poor idiot was not even instructed to use the weapon of the Christian, the sign of the Cross.[41]

After an examination of all the possibilities in such a difficult judgment, "the Court has had regard for the age and imbecility of this child, who is so stupid and idiotic that children of seven or eight years old ordinarily show more judgement, malnourished, and so small that his stature is not appropriate to his age, so that one would think him only ten years old." In order to protect Jean Grenier from society and society from him, the *Parlement* decided to confine him for life in a Bordeaux monastery, where he was already receiving care and instruction.[42]

This account of the Jean Grenier case is significant in many ways. It shows us that the distinguished elite of a wealthy, important city like Bordeaux were not prepared to treat lightly the case of an ignorant, retarded peasant boy who thought he was a werewolf. The courts had considerable discretion in how the law was enforced, but these judges went to extraordinary lengths in this matter to determine the truth as best they could and weighed all the arguments, opinions and facts with great care. This seriousness of approach, combined with a thorough knowledge of law and sense of the importance and dignity of the court, was a crucial factor in the general moderation of the French high courts in these cases.

Another significant bit of information contained in this account is that the court was split in how its members regarded witchcraft. The mention, early in the account, that a faction of the court believed, as did one of the examining physicians, that the whole case was a matter of "fables and false opinions," is of great interest.[43] This is a rare statement of the real existence of some degree of scepticism in areas of witchcraft beliefs on the part of the *parlementaires* of a major provincial capital.

We should not exaggerate the degree or the importance of this scepticism, though. Filesac, who seems to have agreed wholeheartedly with the final disposition of the case, was no sceptic. He stated clearly that he was a believer in the reality and danger of demons and witches. He also was certainly familiar with orthodox Catholic demonology.

The merciful and reasonable outcome of this case could have come only in part from judicial incredulity. Probably much more important was the scrupulousness on the part of the magistrates in the following of correct procedures in these difficult cases involving the occult. There is certainly no hint of bloodthirstiness, contempt or fear of the peasants in this text, or a desire to suppress their culture that could override their valued traditional legal conservatism.

For Mandrou, the prime interest in this case is the divergence in the approaches in the two levels of justice. He contrasted the gullible and severe approach of the local court with the scrupulousness and incertitude of the *Parlement*.[44] But for Caroline Oates, this difference is more apparent than real. She states that the lower court could afford to look tough to satisfy local opinion, and sentence Grenier to death, precisely because they knew that an appeal would follow automatically. If the *Parlement* overturned the judgment, that was not their problem. This let the local court off the hook.[45]

This case is a good example of how the judicial appeal process worked to moderate the often severe penalties of local courts. It meant that, in France, executions for witchcraft and other demonically inspired offences were not very common. This is also a good example of the sort of case that would lead zealot critics to find the mildness and moderation of the *Parlements* objectionable, and lead them to charge the higher magistrates with being soft on witches, to the grave detriment of Christian society.

The interplay between religious politics and the institutions of justice in late-sixteenth-century France is central to the issue of witchcraft in that country. While France's demonologists made strong arguments and called for an intense prosecution of witches, the courts did not respond. Relying on their traditional moderation in legal and religious issues, the high magistrates did not act as the demonologists wanted. Rather than forming a united front with the zealot Catholic polemicists, the judges formed the main obstacle to their program.

Three

Politics and Demonic Possession

After the death of Francis II in 1560 the Catholic zealots came to see themselves as an unjustly spurned minority. Unable to impose their will on the royal government and the administration of justice through political or military means, they had to resort to other methods to increase their support and to make progress toward the establishment of the kingdom of God in France.

They utilized the well-established means of pulpit, press and processions in a very effective way, but more spectacular methods were adopted as well. One such technique was the theatrical public exorcism of possessed women. These spectacles played a significant part in the propaganda war that accompanied the military campaigns of the era. These ceremonies served as vivid demonstrations of the power of the Catholic Church to free possessed people (demoniacs) from their demons. It was one such spectacular event in 1566 that ushered demonological literature into France.

The complex and explosive mixture of religion and politics of the French religious wars forms the context for the development and flour-

---

Notes to Chapter Three are on pp. 157-59.

ishing of demonological literature as one of the forms of propaganda used. Diabolical possession cases played a special role in the ideological contests of the period. They were theatrically staged and highly publicized in order to gain the widest possible audience for the claims of the exorcists that Protestantism (and toleration of Protestantism) was evil, fomented by the Devil, and that the Catholic church was the only true church because only it could successfully force possessing demons to leave their victims.

Belief in the demonic possession of humans is very ancient and widespread. This belief was grafted onto the diabolism and witchcraft beliefs that came to be prevalent in early modern Europe. As the inheritors of Christ's gifts as an exorcist, the Christian churches of the age used ceremonies of exorcism as the way both to free the victims and to prove their claims to be true successors of Christ.

Those people who were believed to be possessed by demons were seen as the victims of the Devil's malice. They were not perceived to be evil themselves and were not regarded as witches. In several French cases in the seventeenth century, discussed toward the end of this chapter, the possessed women accused another person of causing their possession with the aid of the Devil. These people were then accused of witchcraft and tried.

Robert Mandrou devoted much of his work to cases of possession. As William Monter points out, "After reading Robert Mandrou's *Magistrats et sorciers en France au XVIIe siècle* (1968), one finds it hard to escape the conclusion that the French had their own special obsession about witchcraft; they tended to put great emphasis on demonic possession, which seems to have been a relatively unimportant feature of witchcraft in both England and Germany."[1]

Since 1968, several important studies have shown that demonic possession cases occurred all across Europe, and that they attracted considerable attention. D.P. Walker, Erik Midelfort, Philip Soergel and Lyndal Roper have examined cases in England and Germany and have provided a corrective to Mandrou's opinion.[2]

Mandrou recognized the political aspect of the early French possession cases, but saw this as a demonological "confusion," only temporarily uniting witchcraft with heresy. He stated that after 1580, with the appearance of Jean Bodin's *Démonomanie*, the confusion ended and witchcraft recovered its "autonomy," again free of political concerns and manipulations.[3]

William Monter, D.P. Walker and Henri Weber have pointed out the political aspects of demonic possession cases in sixteenth-century France.[4]

These writers have examined the anti-Protestant propaganda element that was central to these incidents. While Walker and Weber have correctly noted this aspect of the big French exorcism cases, their analyses did not go far enough. As much as the Protestants, the uncommitted Catholic majority that seemed to tolerate the new heresy was the target of much zealot propaganda, including exorcisms and the published accounts of them. Clearly too, a special target was the influential Gallican Catholic group, powerful in government and in the law courts. This group, according to the zealots, bore a special responsibility for the growth of heresy. The indifferent could perhaps be converted to a more committed position and mobilized in the combat against Protestantism. The moderate Gallicans, unwilling to go to the limit to destroy the heretics, had to be destroyed along with them, or at least discredited and neutralized.

The focus for the beginning of demonology as part of the Catholic war of ideas in France was the exorcism of Nicole Aubrey (or Obry) in 1566. This case was conducted in public in a glare of propaganda. The widely distributed accounts of the exorcism that appeared several years after the case took place were the first major Catholic demonological works in France. From that time on, demonology in France was exclusively Catholic. The pattern established in the early works proved to be extremely durable, lasting for the life span of demonology as a form of religious literature, about sixty years in France.

The case of Nicole Aubrey began on 3 November 1565, and came to a climax on 8 February 1566. As Henri Weber points out,

> The date of the 'miracle' is significant. It was a period of a fragile peace, in which the two religions confronted each other with intense propaganda that degenerated sometimes into violence. Royal power tried to maintain an equilibrium that was ceaselessly compromised. If Laon was a city with a Catholic majority, the Protestants were very influential in the region. The prince of Condé ... lived not far away, at the Chateau de La Fere.[5]

In November of 1565, Nicole Aubrey, a young woman of fifteen or sixteen, was diagnosed as possessed by demons as a result of the torments she suffered following a vision of her late grandfather. Her body went into such contortions, according to an eyewitness, that it required twelve or fifteen men to hold her down. When Nicole Aubrey spoke, her voice was described as gruff and frightening.[6] These were classic symptoms of possession. She was first exorcized in her home town by a succession of priests, but to little avail. Nicole was eventually moved to the troubled and divided provincial capital of Laon on 24 January 1566. As soon as Nicole appeared there the case took on a political dimension, becoming a contest between Catholics and Protestants. The Protestants tended to scoff at her claims, arguing that the whole business was a hoax. They tried to get the exorcisms halted. Each day Nicole was taken in a great procession to the cathedral to be exorcized in public on a specially constructed scaffold. Ordered to speak by the exorcist, the main devil possessing Nicole revealed himself as Prince Beelzebuth, one of the major demons. Beelzebuth also made it clear that he was Prince of the Protestants, referring to them often as "my Huguenots." The exorcist forced Beelzebuth to talk, and he delivered sermons on the cruelty and infidelity of the Huguenots, a popular theme of Catholic preachers during the religious wars. He even told how local Huguenots had stolen a Communion wafer, cut it up and boiled and burned the pieces. Beelzebuth raged, "I with my obstinate Huguenots will do Him [Christ] more evil than the Jews did!"[7] The charging of the Protestants with this particular offence, and the comparison to the Jews is extremely interesting, since one of the things that Jews had traditionally been charged with in medieval polemical literature was the desecration of the Host.[8]

Many devils were convinced to leave Nicole in the early exorcisms. "The Catholics in great joy gave thanks to God, being more confirmed in their faith; while some Huguenots returned to the way of salvation, others became more and more stubborn, mocking the entire proceeding thing." Some even made threats against her life, according to a Catholic chronicler of the event.[9]

The prince of Condé, one of the leading Protestant nobles in France, then intervened in the case by ordering Nicole imprisoned as an imposter. She was quickly released, however, by order of King Charles IX. The exorcisms continued and on 8 February 1566, Beelzebuth dramatically left Nicole's body. Florimond de Raemond, later a member of the *Parlement* of Bordeaux and an eyewitness, reported,

> Finally Beelzebub, conjured by the presence of the precious body of Jesus Christ [the Host], left and quit his prison [Nicole's body] after having made smoke and caused two claps of thunder, leaving a thick fog that encircled the belltowers of the church, and all those in attendance were delighted at such a great marvel. How long, oh impenitent souls, will you rot in your incredulity and abuse the patience of God?[10]

This incident, widely reported throughout Europe, became known as the "Miracle of Laon" and was regarded as a great victory of the beleaguered Catholic church. As Raemond stated, it was a "Famous miracle, one of the greatest that the human eye has witnessed, and that the devils could not obscure."[11] Again the Catholics rejoiced. And even more important, some Protestants were convinced by the miracle to reconvert to Catholicism, saying, according to witnesses," I believe. Because I have seen it. I will no longer be a Huguenot. Damned are those who fooled me. Now I know the Mass is good and that the priests are virtuous." Those who did not convert "denied the most certain sense of sight, hearing and touch, and were half-mad to see such a miracle."[12]

This dramatic development lent itself naturally to further propaganda exploitation. Jean Boulaese, Professor of Hebrew at Montagu College of the University of Paris went to Laon to gather information on the event in order to produce a book on it. His effort was interrupted by the outbreak of war, and his lengthy study of the exorcism of Nicole only appeared in 1575.

For Boulaese, the lesson was clear: "Outside the Catholic Church there is no salvation. Whatever is said to the contrary is pure invention, either of the Devil, the enemy of God and man, or of pure human ignorance or malice. For true faith and religion makes us know our God and our enemy, the Devil." The reasons for possession were clearly stated by the Devil as he was being exorcized, "I entered into this whore ... by the commandment of God for the sins of the people, to show that I am a devil and to convert or to harden the Huguenots to make everyone one or the other. (We understood this to mean that all men would be Catholics and not heretics, though they tried what they could)."[13]

In the next few years, several interesting possession-exorcism cases occurred, which while they did not become as widely notorious as the Miracle of Laon, carried forward and refined the lines of argumentation established in that case. In 1582 a monk from Soissons, Charles Blendec, published a work on possession. He argued that there were numerous atheists who maintained "that there is no God to take vengeance and punish their iniquities and the enormous sins they commit ... they have believed that He had no need of executioners (which are the devils) to carry out divine justice." Blendec described a case in 1582 in which a twelve-year-old boy was possessed. He stated,

> God sometimes waters a dry branch, to make it green again and bear fruit, as He has done in our time in this deplorable France, by the admirable miracle of Laon ... to extirpate the heresies that grow in our time. In order to induce us constantly to embrace and to have for our mother the Apostolic Roman Catholic Church and receive the holy Council of Trent, through the mistrust of which for twenty years God has given us and visited us with His rods which make us cry to Him for mercy, as the true and good child cries to his father.

In this rather convoluted sentence, Blendec is saying that the trials France was going through were the direct cause of the refusal of the *Parlements* to register the edicts of the Council of Trent. For this act of defiance on the part of the Gallican magistrates, God was punishing the whole kingdom. The boy was freed of his demons by having a Host forced into his mouth. Blendec continued, "that the cross and holy water, together with holy litanies and the relics of the holy martyrs, confessors and virgins fought in this miracle for the Apostolic Church against the heresies and atheism of our times."[14] This is an extraordinarily clear statement of the zealot view and of the way in which the whole panoply of the Church was utilized to defend its claims of unique power and truth.

Another of these cases occurred in 1598 and was reported in a lengthy work by Louis Richeome, a Bordeaux Jesuit who, over three decades published several works on demons, atheism and religious politics. For Richeome, it was a special sign of the truth of the Catholic Church that it could successfully exorcise demons from possessed people. He stated

> There is nothing better known in the primitive church than (its ability) to chase devils out of peoples' bodies, which has been handed down to this day: and this power has always opposed, as a bright star and strong defense of the truth of the Christian religion against the blindness and the calumnies of the unbelievers.... The experience of many demoniacs who have been conjured in our times, serves us as a great torch in order to know the truth.

Richeome stated that Luther had tried to exorcise a demoniac but had failed: "not he, nor any heretic has ever been able to do such exploits as our exorcists do against Devils—believe that this is an evident sign that the spirit of God is not with you and is with us ... if you cannot chase devils and we do chase them, then your religion is vain.... Recognize the truth of our religion by the expulsion of Devils."[15]

By this time, the political situation had greatly changed. The religious wars were over and Henry IV was firmly in power. Duke Henry of Guise, leader of the zealot forces for twenty-five years had been assassinated in 1588, and no successor had emerged who could carry on the fight of the Holy League, which fell apart within a few years of his death. Henry of Navarre, leader of France's Protestants, converted (for the second time) to Catholicism in 1593, and the pacification of Paris and the rest of France followed fairly quickly.

Most historians have assumed that the political pacification, completed by 1596, was accompanied by a national reconciliation and healing of the wounds of the religious wars, and that religious differences became muted or non-existent. This view probably stems from most historians' emphasis on the political rather than religious aspects of the conflict, as well as on a desire to dwell on consensus and unity rather than on violence and hatred.

But the demonological literature of this period shows us that feelings still ran very deep and profound bitterness persisted. The backers of the Catholic League saw themselves, quite accurately, as the major losers of the religious wars. Even though the realm was still legally Catholic, the recognition of Henry IV as king by most Catholics, including the church, and the legalization of Protestantism was exactly what they had fought and died to oppose. The new government had Protestants in high positions, and was firmly anti-papal and anti-Spanish. The Leaguers hated and mistrusted Henry IV and the whole new order of things.

Paris had been the centre of the most militant League Catholicism in the late phases of the wars of religion. The most radical faction of the League—the Sixteen—had dominated Paris in the late 1580s and early 1590s . The explosive mixture of intense religiosity and inclination to violence that characterized the days of the Sixteen did not disappear when the city opened its gates to Henry IV in 1594.

Early in 1598, Henry issued the Edict of Nantes, which recognized the Protestant community as an integral, legal part of the French nation. Resistance to this edict in Catholic circles was intense. In order for the edict to take effect, it had to be registered by the *Parlement* of Paris. The conservative Gallican *Parlement*, some of whose members were still strongly opposed to the legal toleration of Protestantism resisted royal desires for the edict for almost an entire year, until Henry IV had to appear in person to order the registration of the edict, on 7 January 1599.[16]

A vivid insight into the tense and troubled atmosphere of Paris at this time is contained in the journal of Pierre de l'Estoile, a bourgeois of the city and an enemy of the League and its zealot successors. In the winter of 1598-99, his daily entries paint a picture of profound opposition to the edict by the zealot group, which included most of the preachers in the city. In December 1598, he wrote, "All the preachers at this time preached only against the Huguenots and their edict . . . to the point of speaking of bloodlettings that should be renewed in France every twenty five years. [The St. Bartholomew's Day Massacre occurred in 1572.]" In January, a Capuchin preacher stated that "all the judges of the *Parlement* who consent to the publication of the edict are damned, and that they would answer for all the souls of those who converted to heresy from that time." Also in January, "Today a rumour went around of a St. Bartholomew's to be done on the Huguenots. The Leaguers said it was the Huguenots who wanted to do it to the Catholics."[17]

Within a few days of the registration of the Edict of Nantes, the Capuchins dramatically presented a new demoniac to the city of Paris, a young woman named Marthe Brossier.[18] Marthe had been diagnosed as possessed over a year earlier. Her voyage, with her family, through the Loire valley toward Paris must have been something like a travelling carnival, with various priests attempting to exorcise her demons along the way, through all of 1598 and early 1599. During her exorcisms, her primary demon identified himself as the selfsame Beelzebuth who had possessed Nicole Aubrey in 1566. This demon, as L'Estoile stated, "Said marvellous things against the Huguenots." For the embattled Capuchins of Paris, Marthe was a godsend. They arranged great public exorcisms, to which huge crowds of curious Parisians, always eager for novelties, flocked. Her Beelzebuth preached against heresy and the Edict, while the preachers of the city echoed the message.[19]

When fears began to grow that the case might become a threat to public order, the bishop of Paris asked a group of physicians to examine Marthe. Among them was Henry IV's personal physician, Michel Marescot, who subsequently published a *Discours véritable sur le faict de Marthe Brossier de Romorantin, prétendue démoniaque* (Paris, 1599 [*True Discourse on the Case of Marthe Brossier, So-called Demoniac*]). Marescot's examination convinced him that Marthe was a fraud and soon after, the *Parlement* of Paris ordered the exorcisms stopped and Marthe imprisoned. Even though the zealot preachers raged publicly against this decision, the *Parlement* did not relent. Marthe was sent home in May 1599, whence she fled the next year to Rome.

Marescot's book was a wide-ranging attack on the exorcism practices that had been used in Paris and in the earlier case in Laon. He opened by cautioning the reader against too easy belief: "Faith is a sure and certain way to arrive at truth, health and wisdom: too much credulity is a road that throws us into falsehood, fraud, folly and superstition." He also stated at the outset that while he believed totally in the reality of demonic possession and in the efficacy of exorcism in expelling demons, Marthe Brossier was indubitably a fraud. He professed to be surprised and offended that while he and others observed her fraud "other theologians, religious, professors and physicians whether by credulity or to follow popular . . . opinion have said that the evil spirit is in this woman and have calumniated others as infidels and atheists who thought or said that this woman was not a demoniac."[20]

Marescot and his fellow physicians who examined Marthe on 30 March 1599, agreed, "Rien du diable: plusiers choses feintes; peu de la maladie"—(Nothing of the devil—much fakery—a bit of illness). Her contortions and responses to questions in foreign languages were all judged to be within the bounds of the natural. He established a rather neat syllogism to explain his views, "Nothing should be attributed to the demon which is not extraordinary and above the laws of nature. The actions of Marthe Brossier are such that they have nothing of the extraordinary above the laws of nature. So the actions of Marthe should not in any way be attributed to the demon."[21]

The physicians conducted many tests on her, that convinced them of the fraudulent nature of her claims. They found that she did not possess superhuman strength, as they could easily restrain her violent movements. When questioned in foreign languages, like Greek or Latin, she always answered in French. They tried sticking her with large pins, and found that she felt no pain and did not bleed. But Marescot said that all this had natural medical causes, even if the answers were not completely clear. He stated,

> How many things do we see daily that are much stranger, more admirable and incredible, which we do not always attribute to demons, but to occult secrets of nature? . . . There are many things that happen through the secret virtue of nature, that if in order to be secret they must be attributed to the demon to explain questions of physics and medicine, then from the begin-

ning to the end of these two sciences it would always be necessary to have recourse to the demon.[22]

Marescot argued that priests should follow tradition and the instructions of the 1583 Synod of Rheims and investigate any claimed possession very carefully before exorcising anyone. "For often the too credulous are fooled and often melancholics, lunatics and bewitched people fool the exorcist saying they are possessed and tormented by the devil: these always have more need of the remedies of a physician than the ministering of exorcists."[23] This lecture, coming from a royal physician who was instrumental in shutting down the Brossier case enraged the zealot ex-Leaguers who had hoped for a religious revival that would help to block the edict. Their response came from the Pierre de Berulle, later an important reforming cardinal, writing under the penname Leon d'Alexis. Berulle, only twenty-four, was much influenced by both the Capucins and the Jesuits and was part of the intensely Catholic circle which formed around Mme Acarie in Paris.[24] Furthermore he had witnessed the exorcisms. Berulle charged Marescot, who he described as "an impertinent and malicious Physician," with spreading a poison made up of calumny, ignorance and lies against the Church and good people in general. In order to respond to Marescot, Berulle wrote a tightly reasoned brief treatise on the whole question of demonic possession, which he placed in the context of a discussion of the reality of demons.

Angels and demons were important members of God's creation, he wrote, who existed to reward or punish humans after death. The Devil, who attacked humankind because of his special hatred for God, could take over humans' bodies, and "removing the power that was there, substitute in its place his force and his activity." This possession, permitted by God, was to be a "school especially for the rebel soul, which not having learned in the school of nature or that of Jesus Christ and not having learned to believe in God (like the Atheists) or to fear His judgements (like the Libertines) have to learn in this school of the Devil.... God has permitted that the violent possessions by the evil spirit have continued as being useful to conserve the faith as it did [in ancient times] to implant it." Since God lets possessions occur to teach people about the Devil in order to keep faith alive, possession is "a disease and a medicine together to him who endures it and the most useful disease in the world."[25]

Despite this and other arguments, Henry imposed his will, suppressing this exorcism and forcing the registration and enactment of the

Edict of Nantes. Doubtless, because of his interest in religious order, and his demonstrated willingness to exercise his authority in this area, there were no major exorcism episodes for the rest of his reign.

But the sentiments that underlay the political use of exorcism did not disappear. Almost immediately on the death of Henry IV in May 1610, a possession case exploded into a cause célèbre. This case took place in Provence, and resulted in the execution of a priest as the witch who caused the possession. Several other big possession cases occurred in the early seventeenth century that copied elements of the 1611 Provençal case, as well as of the earlier possession cases.

These incidents were major public spectacles that received enormous publicity in their own time. They were different from earlier cases in several important ways. The Marseilles case of 1611, the Loudun case of 1634 and the Louviers case of 1642 all began in convents, involving the possession of several nuns who, while being exorcised, accused a local priest of causing the possession. In all three cases, the priest in question was found guilty and executed.[26] But these cases also had features in common with the great sixteenth-century exorcisms, the memory of which was still very strong. These cases were highly politicized affairs, involving rivalries between religious orders, between secular and religious branches of the Catholic church, and between ecclesiastical and lay authority. They also reflected Catholic *dévot* unhappiness with the toleration of Protestantism.

The attention that historians have paid these notorious cases has tended to distort their significance in the history of witchcraft and demonology in France. These cases were peculiar affairs, not typical of most possessions and exorcisms, and not necessarily reflecting elite beliefs or judicial attitudes of the period. These cases took place at a time when new scientific attitudes were spreading among the elite, especially in judicial circles.[27] During this period, the *Parlements* of Paris and of several provinces were *de facto* decriminalizing witchcraft. Executions of people for this crime became quite rare after 1610.[28]

We will only examine the first of these cases, the 1611 Provençal one, which, while breaking new ground in the French exorcism tradition, constantly referred to the past. This case of the possession of Madeleine Demandols de la Palud and the resulting execution of Father Louis Gaufridy by the *Parlement* of Aix has been described in several recent works.[29]

Madeleine, a young girl of noble birth from Marseilles, was diagnosed as possessed in early 1610 by a local Jesuit, Jean-Baptiste Romillon. Unable to exorcise her demons successfully, he transferred the case to the papal territory of Avignon and put her in the hands of the Grand Inquisitor, Sebastien Michaelis. Michaelis was something of an expert on witchcraft, since he had served as vice-inquisitor during a major outbreak of witchhunting in the region of Avignon. In this series of trials, in 1581 and 1582, at least fourteen witches were convicted and burnt.[30]

All during this time, Madeleine accused Father Gaufridy of sexual misconduct with her, and of causing her possession. He was examined for the Devil's mark, "such as witches are accustomed to having," by Jacques Fontaine, professor of medicine at the University of Aix. Fontaine found the Devil's mark, and just as modern medical researchers do, promptly published an account of the examination, together with a treatise on the Devil's mark. He stated, among other things, that the Devil's mark was one of the best ways to discover a witch. Gaufridy had tried to argue that the marks on his body had been made without his knowledge or consent, but Fontaine scoffed at these claims, declaring that God would never permit the Devil to mark a good person. He also refuted claims that many Devil's marks were really scars. Any competent physician, he wrote, could readily distinguish between a scar and a mark made by the demon's talon.[31] Early in 1611, the *Parlement* of Aix arrested Gaufridy, subjected him to degrading treatment and imprisonment and he eventually confessed. On 11 April 1611, he was publicly tortured and burnt in Aix-en-Provence.

It seems significant that this incident went from being a local matter to a major case just at the time of the death of Henry IV (10 May 1610). It is difficult to imagine it being transferred to a papal inquisitor, outside of the control of the French crown, or the *Parlement* executing Gaufridy, while Henry was alive. According to Mandrou, it was Michaelis who pushed the case from a simple matter of exorcising a possessed girl to a major problem involving a third party, Gaufridy. In the process, Gaufridy was accused not only of being a witch in collusion with the Devil, but of desecrating the sacraments and feeding consecrated Hosts to dogs.[32]

Madeleine's possession was contagious. Her co-demoniac, Louise Capeau, had a demon named Verrine. During the exorcisms, beside accusing Gaufridy of causing their possession through witchcraft, Verrine preached sermons defending the church from its attackers and supporting the devotion of the Virgin Mary and virginity in general, a pet subject of the Dominicans who conducted the exorcisms.[33]

This case, and the other widely publicized cases of the seventeenth century seem to have had, at their heart, a few central issues. Those who conducted and moved the exorcisms forward were Jesuits, Dominicans and Capuchins, the most intense ultramontane Catholic orders, who remained bitterly opposed to the *politique* settlement of the religious wars and of the continued existence of a Protestant community in France. It was these groups that were in the forefront of the campaign to create a Tridentine reformed, papally oriented Catholic church in France. They worked to recreate the French priesthood in the new image. In the exorcism cases of this period, priestly misconduct was publicly condemned and the trials and executions must have served as a warning to parish priests and their superiors throughout the kingdom. These cases all depended on the testimony of the demons who possessed the girls who, under orders from the exorcist, revealed much hidden information.

The proponents of the political use of demonic possession invariably reacted very strongly to any attempt to criticize their tactics. Even remarks that would seem cautious and mild to a modern reader were refuted with violence. Berulle's refutation of Royal Physician Marescot has already been discussed. An earlier critic of the Catholic zealot use of demonic possession was Jean Bodin. Bodin devoted a chapter in his *Démonomanie* (Book 3, Chapter 6) to demonic possession, in which, through many anecdotes and examples, he defended the reality and seriousness of the possession of innocent people by demons. But he also criticized, in strong terms, the exorcism practices of his contemporaries. He stated,

> It is remarkable, the exorcisms which many resort to, since the holy prophets never practiced them: they abhorred questioning or asking anything of Satan, or doing anything he commanded. Rather, the presence of holy persons drove out the evil spirits, along with the praise of the one, sole God. In St. Augustine . . . we read that people did nothing but pray to God to cast out demons, without becoming familiar or trifling with them, and without in any way questioning Satan, as happened to some people in Germany: they even believed Satan's words, and others carried out his commands, which is a despicable and damnable impiety.[34]

These remarks were sharply resented by the Catholic demonologists. First of all, it came very close to the Protestant rejection of Catholic exorcism ceremonies as superstitious necromancy and wizardry, and their emphasis on prayer as the only remedy for demonic possession.[35] Furthermore, in making this particular criticism, Bodin was strongly condemning the very practices that made exorcisms important in France—the public questioning of possessing demons in order to uncover and reveal the ties between the Devil and the Protestant heresy. For this, and other similar views, Bodin's work on demons was roundly condemned by zealot Catholic writers.[36]

For these writers, the defence of their exorcism practices was of central importance. Father Jean Benedicti, a well-known author and preacher from Lyons acted as an exorcist in a possession case in 1582. His account of this exorcism was not published until 1611, when the Gaufridy case was going on. In this work he repeatedly attacked those who criticized exorcisms, especially those of the medical profession, who attempted to argue that the signs of possession were actually symptoms of medical disorders. He repeatedly refers to "Many mockers and unbelievers who cannot believe that there are possessions, or who say that it is fakery or abuse." To disbelieve in possessions and exorcisms was to disbelieve in God and His church, according to this writer. This defence of the zealot position helps to give an insight into what Benedicti, at least, felt was widespread learned scepticism in the area of demonic possession, and opposition to the use of exorcisms as political propaganda. Like Berulle, he stated that any criticism of these practices brought the world closer to heresy and atheism.[37]

We cannot, with any precision, know what sort of things ordinary people said about possessions and exorcisms, or about witchcraft in general, in this period. Certainly published criticisms of the zealot position were rare, and seem to have been written very carefully to establish the Catholic *bona fides* of the author and to avoid any hint of heresy. However, around 1620, two works appeared, both written by members of religious orders, which were serious attacks on the kinds of exorcism practices being discussed. In 1618, Sanson Birette, an Augustinian, published a discussion of some exorcisms in his home town of Valonges, in Normandy. Birette's main concern was that common people, "the vulgar," gave too much credence to what was said by devils under exorcism, and that it led to accusations of innocent people. His account depicts the opinions of his contemporaries sharply:

Everyone knows how, in the last few years, there has fraudulently grown in this diocese the belief among the vulgar, that everything that comes from the mouth of a devil being exorcised should be held and received as truth as if it came from the mouth of God.... Some are of the opinion that we must believe and receive as truth all that devils say while being exorcised. Others believe that we should have no regard for it since he (the Devil) is the father of lies: these propositions have been argued over the whole diocese, so that most of the vulgar hold the affirmative and this erroneous belief took such root in the brains of the people that it is very difficult to pull it out.[38]

While Birette repeatedly reiterated his belief in demons, in their ability to possess people and in the unique ability of the Catholic church to exorcise demons, the exorcists in the Valonges case had exceeded the appropriate exorcism traditions and practices. They had questioned the possessing demons on all sorts of issues, "on illnesses, death, accidents, losses of livestock, occult crimes and other things which did not lead at all to the expulsion of the devils." This had led to accusations against innocent people. Birette stated that for pointing out these excesses, he had been called "a preacher of falsehood and an enemy of the power and truth of exorcisms."[39] So he wrote his book both to make public his views on exorcism and to clear his name of these charges.

A similar case, a few years later, led Claude Pithoys, a Minim friar in Lorraine to address the problem in a similar way. He argued that a local demoniac, Elizabeth Ranfaing, was a fraud, but he had been overruled by his bishop. Before publishing his exposé, he was careful to get approval and support from the Minim abbots of Dole, Champagne and Paris.[40]

Pithoys began by stating, "It is a very certain and well-known thing that there are devils and that, God permitting, they can take over a person and possess him.... Christian faith does not permit doubt on this point." But he moved quickly to a more controversial position. By the next page, he arrived at the heart of his argument. "But a very difficult thing, where the wisest doctors find themselves blocked, is to discern and recognize a true and real possession from a ruse or diabolical illusion." Sometimes false possessions were a devil's trick, but sometimes they were pure fakery. For example,

> It is an extraordinary thing that Marthe Brossier, who fooled so many noted personages even in Paris, in feigning and simulating being possessed was exorcised as such by Doctors of religion of great renown who,

under the influence of alleged signs wanted to mortgage their souls for assurance of a true and real possession, for which they were covered with shame when the august *Parlement* of Paris made them see, to their great surprise, that the girl mocked them for their stubbornness to exorcise her; and that in effect she was not at all possessed, except by a malicious passion.[41]

Pithoys expressed surprise that so many people would accept claims of possession, "I am surprised that these people, though serious and recognized as wise in all other affairs, let themselves be so easily fooled in this matter, to say, on I don't know what signs of devilishness at all, that they believe firmly and stubbornly that there is certain diabolical possession in people, even though experience makes us see there isn't really any at all."[42]

Some people were genuinely gullible, while some few others wanted to use the widespread belief in possession in cynical self-serving ways. For both, Pithoys expressed scorn. He wrote of those who "are so light of wit, that they believe easily that fables are history and admire tricks of sleight of hand as great miracles and persuade themselves easily that dreams and reveries are divine revelation." Probably worse was the "zealous exorcist who is dying from the desire to exorcise, in order to show off his grave eloquence and Christian boldness in combatting demons." He repeatedly addresses "Monsieur le zélé" and "Monsieur l'exorciste" in a derogatory, scornful way.[43] Clearly, he was not trying to ingratiate himself with the zealous exorcists.

Central to the zealot tradition of exorcism, as we have seen, was the interrogation of the possessed person, or to be more precise, of the demons possessing the demoniac. Pithoys attacked this practice, repeatedly pointing out that fraudulent demoniacs could denounce and gravely harm innocent people. He stated, "I say with the most sensible doctors that exorcisms are not instituted to make devils tell the truth" (since devils are not to be believed in any case) but only to free the victims from the Devil's clutches. It was a mortal sin, he declared, to question demons to obtain accusations of crimes of witchcraft.[44]

By this time, witchcraft was beginning to recede as an issue, at least for the French social and intellectual elites. Few demonological works were to appear after this date, and the *Parlement* of Paris and some of the provinces had, in effect, decriminalized witchcraft. But one direct attack on Pithoys' work did appear, composed by a Lorraine physician, one Remy Picard. His attack was very direct. He called Pithoys' work a "defamatory libel" and a "chaos of absurdities and impertinences," full of "horrible blasphemies." "What he has told of Marthe Brossier is so far distant from the truth that I blush for this assured liar." It is interesting to note how fresh was the memory of this case, which had occurred twenty-three years earlier. Picard condemned his foe, "The children of confusion would be content to see all things upside down, pell-mell the bad and good, vice and virtue, light and shadows, heaven and earth, all together."[45]

One very interesting passage in this broadside deserves to be quoted, as it shows the extent to which new information and opinions were developing at this point. It also demonstrates, that in this very complex period, knowledge of the new did not necessarily mean any dramatic shifts of opinion. Picard related,

> An excellent mathematician of our age complained to me that, at high noon, having looked fixedly at the Sun through a telescope of Sieur Galileo, he felt such a discomfort in his eyes that the objects he contemplated appeared all white to him. He asked me the reason, which I thought were furnished by Aristotle, *excellens sensibile corrumpit sensum*. Brother Claude Pithoys has such strong and penetrating vision to see not only the Sun, which everyone can see, but into the souls and devils that none can perceive.[46]

For Robert Mandrou, the case involving Louis Gaufridy in 1611, Urbain Grandier in 1634 and a few others, were crucial in sharpening the issues and creating a public debate that eventually ended persecution for witchcraft in France in the 1630s and 1640s. There is no doubt that those cases were widely publicized and discussed, and helped bring scepticism on the subject of witchcraft and demonic possession to the surface.

But it is important to remember that, from the beginning, demonic possession was encouraged and used by the zealot fringe of the Catholic political movement for their particular political purposes. The political aspect of these incidents was recognized by contemporaries and there was always controversy attending the public exorcisms of possessed women. While the proponents of the reality and orthodoxy of the possession cases published more than their adversaries on the subject, it must be remembered that these demonological writers were part of a beleaguered minority, defending a minority view. The aggressive defensive tone of French demonological literature is the reflection of this context of violent party politics.

Four

The Jesuits, Maldonat and the Development of French Demonology

The exorcism of Nicole Aubrey introduced demonology to France as an aspect of the propaganda wars of the period. From these theatrical beginnings, political demonology was refined, given structure, intellectual rigour and respectability through the efforts of well-known Jesuit scholars, teachers and polemicists and their allies. France's demonologists were not a random group of unknowns who happened to share a particular obsession. They were, rather, a network of noted people who were committed supporters of the Catholic zealot party in the wars of religion. Many of these writers were intimately connected by personal relationships as well as by education and religious sentiment. We will examine in this chapter the early experience of the Jesuit order in France and especially the controversial foundation of the College of Clermont in Paris, for this is the context for the development and refinement of French political demonology. We will then look at the network of demonoogical writers that was directly involved in or influenced by this Jesuit experience.

From their origins in the 1530s, the Society of Jesus has been controversial. The historian whose goal it is to understand the role of the

---

Notes to Chapter Four are on pp. 159-61.

Jesuits in early modern Europe has to tread warily through a minefield of bitterly anti-Jesuit polemic on one hand, and partisan defense of the order on the other. A principal source for the early history of the Jesuits in France is a group of nineteenth- and early-twentieth-century works, written by scholarly French Jesuits.[1] These works tend to picture the Jesuits as saints and martyrs, and their enemies as cruel oppressors. Once the biases of these works are recognized though, they still can have great value for the historian, in presenting a detailed narrative of the Jesuits' experience and in extensive quotations and paraphrases from primary documents. These Jesuit scholars were *engagé*, but were still good historians. Also, a few studies on these matters have appeared in recent years, that are very helpful as well, though not entirely without their own biases.[2]

The Jesuits were established in Paris by their first French patron, Guillaume du Prat, bishop of Clermont, around 1550. From this time on, the new arrivals were embroiled in bitter jurisdictional controversies. The Jesuits found support from successive monarchs. Royal letters patent establishing the order in Paris were opposed by the *Parlement*.[3] The letters of Henry II and Francis II stated that the Jesuits should be in Paris for the good of the kingdom, while the *parlementaire* opponents argued that they should be kept out of Paris for the same reason.

In the 1550s the Jesuits began to found colleges in France for the education and religious formation of the Catholic elite. As early as 1551, royal letters patent were granted for the foundation of a Jesuit college in Paris, and this became a key ingredient in the long war of words and lawsuits that made up early Jesuit history in Paris.

The Colloquy of Poissy, a national church council organized by Catherine de Medici, recommended acceptance of the Jesuits and their plans to start a new college in 1561 . This was seconded by the king, and eventually accepted by the *Parlement* of Paris early in 1562.[4]

With a legacy from the bishop of Clermont, the Jesuits bought a building in the rue St. Jacques near the Sorbonne. They named their new college the College of Clermont, after their benefactor. The opening of classes, originally planned for the fall of 1562, had to be delayed because of a plague epidemic that ravaged the area, so that classes did not get under way until early in 1564.[5]

Immediately, the new institution found itself embroiled in another bitter and protracted legal fight for its existence. This time the main adversary was the university of Paris. At this point, many officials of the

University were Protestants, or were sympathetic to Protestantism. The best known of these was the brilliant Protestant philosopher, Peter Ramus, who became a leader in the fight against the Jesuit college.[6] Complex legal manoeuvres went on through 1564, accompanied by pamphlet warfare and occasional physical violence in the streets of the Latin Quarter.

The case finally went to the *Parlement* of Paris, as a lawsuit on the part of the University against the Jesuits. The *Parlement* eventually ruled in favour of the Jesuits and decided to permit the College of Clermont to continue its teaching.

It is not surprising that the issue of the foundation of a college was the centre of such controversy. The sixteenth century was a great age of educational reform and expansion. Both Protestants and Catholics shared an intense interest in improved education and both groups saw it as an essential aspect of the religious struggles that marked the age. The proper education of the Catholic elite was a principal aspect of the Jesuit mission in France. For the Jesuits, education was an essential ingredient for "the reform of morals, the destruction of heresy, the Christianization of society, the Catholicization of France—in short, the salvation and perfection of souls."[7] In their colleges, the Jesuits combined a classically based humanist curriculum with an intensely active religious life. "If the same profane culture united Catholics and Protestants at the end of the sixteenth century, their religious expression differed strongly: to Protestant modesty was opposed Jesuit triumphalism."[8] The Jesuit colleges stressed the triumphant, mystical aspects of Catholic Christianity; candles, fasts, rosaries, images of saints, processions. Their students often acted in the community to stimulate religious revival.[9] Intentionally, the Jesuits used their colleges as "citadels against Calvinism."[10]

The opening of classes, and the early years of the College of Clermont took place in a highly emotional, sometimes violent atmosphere. The new college seems to have been, from the first, an enormous success.

One of the most important and popular teachers at Clermont was its new professor of philosophy, the young Spanish Jesuit, Juan de Maldonado, or Jean Maldonat, as he was known in France. Maldonat's courses were central in the development and refinement of demonological thought and its use as a political weapon in the religious civil wars. As an educator of elite students and a popular public lecturer, his ideas were widely disseminated and his influence was extraordinarily long-lived. The direct influence of his teaching can be seen for over fifty years following the presentation of his lectures, lasting for virtually the entire life span of political demonology in France.

Maldonat (1534-83) was a native of Seville of noble origins who joined the Jesuits around 1560 and became a professor at Salamanca in 1562, the same year that he was ordained in Rome as a priest of the Jesuit order. Not long after that, he was ordered to Paris to take up the chair of philosophy at the College of Clermont. When a new chair in theology was created in 1565, Maldonat became professor of theology.[11]

Many accounts confirm that the new professor was an enormously successful and popular teacher. From the outset, his lectures drew huge numbers of auditors. It was not unusual for four hundred people to gather for his lectures. He seems to have attracted a broad spectrum of the Parisian elite. Students, priests, abbots, magistrates, lawyers and nobles crowded in to hear him speak. Reportedly, even Protestants came, though in disguise, for fear of being recognized.[12] When the weather permitted, lectures would have to be moved outside into courtyards in order to accommodate the crowds. People would send their lackeys hours ahead to save seats. Scribes wrote out the lectures and their notes were sold to those unable to attend. This popularity continued throughout Maldonat's time in Paris, and was, without a doubt, one of the prime motivations for the Jesuits' enemies' eagerness to close the College of Clermont.[13] Maldonat earned high praise from a life-long opponent of the Jesuits, Estienne Pasquier. He described Maldonat as, "versed and nourished in all sorts of languages and disciplines, a great theologian and philosopher . . . (who) attracted a great number of scholars to himself."[14]

To a significant extent, much of Maldonat's teaching career at Paris was an intellectual duel with Ramus. Each man personified the extremes in religious thought at the time. Ramus, the Protestant anti-Aristotelian, condemned the scholastic tradition and called for a simplified theology based on scripture while Maldonat set out to present a vitalized Aristotelian scholastic Catholicism. It is no accident that the centre of Maldonat's teaching in the 1560s and early 1570s was the philosophy of Aristotle and its fundamental importance to Christian philosophy.[15]

Maldonat's primary intellectual concern through many years of lectures, working through Aristotle's *De Anima*, was to define and defend the notion of the immortality of the soul, which he saw as central to Catholic theology, and in danger of being undermined by Protestants and other unbelievers. He proceeded from the point of view that faith was the necessary precondition for the study of theology, as opposed to the other sciences, where reason was supreme. Without belief, one could understand nothing. He stated that heresy had grown as a result of the impious attempt to understand the divine through the use of human reason.[16]

Maldonat's inaugural lecture as professor of theology in 1565 was a call to arms to all Catholics to join in the fight against heresy. He stated that theologians were soldiers in the battle for Catholicism, and had to cease being nit-pickers. They had to understand the major issues in order to press the attack on heresy.[17] There was to be no such thing as academic study for its own sake, but only for service to the cause of the restoration of the Catholic church to its proper place in society. Maldonat's lectures were, from the beginning, combative, directed against the Protestants, to whom he always referred as heretics.

After several years of uneasy truce, open warfare between Protestants and Catholics broke out again in 1567. The second war of religion (September 1567-March 1568) and the third war (September 1568-August 1570) were very violent, during which massacres of civilians and all sorts of atrocities became common. In large regions the rural economies were wrecked, and thousands of churches of both faiths were sacked.[18] Although the treaty that settled these wars granted continued concessions to the Protestants, the military and political balance was shifting strongly in favour of the Catholic forces.[19] It was during this period that the royal government of Charles IX moved from a neutral, tolerant, even pro-Protestant position, to an active pro-Catholic role. The king's brother, later King Henry III, earned wide acclaim and admiration for his participation in the victorious campaigns in the Catholic-royalist army in 1569.[20]

One of the principal theatres of warfare in the third war of religion was the Poitou, in west-central France. The lower Poitou was the centre of French Protestantism through the whole early modern period. Poitiers, the capital of the province, was reformed by Calvin himself in 1534. By 1560, there were sixteen reformed churches in the province. Violence between Protestants and Catholics was ferocious in this region. In 1562, Poitevin Protestants went on a rampage of destruction of Catholic churches and relics. Bitterness between confessional factions was very deep.[21]

The campaign of 1569 in the Poitou was devastating. Both sides had assembled very large armies for the time, numbering around 40,000 each. This campaign cost the Protestants the Prince of Condé, killed at Jarnac in March, following a major Catholic victory. Another Catholic success was the defence of Poitiers in the summer of 1569. The city was besieged by Coligny's army for three months. The young Duke Henry of Guise inspired the population in its resistance and his popularity and reputation grew. When the seige was lifted, the joyful inhabitants of Poitiers conducted a great procession of thanksgiving, and the anniversary of this date was marked in Poitiers up to the Revolution.[22]

The Protestant armies withdrew from the upper Poitou and tightened their grip on the lower Poitou, where Protestants were in the majority. This region, with the cities of La Rochelle, Montaubon and Cognac was the centre of French Protestantism up to the abrogation of the Edict of Nantes by Louis XIV.[23]

The king and the powerful Cardinal of Lorraine (Guise's uncle) organized a religious follow-up to the military reconquest of the region. The College of Clermont, long favoured by the Cardinal, was asked to send missionaries into the area, and Maldonat was one of six who were dispatched.[24] The Catholic church had been all but destroyed there after years of Protestant domination. The Jesuit mission, which emphasized preaching, teaching and catechising was the beginning of the rebuilding of Catholicism in the upper Poitou, and was also part of the beginning in a major shift in the fortunes of the warring factions.

Maldonat and his fellow missionaries arrived in the early winter of 1569, and stayed until September of 1570. They found a weakened church, a people in whom ignorance was rampant, and a clergy in a sorry state.[25] Professing pleasure at being away from the politics, rivalries and hatred of the Paris scene, Maldonat threw himself into the effort to bolster the beleaguered Catholics of Poitiers and to instruct and convert the Protestants. He gave a series of lectures that drew large crowds of both Catholics and Protestants. Maldonat made a point of lecturing in a college auditorium, not in a church, so that Protestants who would not enter a Catholic church could come and hear. He and his colleagues reported great success, Maldonat reporting that he had personally been asked by over fifty Protestant families to convert them.[26]

The mission also had its aggressive aspect. The practice of the Protestant religion was banned, the selling of their books was forbidden and burnings of heretical publications were organized.[27] As Maldonat's most recent biographer states, "The mission was incontestably a success" with Protestantism virtually disappearing from the region.[28]

Even though the Protestant forces had been defeated in battle, Coligny managed to move his army across the country and defeat a royal army in Burgundy in June of 1570.[29] Thus, the Peace of St. Germain of August 1570 did not result in the total triumph that the Catholics expected. The Protestant forces had survived and were able to win substantial concessions from the weak royal government. Coligny emerged more powerful than ever and the Protestants returned to many areas they had had to flee during the fighting. Protestants were guaranteed open worship in designated towns and kept their ability to occupy important fortified cities, including La Rochelle.[30] The militant Catholics saw this treaty as a sell-out and a deep injustice, and resented it angrily. The young duke of Guise, though now out of favour at the royal court, was the darling of Paris, and peace was very shaky in the city.[31] Janine Garrisson summed up the situation well, "In August 1570, after three civil wars, and after two Huguenot defeats in pitched battle, the Treaty of St. Germain reintegrated into the kingdom those who had until recently been sacrilegious rebels against it. This the Catholic masses could not understand. They could not accept the tortuous policy of the monarchy...."[32] Responding to provocative partisan sermons, Paris' zealot Catholics committed many acts of violence against Protestants between 1570 and 1572. Anti-royal feelings also boiled to the surface, aggravated by economic grievances, contributing to a general sense of chaos.[33] The sense of betrayal from above is very strong throughout the polemical literature produced by Catholic zealot writers, and even stronger in their demonological works. It is crucial in attempting to understand the Catholic zealot mentality of the next several decades.

When Maldonat returned to Paris for the new academic year, he must have been exhausted but tremendously exhilarated from his experience on the front lines. His lectures for the next few years were shaped by that experience. It was in these lectures, specifically those of 1571 and 1572, that a theologically refined and sophisticated Catholic demonology was presented to a large Paris elite audience. Again, these lectures were tremendously popular. The lectures concerning demons were delivered on Sundays and holidays and were deliberately presented in a simpler-than-usual Latin style in order to appeal to as wide an educated audience as possible.[34]

It is a godsend for the historian that full notes to these lectures were published some thirty-five years later by a former student, one François de la Borie, canon of the cathedral of Perigeux. La Borie translated his notes into French for a wide lay public audience as a *Traicté des anges et demons* by Maldonat.[35] This publication should not be considered as Maldonat's own work, according to J.M. Prat, Maldonat's nineteenth-century biographer. Prat did a detailed comparison of this publication with the Latin manuscripts of Maldonat's courses and stated that while there were some errors and omissions in la Borie's work, he seems to have been a good and serious student, and his work is very helpful in revealing Maldonat's arguments.[36] Other evidence supports the accuracy of la Borie's work. Another of Maldonat's students, Martin del Rio, was later a well-known authority on demonology and authored a major work in the field. Del Rio's 1599 work has large chunks that compare closely with la Borie's text and obviously were based on his notes from the same 1570-72 lectures.[37]

Many of the principal themes presented by Maldonat may have already been present in thinking and writing about the Devil and his place in the world. Maldonat, like most theological thinkers of this time, did not intend to be original. The importance of these lectures in the history of demonology in France lies not necessarily in their originality, but in the strength and unity of Maldonat's arguments, in his tremendous prestige as an authoritative orthodox Catholic theologian and his popularity as a learned lecturer. We must keep in mind the intensely inflamed atmosphere of Paris between 1570 and 1572 as the necessary context, that meant that these lectures were calculated and formulated to have a powerful effect.

From the beginning, Maldonat stuck to the theme of the battle of ideas, parallelling the military conflicts. He stated, "We are accustomed to disputing theological issues against Atheists, Jews, Philosophers and Heretics. These are the sorts of adversaries the theologian must oppose to defend religion."[38] Maldonat enlarged on the theme, recently exposed in the exorcism of Nicole Aubrey in Laon, of the intimate connection between heresy and demons. He stated authoritatively that witches had always accompanied heretics. "In Bohemia and Germany, the Hussite heresy was accompanied by such a storm of demons that witches were busier than heretics." Then Geneva was infected by witches, and they spread thence to France. He enumerated the reasons that "magical arts follow heresy": Demons live with heretics; after a violent outburst, heresy degenerates into atheism and magic; the "curious arts" follow heresy like a plague; demons use heretics to deceive mankind. All this was made possible and worsened through the negligence of unfit or undedicated priests.[39]

A sin that helped to connect heresy with witchcraft was curiosity. "For there is nothing that helps the devil more than curiosity, in which he is well studied. That is why there are more women than men who are witches, since women are more inclined to curiosity."[40]

Maldonat charged that his contemporary heretics, like those of ancient times, denied the reality of angels as well as of demons.[41] This was a great sin, equal to atheism. He claimed to be steering a middle course, through opposing intellectual extremes:

> Some believe that the devil appears to no one. Others on the contrary are so credulous that whatever presents itself to their view, they believe it is a demon. Both are in error: the first derives from various causes, like the impiety of some who do not believe in either God or the Devil. There are many of these today, who boast openly that they would give all their goods to anyone who could show them a demon. . . . For others the error is too much faith—that is to say indiscreet faith—supported by great stubbornness.[42]

Maldonat also confirmed the theological correctness of many elements of current witchcraft beliefs, such as the reality of the transportation of witches to sabbats, sometimes through the use of ointments, and that witches sometimes murdered infants to produce these ointments.[43] Throughout the lectures, he emphasized that the Calvinist heretics denied these facts, and that this denial was a significant aspect and sign of their heresy. For example, he stated that witches could make themselves invisible, with the help of the Devil. But "It is easy for Calvin to respond that they cannot, since he denies that our Lord Jesus Christ was often rendered invisible . . . demons can do it too." These transformations were denied by the Protestants, who also denied the mystery of transubstantiation.[44] It was important to point out though, that the Devil could not do real transformations. This was reserved for God. The Devil could only alter the appearance of things, or fool the judgment of an observer—what Maldonat called "false miracles."[45]

Throughout the lectures, then, Maldonat defended the reality and the importance of the Devil and of demons, of the underworld, and of many aspects of witchcraft beliefs, like the sabbat. He emphasized that these were correct and to disbelieve in them was heretical in itself, and was part of the Protestant heresy as well. He cited the famous fifteenth-century German demonological text, the *Malleus Maleficarum* in the lectures, and it was clearly an important source for him. He presented a detailed and learned account of the intimate connection that tied the Devil, witches and heretics together. This line of argumentation became a central theme in French demonology for several generations.

Jean Delumeau, in his brilliant study *La peur en occident*, points out a connection between heresy and demonology in early modern Europe. His argument centres on a general fear of heresy that, as early as the fourteenth century, became a near obsession of certain Catholic writers. According to Delumeau, the demonologists, from the fifteenth century on, took over these fears and incorporated them into their works. They tended to call witchcraft a heresy, and treated witchcraft and heresy as aspects of a single horrendous crime.[46] But what Maldonat did was subtly but significantly different. He, as other Catholic polemicists, labelled the Protestants as heretics and always referred to them as such. Then he argued that in their heresy, they were inspired by and allied to the Devil. He always stressed the intimate connection of witchcraft and heresy, arguing that the Devil made both possible and benefitted from their growth. In other words, rather than only saying that witches were heretics, Maldonat inferred strongly that the modern Protestant heretics were witches.

Maldonat's influence was powerful. For what he presented in a thorough, respectable and scholarly form, was a detailed diabolization of Protestant heretics. The diabolization of heresy in the 1571-72 academic year in Maldonat's lectures must be included among the factors contributing to the fury of the popular pogrom phase of the St. Bartholomew's Day Massacre in Paris, which began on 24 August 1572. In three days of bloodletting, some 3,000 Paris Protestants were murdered by Catholic mobs, led by the Paris militia. The close identification of heresy with the Devil—that the Devil encouraged the development of heresy in the first place and benefitted from its growth and spread must have been a significant aspect of the process that Janine Garrisson calls the "marginalization" of the Protestants.[47]

Modern historians have discussed many aspects of this most dramatically violent incident in the French Wars of Religion. Economic, social and political factors underlying the massacre have all been analyzed in recent studies. Natalie Davis has pointed out the imagery used by Catholic propagandists to describe the Protestants as polluting vermin, and the Catholic crowds of Paris' sense of rightness in the murder of heretics, the sense that they were only imposing proper justice in the name of the king.[48] Garrisson emphasized the sense, among the Catholics of Paris, that the Huguenots were rebels who had caused years of violence and instability and that they were outsiders from the general community by their dress and comportment. According to Garrisson, these factors helped to produce violent hatred of the Protestants, and fuelled the popular pogrom against them.[49] To these factors we should add the possible effect of Maldonat's very popular lectures during the year leading up to the massacres. That the Protestants were also described as allies of the Devil, and participants in witchcraft, must have helped to focus and solidify the hatred that many Paris Catholics felt.

Maldonat's lectures had been delivered to an elite, though fairly broad audience, in easy Latin. We must assume that many preachers of the city must have taken Maldonat's message, heard first- or second-hand, and integrated his political demonology into their sermons. In this way, the vivid image of heretic as demon worshipper was widely broadcast. Paris preachers were a violent lot, and they called over and over again for the extermination of the heretics.[50]

The royal court, too, was deeply affected by the demon-heretic connection. A chilling preview of the massacre took place on 20 August 1572, as part of the celebration of the marriage of the young Protestant prince, Henry of Navarre to Marguerite de Valois, the daughter of Catherine de Medici. At the Hôtel de Bourbon, a masque called *The Mystery of the Three Worlds* was performed. In it, knights representing Condé and Navarre, the leaders of the Protestant forces, attempted to gain entrance into the heavenly Eden. They were repulsed by angelic knights representing the king and his brothers, who threw them down into hell, where they were locked in by demons.[51] Symbolically, the Protestants were murdered and sent to hell, where they belonged, to lodge with their master, the Devil.

According to Paul Schmitt, neither Maldonat nor the Jesuits of Paris were directly involved in the massacres.[52] However, many of them rejoiced at news of the massacre, interpreting it as God's providence at work, dispensing justice to the heretics. One French Jesuit, Father Ponce Corgordan, described the massacre as "a very happy event, very much desired by all Catholics."[53] The Jesuits of the College of Clermont could not have been very sorry to learn of the murder of their long-time enemy, Peter Ramus, at his College of Presles on the third day of the massacre.[54]

A month after the Paris bloodletting, a well-known fervent zealot Jesuit priest, Emond Auger, preached a series of violent sermons in Bordeaux, explicitly calling for the extermination of the heretics. His sermons had their desired effect, touching off a three-day bloodbath in which several hundred Protestants were killed. It is not clear if he knew Maldonat's message directly, but his imagery at times seemed to reflect a similar message. A contemporary noted, "Speaking of angels, through whom God had executed his threats and vengeance, he cried, 'Who has carried out the judgement of God in Paris? The Angel of God. Who has carried it out in Orléans? The Angel of God. Who has carried it out in many other cities of the kingdom? The Angel of God. Who will carry it out in the city of Bordeaux? It will be the Angel of God.' "[55]

If we must hypothesize about the influence of Maldonat's lectures on the St. Bartholomew's Day massacres, their centrality to the development of demonology in France is clear and undeniable. Several of France's major demonological authors of the next generation were students at the College of Clermont between 1565 and 1572, knew Maldonat and heard his famous lectures. These authors acknowledged their debt to Maldonat, and cited him frequently in their own works. Martin Del Rio, Louis Richeome and Pierre de Lancre were among this number.

Del Rio (1551-1608) published a wide-ranging, encyclopedic work on demons and witchcraft in 1599. It was an enormously popular work. Brian Levack states, "Printed twenty times and translated into French in 1611, Del Rio's work became the most popular and authoritative witchcraft treatise of the seventeenth century."[56] So much of Del Rio's work was based directly on the 1570-72 lectures of Maldonat that, to a large extent, it represents the further dissemination of Maldonat's ideas and formulations. Much of the work reads like a paraphrase of Maldonat, with many passages quoted at length. For example, Del Rio reproduced Maldonat's reasons for the relationship between heresy and the Devil in virtually the same terms as la Borie's version of Maldonat.[57]

Del Rio's demonology was highly political, as Maldonat's had been. Early in his work, he stated that his age suffered more from witches than had any other. The principal reason for this "is the languor and distrust of the Catholic faith among us. For it is faith alone that is capable of breaking the counsel and artifice of the Devil." Where the faith is weak, the Devil is strong, as in Africa and Asia among the Mohammedans, in Italy and other countries among lukewarm Catholics called *Politiques*. In all these places, I say, magical superstition has planted its roots.... Certainly that the filth of magic accompanies heresy and follows it like a shadow follows the body is such a clear fact that whomever doubts it doubts the day and makes night out of high noon. The principal heretics have been magicians.

In Germany, it was the Lutherans, while Switzerland, England, Scotland, France and Flanders "have been mainly poisoned with this venom by Calvinism."[58]

Del Rio also followed his master in his discussion of the powers of the Devil. He emphasized that the Devil could not perform real miracles, but only create appearances of miracles through illusion or occult effects. He stated, "No one can change the order of nature except the Author of Nature himself, and no one can annul the laws of the Universe, except He who has made them. There is common assent among theologians that the Demon cannot carry out anything that surpasses nature." Those who granted the Devil too much power were in danger of condemnation, as were those who denied his power. He pointed out that "Luther so highly magnified the power of the Devil that he made him Lord and King of the whole world." This was a "damnable superstition."[59]

Del Rio was extremely severe as to the treatment witches deserved. He called witchcraft "an enormous and very grievous crime, since in it alone is found all the aspects of the grievous and enormous crimes of apostasy, heresy, sacrilege, blasphemy, homicide, even parricide, unnatural carnal couplings with spiritual creatures and hatred against God." Del Rio's demonology was part of the larger religious war going on all over Europe, in just the same way that Maldonat's was. The fight against heresy was an essential part of his demonology. For example, when listing the proofs against those accused of witchcraft, Del Rio stated, "The third index is that witches are, for the most part, heretics, and those who knowingly defend them and their errors are worse than the witches themselves and should be regarded as accomplices in their crimes." A few pages later, he reiterated, "Witches are almost always suspect of heresy."[60] He stressed that it was the responsibility of judges to believe in the reality of witches and to deal with heretical witches severely. It was their job "to destroy and exterminate this sect."[61]

Another important religious writer of the day who was profoundly shaped by Maldonat's lectures was Louis Richeome. Richeome (1544-

1625) had a long career as a Jesuit priest and writer. He joined the Jesuits in 1565, was professor of Greek at Bordeaux through the 1570s, rector of Dijon 1581-86 and provincial of Lyon 1586-92. Claude Sutto calls Richeome a "renowned preacher and talented polemicist," who assumed the role as chief defender of the order in the difficult times of the 1590s and beyond. In a recent study of the history of Bordeaux, Robert Boutruche calls Richeome, "One of the best representatives of 'dévot humanism,' his human and optimistic spirituality prefigures St. Francis de Sales.... A solid and well-researched apologist, he was a serious adversary to the Protestants."[62]

A. Lynn Martin includes Richeome in his list of Jesuits who were Gallicans in the 1580s. But his writings were a fierce defence of zealous Catholicism, that reveal deep sympathy for the Holy League.[63] Throughout a long writing career, Richeome defended the Jesuit view of Catholicism, as had been defined by Maldonat during the wars of religion. He consistently returned to the same themes, identifying anti-Jesuit opinions as heretical and inspired by the Devil.

Richeome's debt to Maldonat was enormous and he acknowledged it often and at some length. He was Maldonat's student at the College of Clermont in the 1560s. In praise of his master, he listed Maldonat as one of the great philosophers of the age,

> renowned in France for his lessons and doctrines, in all Christendom for his writings, thoughts and religious virtues, loved and honoured by all those who saw him and knew him privately. He was my first regent in our company in his lessons on philosophy in Paris which he began in 1564. He was also my first master in my devotional exercises.... He was the principal personage in this dispute on the immortality [of the soul].[64]

He pointed out that, from the beginning, the Jesuits in general, and Maldonat in particular, had directed their teaching to the problem of the growth of Protestantism in Europe. He stated,

> France, like Europe, was vexed by several heresies and wars ... [When] the Company of Jesus began to open schools in Paris in 1564.... Virtue was so mistrusted and all the vices reigned, namely ambition, rebellion against princes and licence to all excesses were carried out with applause and honour, called freedom of conscience in which each believed according to his own fantasy and only obeyed his own senses: each shaped his own religion and carved his Gods ... the most impudent and dissolute Lutherans professed their heresies with inflated necks and raised foreheads as a reformed religion.... Among the errors was that of the

mortality of the soul, a muffled heresy and less bold to speak of in public than Lutheranism, but no less pernicious, an old evil, sown by Satan quietly in the fields of the world since its beginning and freely advanced by him during the dark times of paganism.[65]

Richeome went on,

When Father Jean Maldonat began his public lectures, exposing the work of Aristotle on the soul, with great attendance and approbation, not only of scholars, but also of Doctors and regents who came to hear him, he delivered a direct blow to this heresy and worthily sustained with dignity the assertion of the immortality of the soul according to true philosophy and the Catholic faith.... I had the pleasure that year to be his student, not yet being of this Company.[66]

Richeome's major theological work, published in 1621, was a defence of the immortality of the soul, and was clearly based in very large part on the instruction he received from Maldonat from 1564 on. Through Richeome's work, we can again see how Maldonat's defence of an important doctrine—the immortality of the soul—fed into his interest in demons, and the extent to which the defence of Catholic orthodoxy in Jesuit teaching in the 1560s and 1570s involved the identification of Protestantism as a diabolical heresy. It is also of great interest to see the relevance and the strength of these arguments some fifty years after Maldonat spoke on them.

Richeome stated that the belief in the resurrection and immortality of the soul is an article of faith and whomsoever denied it was "an infidel and without God." Calvin was such a one. "Certainly I believe that Calvin's impudence surpasses that of the Devil. . . . The principal causes of heresy are the desires of the Devil, the second is the familiarity of the body and soul, and third the corruption and perversity of man." Heretics were like madmen who were sick in mind, but didn't know it.[67]

The relationship between the immortality of the soul and the importance of demons is crucial. The souls of the dead would be resurrected and since they were immortal, they would be sent to heaven or hell after being judged. The souls of the saved would be rewarded in paradise by the angels to eternity, while the souls of the damned were to be tormented by demons in hell.[68] Thus, folkloric medieval Christianity was wedded to Aristotelian philosophy in the war against heresy to become an important theological underpinning of demonology.

One of the best known, indeed notorious, French demonologists, Pierre de Lancre, was directly influenced by the Maldonat lectures and

Jesuit approaches to theology as well. De Lancre (1553-1631) was a student at the College of Clermont in the years before 1575 and it is highly probable that he heard the Maldonat lectures first-hand. In 1609, as a member of the *Parlement* of Bordeaux, de Lancre conducted the only mass witchcraft trial in early modern France, in which he sentenced around eighty people to death. A prolific writer and well-educated humanist scholar, he wrote at great length about witchcraft, based on his educational and judicial experiences. More than being auditors of the famous Maldonat lectures unites this group of demonological writers. Florimond de Raemond, Martin del Rio and Pierre de Lancre were intimately connected by ties of kinship and friendship. They were related as well to Michel de Montaigne. Raemond bought his seat on the *Parlement* of Bordeaux from Montaigne in 1570. De Lancre was Raemond's brother-in-law and a cousin through marriage to Montaigne and Montaigne was a witness to de Lancre's marriage contract. De Lancre was a friend of Camain, who was Montagne's brother-in-law. Del Rio, though Flemish, was a nephew of Montaigne. Much of Montaigne's family was close to the Jesuits, and another of his nephews was a member of the order as well as Del Rio.[69] As contemporaries and members of a large extended family and members of the small elite of a provincial capital, de Lancre, Del Rio and Raemond must have known each other fairly well.

De Lancre and Del Rio must have known Richeome as well. Though a few years older, Richeome was Maldonat's student, and the world of the embattled College of Clermont must have been a small and close one. Richeome served in Bordeaux for several years at the Jesuit college founded there in 1572, and Boutruche considers him a Bordeaux writer. Another writer of note that we will discuss later is Jean Boucher (1550-1641). Boucher, descended from an important Paris family, was a devoted Leaguer and a central member of the Sixteen, the radical Catholic group that dominated Paris in the later days of the wars of religion. Though not a Jesuit, Boucher was a theology student in Paris at the time of the Maldonat course of lectures, and probably attended them.[70]

That Maldonat's lectures had a very wide influence is borne out by an interesting hostile reference as well. France's one Protestant demonologist, Lambert Daneau, mentioned the lectures in his work published in 1574. This book is in the form of a dialogue in which "Antoine" poses questions and is enlightened by "Theophile." Early in the work, Antoine says that he had heard of "a certain Spanish Jesuit, named Maldonato, a man of evil and unhappy name and sign, disputing on demons for so long that everyone was angry to hear so much said on the nature of demons." Theophile pointed out in response that the elaborate Aristotelian scholastic treatment of such a subject was wrong and led to dangerous and evil curiosity, the "mother of true folly."[71] For Daneau, using a typical Protestant line of argumentation against the Catholic intellectual tradition, the reality of witches (which he did not question) depended on Scripture and human experience, not lengthy, complex arguments.[72]

Maldonat's indirect influence must have been very wide as well. Many other writers, who cannot be definitely placed at the lectures of 1571-72, seem to echo arguments made by Maldonat, or particular ways that he formulated issues. We can be certain that a number of French demonological writers attended the lectures, or mention Maldonat in their works. Even if this is the absolute limit of Maldonat's influence, and this is not likely or realistic, this would still constitute a crucial aspect in the development of demonology in France and its use as a weapon in the religious wars. The authors discussed in this chapter wrote many influential, widely read books. Del Rio and Richeome were major Jesuit authors of impeccable theological reputations, and Raemond and de Lancre were well-known magistrates. Since they were exposed to Maldonat's influence in their youth, and lived long lives, they were still publishing work influenced by Maldonat well into the seventeenth century. Through their works, many other like-minded writers were acquainted with these views and adopted a position that integrated politics and demonology. This combination was used by Catholic propaganda warriors well into the seventeenth century.

Five

Politics, Morality and Demonology

While Maldonat developed and refined the connections between Protestantism, heresy and the Devil in France, he did not invent them. These themes were already being exploited by the exorcists at Laon and were being spread by preachers before they were given theological rigour and respectability by Maldonat and his students. In the two generations following Maldonat's famous Paris lectures, the Protestant-heretic-devil scenario was so frequently used in works of demonology and politics that it is clearly a central theme in the polemical literature of this period. There are times when the dividing line between politicized demonology and demonized political writing are indistinct in the propaganda wars of the civil war and post-civil war period.

The political thought of the Catholic zealot party (the Catholic League after 1584), as it developed through the religious wars, was always a mix of religion and politics.[1] As Miriam Yardeni pointed out, "the state is the political and civic expression of religion" for the Leaguers. For them, the concept of France as the "eldest son of the church" and the "Most Christian Kingdom" was powerful and impor-

---

Notes to Chapter Five are on pp. 161-63.

tant. Little wonder that they saw the Protestants as intruders and perturbers of society who deserved to be treated as traitors.[2] Elie Barnavi writes, "Who then is Catholic, in the eyes of the Leaguers? The Leaguers, since as Dorleans says, the League is 'the true religion of Frenchmen and the true state of France.' And who is a heretic? He who is not a Leaguer.... To leave the [League] party is to abandon the Catholic religion."[3] Thus the Leaguers condemned all those who did not actively back them as traitors and heretics who were betraying God, His church and France.

Denis Crouzet stresses the violent nature of the written works of Catholic partisans. For them, the Protestant heresy was an integral part of the Devil's attack on the world which presaged the Apocalypse. The violent repression of Protestantism was seen as necessary, as the only way to assuage the anger of God and save the world.[4]

It should not be surprising that demonology and politics were so closely tied in late-sixteenth-century France. As we have already discussed, demonology was the preserve of a clearly defined faction among the combatants of the time who were active propagandists. But in addition, it should be pointed out that by its very nature, witchcraft was far more than a purely religious or moral crime. It involved, according to the demonologists, heresy, treason, murder, injury, sexual offenses and property damage as well as renunciation of God and the church. In France, all these heinous crimes came under the purview of the civil court system. Among the demonologists, there was a strong belief that the king, his court, the nobility and the judges of the high courts were important in providing the moral and religious tone for all of society. Things would certainly be much better, according to these writers, if the king and his nobles led moral lives and insisted on severe treatment of witches, heretics and the host of evildoers associated with them. Ideally, the king of France was the defender of the true church. Only the monarch could, in the troubled context of the late sixteenth century, ensure the purity of religion and the destruction of heresy. That he did not seem to do so was a profound disappointment to the Leaguers and their allies and helped engender a sense of betrayal from above that is an important aspect of the writings of the demonologists. The heresy-witchcraft connection made in these works and preached from hundreds of pulpits by pro-League pastors was a profoundly political doctrine.

Many of the writers of these texts also reflect an interesting moral stance, best labelled Catholic puritanism. The new religiosity of this period, much influenced by Jesuit revivalist activism had strong elements of triumphalism and ostentatious display on the public level, combined with moral renewal on the personal level. This is what Philip Benedict called "ligueur spirituality" in his study of Rouen. Benedict correctly points out that this spirituality was "an aspect of the religious controversies of the civil war period that has been largely overlooked by historians, or contemptuously rejected as 'fanaticism.'"[5] A strong thread of disapproval of contemporary immorality runs through many demonological works, in which the Devil and his heretical allies were blamed for a perceived profound moral decay. If regarded seriously as a significant historical situation, we can begin to place this religious attitude and the demonology which helped to convey it in a meaningful context, and help to free this subject from the weight of modern historians' distaste.

This chapter will examine these areas of politics and morality in French demonological literature. They are intimately connected and together provide a key to the power of this literature, its appeal to some readers, but also to its lack of general authority in society. Ultimately, the devotees of demonology were only a small minority of the learned elite, and one that became increasingly marginalized as time went on into the early seventeenth century. This is why so much demonological literature is strident in tone and defensive, and also part of the reason that the witchcraft crisis was not as severe in France as in many other parts of Europe.

There have been some interesting studies of the religious propaganda of this period. Before the outbreak of bloody religious strife in 1562, while much anti-Protestant propaganda had been generated by Catholic writers and printers, the diabolical aspect of the Protestant heresy did not seem to be a strong theme. French Catholic polemicists attacked Protestantism from at least the 1530s, stressing that the Protestant version of Christianity was not truly reformed. They dubbed it the "so-called" or "pretended" reformed religion. These writers concentrated on the moral depravity of the "so-called" reformers, describing them as debauched lechers, gluttons, sodomites, murderers, whores and the like. Geneva was described as the birthplace and refuge of this depraved, debauched sect. The Catholic propagandists blamed the spread of Protestant heresy in France on her weak, compromising rulers, especially Catherine de Medici and Henry III, who were depicted as archenemies of the church.[6] The Protestants were also depicted as seditious traitors, who undermined the repose and security of the state. In Paris and Rouen, for example, these charges were made from the pulpit by preachers who incited their flocks to riot and violence against the reformers and their followers.[7]

Still, the idea of equating the rise and spread of Protestantism with the work of the Devil was present in France by the mid-1560s. We have seen it used with considerable power in the exorcism of Nicole Aubrey in 1566. It also shows up in an interesting doggerel poem that circulated in Rouen around the same period:

> Those who want to read (these words)
> Will know full well
> That the devil and the huguenots
> Are of the same will.
>
> The devil is in great horror of the mass
> The huguenots want to see it ended.
>
> The devil wants to destroy the church
> For the huguenots, this is their principal goal.
>
> The devil hates all religion
> The huguenots want to destroy them.
>
> The devil hates saints' images
> The huguenots break them in the villages.
>
> The devil hates the cross of wood or stone
> The huguenots throw them to the ground.
>
> So it is very true
> That the huguenots and the devil are very alike.[8]

The Catholic zealots' depiction of Protestants as moral and political subversives who were allied with the Devil and doing his evil work was a potent weapon in the conflicts of the era in France. This connection was intellectually sharpened and given a solid theological basis, emphasizing the defence of the immortality of the soul, by the Maldonat lectures that began in Paris in 1570 and went on for several years. From that point on, most of the demonological works published in France were highly politicized. It is probably justified to state that "pure" demonological works, that is works primarily concerned with the Devil, his role in the universe, and his relations with witches were a very small minority of the total output by French demonological authors. For most of these writers, using the ideas developed by Maldonat and his students, politics and religion were inseparable and the demonic aspects of the spread of heresy were a grave problem that had to be made evident to the apathetic, uncommitted public.

These themes turned up in a lengthy treatment as early as 1578 in a violent partisan work by Pierre Nodé, a Minim friar. Nodé was a colourful writer and he used his rhetorical talents to attack "the execrable error of Evildoers, Witches, Enchanters, Diviners, magicians and their accomplices ... who commit a crime so great that everyone should have such horror that it should make their hair stand on end, grind their teeth and make their knees tremble ... [it is] a true apostasy, a sin of blasphemy, a crime of divine treason."[9]

Nodé saw his troubled time as an age of crisis and woe, writing, "this storm of bedeviled men has fallen on the weak shoulders of this deplorable century ... such a great number of men and women have quit the faithful troop of true Christians, to make war against them under the ensigns deployed by I know not what spirit of error.... Alas Christians and dear fellow Frenchmen," he lamented, "seeing these strange signs mixed with so many heresies and an infinity of vices and abuses."[10]

Much of the problem for Nodé was the lack of political will to take the tough measures necessary to address France's grave condition.

> Where is the prince, who strongly and for the name of God, or through zeal for his ancient religion, will wed the cause and take up the fight for his God and for his Church? What good is the sword hanging at the flank of a gentleman, if it is not used by a strong arm for the teaching of virtue and the defence of the paternal faith against these mutineers and rebels, enemies of God, of the Church, of piety and holiness?[11]

Heretics and witches were interchangeable terms for Nodé. He stated that Satan's curse on France "is made evident by the abominable doings of his own agents among us, these witches, false Christians and heretics." These evildoers were the advance party for the Antichrist, in this heavily apocalyptic work. He called on the authorities to act strongly, "Forbid, Judges and Lords, all these evils if you can, for you have the power.... Cut the thread of the abominable life of such people.... Civil law wants their bodily death, the holy Canons ... order their spiritual death and God commands both against them, so that this race of such perverse malefactors is exterminated from heaven and earth." Negligence in this task, or "indiscreet pity" that led to mild treatment of witches and heretics would inevitably bring ruin to France, for God would punish her as he had the kingdom of Israel. "How much better would it be to exterminate such people from the earth and wipe out their memory, than to await such a great disaster and calamity."[12]

These arguments, repeated over and over again, were intended to bolster the League cause, to rally the majority of Catholics who were not Leaguers to the cause, and to incite the Catholic elites to lead the masses in the extermination of the Protestants.

The presses controlled by the League turned out hundreds of propaganda pamphlets that broadcast these violent sentiments to a larger audience. An important theme in many of these brief works was the betrayal of the Catholic cause by the leaders who should have promoted it, especially in the 1580s, King Henry III. As the Guise-Henry III struggle for power became more intense, this propaganda intensified as well. When Henry III had Guise assassinated in December of 1588, the League documents became truly hysterical. Henry became the antiprince, associated with the Devil in his plot to ruin the kingdom.[13]

The titles of the League pamphlets tell the story: "The atheism of Henry of Valois: in which the real goal of his lies and cruelties is shown." This pamphlet accused Henry of being an atheist, heretic and witch and working with Satan to pervert the world: "The sorceries of Henry of Valois," in which the king was accused of practising black magic using, among other things, a piece of the true cross and a dead baby's skin. "Comparison of two parties, to teach all true Frenchmen to embrace the party of Jesus Christ which is the Holy Union of Catholics, and chase away the tyranny and hypocrisy of Henry of Valois, associated with the heretics, who are the party of Satan."[14]

This violent tone is strongly evident in a work by Pierre Crespet (1543-94). Crespet was well known in his day as a League writer and preacher in Paris. He was a fervent advocate of the League, from its first formation in 1576, and was the prior of the Celestine abbey in Paris when he published his *Deux livres de la Hayne de Sathan et Malins esprits contre l'homme* in 1590.[15] For Crespet, all the troubles of his time were to be attributed to the Devil and his supporters, the Protestant heretics. He stated,

> Lucifer [was] the first chief of the heretics and apostates . . . never has the devil left the church of God in peace, for always he has vexed and molested it. He has always tried to uproot faith in order to sow infidelity, pull up virtue to plant vice and exchange good works for bad. . . . Today he tries to uproot faith from our hearts and introduces atheism by means of heresy and the evil arts which are practiced with impunity in France.[16]

Crespet explained that the heretics of his day were the followers of the most pernicious of all Christian heresies, Arianism, an early Christian heresy that denied the divinity of Christ. "Never did the pagans dream," he wrote, "of such cruel and execrable tragedies that are renewed in France and other places by the heretics, evil race and seed of the first Arians." Continuing his historical analysis of heresy, Crespet found that medieval heretics like the Vaudois and Albigensians were also

> the true patrons of the Lutheran and Calvinian heresy.... The Albigensians committed the same insolences that the huguenots have perpetrated in France and have blasphemed the Virgin Mary, massacred priests, pissed on the holy vessels, left their excrement in the sacred altars, denied the Roman church, condemned all its sacraments and broken images, in brief we have seen all their cruelties revived in France, so that we know it is the same demon that agitated these [heretics] today as well as those in the past.[17]

While Crespet repeated the charges that the Protestants were hypocrites, his work was heavily larded with the connections between the heretics and the Devil, and emphasized the heretics' rejection of the immortality of the soul as a primary sign of their wickedness.

He stated,

> There is nothing more certain than that the Devil makes himself familiar with those who have lost faith, forgotten God and abandoned his Church or live like Atheists without God.... [T]hose who adhere to the Devil's counsels are declared apostates of the faith, heretics and [are] excommunicated and chased from the flock of Jesus Christ... they have renounced the holy agreements they have made with Jesus Christ in order to give themselves over to diabolical superstition in the hope of gain.... Satan prances in the places where the Faith is abandoned and the exercise of sincere Catholic religion is rejected.

Crespet even stated that monsters could be born of the union of Catholics and heretics.[18]

He darkly conjectured, "I do not know what so many Demons, witches and magicians who reign without contradiction, so many atheists and heretics who establish Epicureanism presage for France, unless it is a prognostication of future desolation and abolition of the faith, so that Satan can establish his throne here as he wants to do."[19]

For Crespet, the Protestants, as well as "*Politiques*, Machiavellians, Atheists and Libertines" just wanted to follow their own depraved wills in order to do whatever they wanted. Like many other writers discussed in this study, he perceived his age to be the most unhappy time, beset by evil, impiety and maleficent magic.[20]

Crespet stated that the only way to save France was to wipe out heresy, through the severe punishment of witches, heretics and all their allies. The civil authorities had the responsibility and the power to do that, while the religious authorities were enjoined to encourage and increase the faith through spreading the appreciation and veneration of the cross, the saints and the sacraments.[21]

Many of these themes were carried on after the winding down of the civil war in early 1596. While France remained officially Catholic, the zealots who had constituted and supported the Holy League could not accept Henry IV's second conversion to Catholicism as sincere, and were profoundly bitter at the toleration of what they saw as demonically sponsored heresy. If the writers of the postwar period were a bit more muted in their rhetoric than the violent polemicists who preceded them, they were no less determined in their goal to undermine the new order imposed on them through military might, to reanimate the revival of Catholic militancy and to destroy the Protestants.

A good example of this was Florimond de Raemond, a member of the *Parlement* of Bordeaux, and relative and friend of Pierre de Lancre, Martin Del Rio and Michel de Montaigne.[22] Raemond's published works were primarily concerned with the politics of religion and the condemnation of heresy, but he made frequent reference to demonological matters including demonic possession and witchcraft, demonstrating the penetration of demonology into politics in this period. His first published work was a refutation of Protestant charges that the pope and the Catholic church were the Antichrist. Raemond, in establishing his credentials to deal with such a weighty subject, stated, "You will say, perhaps, that I should not involve myself in the occupation of another. But do you not know that jurisprudence and theology have a connection and an affinity?"[23]

Since the growth of modern heresy, he argued, "atheism, impiety, irreligion, every excess of sacrilege, horrible blasphemies and incest, massacres, perfidies, treason and rebellions: in brief every kind of vice and evil triumphs immodestly, not hidden away, shameful of its ugliness as in the less corrupted times of our fathers, but in open theatre."[24]

Raemond bemoaned the ferocious cruelty of the religious wars. While other writers, like Crespet, accused the Huguenots of unspeakable acts against the Catholic church and its forces, Raemond, in an unusual and revealing passage, regretted the violences committed even by Catholic soldiers. He wrote, "We have often seen our soldiers return victorious, with their hats decorated with the ears (of their enemies), in place of the medals and signs that our nobles wear in their bonnets.... Our soldiers (oh unhappy France! can you support such monsters) have tied and garroted living men together."[25]

According to Raemond, the *Parlement* of Bordeaux had heard many witchcraft cases. He reported,

> all those who have left some marks concerning the time of the arrival of the Antichrist have written that witchcraft will be spread everywhere then. Has it ever been so in vogue as in this unhappy century? The benches for the accused have all been blackened. There are not enough [judges] to hear them. Our prisons are full of them and a day does not pass without our bloody judgements. We return unhappy to our homes, terrified by the hideous and horrible things that they confess. And the devil is such a good master that we cannot send such a great number to the fire, that their cinders do not give birth again to others.[26]

It is difficult to corroborate this strong statement, but it would appear likely that Raemond was exaggerating considerably in order to make his point.

Another of Raemond's books was published posthumously in 1605. According to the printer, the work had been written ten years earlier, perhaps in the closing days of the civil war. It is a bit surprising that it received official permission to be published in 1605, since it is a bitter attack on the Protestants, who Raemond calls "Raging lions, ravishing wolves, monstrous dragons and deadly vipers." He declared, "An unhappy defrocked monk, born in Germany (a land fertile since then in all sorts of impieties) was the godfather of this monstrous birth." The Protestants were "the army of Satan ... an infernal monster" who had committed "crimes of divine and human treason, infinite evils and strange impieties."[27]

In this work, Raemond examined the connection between the growth of heresy and the Devil's work. He accused Luther of being "if not the Antichrist, at least his advance rider." He repeatedly called for more severe treatment of heretics. He praised the *belle police* of the Spanish Inquisition. The active role of the Inquisition in quashing heresy had resulted in "the maintenance of the lustre and natural beauty" of the Catholic church in Spain. "If such an Inquisition as that of Spain had been established at the beginning in this realm, all this would not have happened and France would not have suffered so much destruction in religious matters."[28] These are unusual sentiments for a member of a corps that had successfully fought to end effective ecclesiastical courts, and to create an exclusively lay system, one that was free from interference from outside. Undoubtedly, Raemond's views that heresy was a "pestilential venom" that had poisoned the realm overrode his attachment to *parlementary* traditions.

The only good that the Bordeaux counsellor could find in all the destruction, evil and unhappiness of his day was that God had provided an antidote for the evil infection of heresy. That antidote was the Jesuits, provided as a balancing remedy that would help to roll back the enemy's advance.[29]

An important learned Jesuit who Raemond must have known well was the defender of the order and opponent of heresy, Louis Richeome. As already mentioned, Richeome was a student of Maldonat's in Paris, who spent several years at the Jesuit college in Bordeaux after his time at university.

Over some three decades, Richeome published many works, in which he blended politics, theology and Maldonat-style demonology. His first published work appeared in 1598. It is a defence of aspects of the Catholic tradition, entitled *Trois discours pour la religion catholique et miracles et images*. His goal was to defend miracles, both ancient and modern, from what he described as heretical Protestant opposition to the miraculous. This work shows a serious concern with the Devil and his alliance with the Protestants. He distinguished between true divine miracles and the Devil's "illusions, using natural agents, that make them pass as true miracles" that could fool the unwary. Much of this work is a defence of Catholic exorcisms, in refutation of Protestant charges that Catholic exorcists were themselves sorcerers and enchanters. He wrote that it was a calumny "to name as sorcerers and enchanters those who have always fought against the devil, father of enchanters and sorcerers, to call preachers liars and writers of falsehoods and trumpets and tricks of Satan those who, by their preaching, by their writings, and by their lives, by their actions have ceaselessly combatted against the devil, vice, heresy, superstition and atheism."[30]

In December of 1594, a former Clermont student, Jacques Chastel, attempted to murder Henry IV. This act brought out all the old hatreds against the order. The *Parlement* of Paris, never well disposed to the order (except during the domination of Paris by the Sixteen) proceeded harshly with the Jesuits. Chastel was executed and one of his old teachers, Father Guignard, was executed as well for teaching treason. The order's goods were confiscated and the Jesuits were expelled from the Paris region. Henry IV, perhaps understandably, was not a friend of the Jesuits at this point. In 1597 he stated that the Jesuits "excited my subjects against me. They treated with the king of Spain against our kingdom." He publicly disapproved of their theological style as well. In 1599, during a speech ordering the *Parlement* of Paris to register the Edict of Nantes, he stated, "I am a Catholic, a Catholic king, a Roman Catholic, not a Jesuit Catholic. I know the Jesuit Catholics and I am not one of those."[31]

In 1603, Richeome came to the defence of his order. He argued that Pasquier and the other enemies of the Jesuits were "the most noteworthy calumniators seen in France since Luther gave birth to monsters extreme in their impudence, ignorance and malice." He charged them with being "atheists, machiavellians, and other soulless men, associated and sworn to fight against us, and through us the Catholic religion."[32] In this wholly political tract, Richeome again echoed the language of the characterization of Protestantism as devilish heresy that was so common in Catholic civil war propaganda. In any case, the Jesuits were recalled in 1604, at a point when Henry needed to improve relations with the papacy.

In Richeome's major work on the immortality of the soul (1621), the connection between the Devil and the heretical followers of Luther and Calvin who denied that the soul is immortal, underlays the whole work. For Richeome, the Protestant reformers were the willing tools of the Devil in his attempt to debunk the mysteries and miracles of the Catholic church and lead humans to perdition. Richeome stated that the heretics were "worthy of punishment and not refutation."[33]

The writer who perhaps best demonstrates the interpenetration of politics and demonology is Jean Boucher (1548-1644). Boucher was descended from a wealthy and well-connected Paris family. He was a student at the University of Paris at the time of the Maldonat lectures, and most likely heard them. He had a rapid rise in academic-theological circles in Paris, becoming rector of the university at only thirty years old. He taught theology in the university and was the curate of the parish of St. Benoit. Boucher was a fiery preacher and writer. He represents the furthest extreme in Catholic zealot sentiment, sometimes beyond that of the League. He was a violent opponent of Henry III and Henry IV and even of the duke of Mayenne, Guise's brother and head of the League after 1588. He was the best known of the League preachers, and was popularly known as the "king of Paris." He was a central member of the Sixteen, the radical League faction that dominated Paris between 1588 and 1593. In the pro-league *Dialogue d'entre le manant et le maheustre*, he was called the "first pillar of the league" in Paris.[34] Under the Sixteen, Paris was a bastion of intense Catholicism and opposition to any attempt at moderation. Through intimidation and violence, opposition to the Sixteen was stifled in Paris.

After the expulsion of Henry III in the famous "Day of the Barricades," in May 1588, the Sixteen controlled Paris. In preparation for an Estates General that had been called to meet at Blois in December of that year, the leaders of the Paris League drew up their *Cahier de doléances*, in accordance with traditional practice. There can be little doubt that Boucher was an important participant in this process. Barnavi points out that this document is significant because it was "the Platform of the League party," not intended for publication.

The section entitled "State and Church" is very revealing and shows the extent to which demonological thought and imagery had been absorbed into politics. The first seven articles of the section state that all heretics should be burnt alive, and their properties seized. This included all who expressed doubts concerning the faith and the Council of Trent. Article Eight sums up the tradition of demonological politics. It reads:

> And because witches have a great affinity with heretics, and that both having the same father they have wasted and infected this poor kingdom, in order to uproot all the impiety that Satan has sown and to cut short the perverse dissimulation of some judges, it should also be ordered that all divines, witches, enchanters, tiers of knots or turners of sacks, who teach lost things having had communication with evil spirits shall be burnt alive.[35]

During these years, Boucher and his fellow preachers preached violent sermons against the heretics and their *politique* allies. Pierre de L'Estoile noted that Boucher preached "nothing but killing." He also said, of the one-eyed Boucher, "In the kingdom of the blind, the one-eyed are kings."[36] In 1591 he recorded, "His sermons were even worse than the others, containing blood and murder even against the court." L'Estoile stated that a friend of his said he was afraid "that in his rage [Boucher] would come down from the pulpit, jump on some *politique* and eat him raw with his teeth." De Thou wrote a few months later that Boucher was "the most violent and injurious of them all."[37] While the

Sixteen's influence declined after 1591, until its suppression in 1593 by the League leadership, Boucher kept up his virulent attacks.

Boucher and his fellow preachers enjoyed tremendous popularity and power in Paris during this period. Boucher condemned Henry IV, defied Mayenne and threatened to slaughter the League's opponents in Paris. During the "League" Estates General in 1593, he was the champion of Spanish interests, arguing in favour of the marriage of the Spanish Infanta and the young duke of Guise, Charles of Lorraine. Charles was also his candidate for the crown of France.[38]

When Henry IV finally entered Paris without a battle in March of 1594, he declared a general clemency for his old opponents. It was Henry's style to pacify and buy off his former enemies rather than punish or ruin them. But a few, notably Jean Boucher, were specifically excluded from the royal pardon. He left the city with the Spanish garrison that filed out as Henry made his triumphal entry, never to return. He spent the rest of his life, fifty more years, in exile in the Spanish Netherlands, where he taught at Tournai. He continued to compose violent tracts against the toleration of the Protestant heresy in France.[39] His writings should not be primarily regarded as demonology, but the demon-heresy connection is always present in them. For Boucher, as for most of the leaguer propagandists, there was no separation between politics and religion. The Devil had inspired the heretics and the politiques and was thus the author of their takeover of the kingdom. The victory of Henry IV was the victory of the Devil. His violent treatise *De Justa Abdictione* attacked Henry III as a tyrant who deserved to be deposed, and is a key document in the development of Leaguer political thought.[40] The writings of Jean Boucher, stretching well into the early seventeenth century help to provide some insight into the continued bitterness and refusal to compromise on the part of the *dévot* ex-leaguers. Many of them eventually made their peace with the new order. But some, at least in their hearts, never accepted it.

In 1594, before he was forced into exile, Boucher attacked Henry IV's second conversion to Catholicism. This was not a trivial matter. Conversion was profoundly serious for the Catholic writers of this period. Every sincere conversion to Catholicism was victory in the war against heresy and was exploited by the propagandists. The conversion of a king was a complex combination of private commitment and public policy. As Michael Wolfe put it, "If sincere, the conversion of Henry IV held out the promise of not only an end to the wars that devastated France, but also to the possible reunification of Christendom under the Roman Catholic church, and its eldest son, the king of France. If insincere, however, the dangers that Henry IV could pose to France and mother church were too horrible to imagine."[41] Boucher strongly argued the latter case.

While most of the leaguers, even the intense ones, eventually accepted Henry's conversion, Boucher called it false and hypocritical. He charged that Calvin, the father of the heresy that so troubled France, was a hypocrite as well, and a follower of the Devil. Boucher called the heretics of his day "the seed of the Devil ... [as] the Catholics are the seed of the church." He stated that Catholics had had to join together to defend their church, writing, "The Catholics were obliged by divine right to form a league against the heretics. The people of God were a League, to exterminate Canaanites, Jezubites, Amorites and such a plague of infidels and precursors of heretics." Why, he demanded, should the French nation support Henry of Navarre,

> a heretic, a relapse, chief of heretics, a sacrilege, and burner of churches, a corrupter of nuns, one who massacres monks and priests, a sworn enemy of the Church, who has spent his life doing nothing else than making war on the Church and shedding the blood of Catholics.... [He is] the chief, patron and support of the heretic rebels, whose life has only been rebellion against God, against the Church and against Kings Francis II, Charles IX and Henry III ... he has diminished the honour of the Holy Father and of their Catholic Majesties, he has sustained in his own words that of the Devil.

In order to be a genuine king and Catholic, Henry had to do more than hear a Mass. "He must ruin heresy, punish the heretics, purge the kingdom of heretics and totally exterminate them." Boucher then reiterated that heresy was a diabolical plot, and could not be confused with real religion.[42]

There can be little doubt that it was this sort of statement that led to Chastel's attempt on the life of Henry IV. Chastel must have been convinced that he would be carrying out a godly act, in murdering the falsely converted heretic tyrant who had done such evils to the true church. So it is not surprising to see that an impassioned defence of Chastel from Jean Boucher appeared not long after the act. This is an extremely violent polemic, which is full of references to the Devil, and is an excellent example of demonized politics. The Devil, Boucher wrote, "pulls behind himself heretics full of vanity and filled with self-love." He uses tricks to make evil things appear good, and vice versa.

According to Boucher, Chastel's act was "purely just, virtuous and heroic." It is permitted to kill certain kinds of people, especially heretics and tyrants, "but even more so when the two are joined together." Since Henry of Navarre had done so much to establish heresy in France and to damage the Catholic church, Boucher stated, he deserved to be murdered. Henry was "a notoriously adulterous bastard and heretic who was born, nourished and raised in heresy, among heretics." The divisions of religion that had torn France apart and caused thirty-five years of civil war were "a diabolical invention, that makes friends into enemies in wars of religion."[43]

Boucher came to the defence of the Jesuits as well, in this work. He condemned "the barbarous fury that has been vomited at them and against the church and religion altogether" by the *politiques* and other enemies of the league. He saw betrayal in the actions of the *Parlement* of Paris who tolerated heretics and punished good Catholics.[44]

Boucher kept up this sort of thing for decades. In his *La mystere d'infidelité* (1614), the parallels between witches and heretics were again explicitly made when he stated that the heretics "were marked on the hand with the mark of the Antichrist, are enemies of God and his church... traitors to religion." Boucher explained, "The devil, having resolved to make, in recent times, a great effort against the Christian church and to attack this time the most divine and highest mysteries of religion... needed to drag Luther from the Augustinian cloister at Wittenberg... he and others, including Calvin, Zwingli, Ochino and Knox, seemed most appropriate to Satan for the execution of his design."[45]

"The devil," he continued, "is the father of the one and the other [witchcraft and heresy] and has engendered them in the garbage of lust, in order to oppose them to the purity and cleanness that God requires of those who serve him." He reiterated this as the close of this work, addressing his enemies, "Am I not right to have said that you are heretics, that your heresy was born in lust and that the devil engendered it in immodesty?"[46]

The work of Boucher's that comes closest to real demonology was published in 1624, by which time the *Parlement* of Paris, and a number of the others had practically halted the prosecution of witches. But this did not blunt the violent sharpness of his attack. The themes and the extreme style of writing are the same as in his earlier works. Time and exile did not mellow Jean Boucher.

In this book, Boucher condemned the Protestants' show of piety as hypocritical. It was like "the luckless and unhappy tree that gives its leaves to God, and keeps its fruit for the devil." Boucher accused the Protestants of debunking miracles. This led directly to atheism. He expressed special horror that these atheistic heretics denied the immortality of the soul, and thus the reality of heaven and hell. Those who were not under the protection of the Catholic church "are exposed to the mercy of the birds of the sky, that is to say the devils, who devour and tear the hearts out of those who are outside the obedience of the church."[47]

Boucher called magic and witchcraft "the horror of horrors, the crime of crimes, the impiety of impieties.... This abomination is the consequence of atheism and the sovereign degree of atheism." The tremendous and tragic evils of his age were all the result of the hypocrisy, doubt, infidelity and atheism introduced by the Devil. In this work, Boucher discussed the whole world of spirits, elves, and goblins that vexed men of good will. They were, he stated, the direct result of the impiety and heresies of the age. He defended the reality of signs and omens of future events, although he condemned judicial astrology as an ungodly science fathered by the Devil.[48]

Noel Taillepied, canon at Pontoise, published in 1616 an extended attack on the leading Protestant reformers. After dealing with Luther, "an arrogant heretic, full of enormous blasphemies and execrable heresies," he turned to Calvin. He stated that his discussion of Calvin was based on Jerome Bolsec's vengeful biography of Calvin, published in 1577.[49]

In Taillepied's hands, Calvin's history was a perfect example of political demonology:

> Among all the unhappiness introduced into the world by the father of lies and the author of sin after the fall of our first parents, heresy has brought most troubles and seditions ... this horrible and pernicious monster has engendered the pride of ignorance.
>
> Since the reception of the evangelical law, several heretics have risen through diabolical suasion.... But it seems that in our time this enemy of God and of Christian unity has gathered more of these heretics and false doctrines, long since refuted and condemned. And he has put them in Geneva by means of John Calvin of Noyon, among all men the most ambitious, presumptuous, arrogant, cruel, evil vindictive and most ignorant.... (Calvin's followers were) poor ignorant people and idiots who were turned away from the true way of well-being and fallen into false opinions by the frauds of Satan."[50]

It is interesting to see, over fifty years after they were delivered in Paris, so many of the themes of Maldonat's lectures continue to appear. It must be remembered that many of the writers of French demonology books in the second and third decade of the seventeenth century were, like Richeome, Boucher and De Lancre, men of the generation of 1550. They grew up during the civil wars, heard Maldonat's lectures and spent long lives carrying on the arguments of their youth.

The writers of these politicized works of demonology and demonized works of politics also campaigned in their works for a moral and religious renewal for Catholicism in France. An integral aspect of the Reformation was a heightened sense of personal moral responsibility and of the need for the religious elites to control popular morality and sexuality. The effort to establish a proper discipline of morals was part of the fight against the Devil.[51] Many zealous Catholics of this period, including the Jesuits, promoted a purified, austere religious life and condemned the blasphemy, swearing, drinking, dancing and participation in carnivals that was perceived as widespread and harmful to public morals and order.[52] They encouraged extreme austerity, mortification of the flesh, constant prayer and contemplation of Christ's sufferings and frequent communion.[53]

The zealots argued that their world was full of moral chaos and had to be cleansed in order to appease God and avoid his wrath. They saw this moral disorder as caused by Satan, as part of his attack on godly religion. The zealot Catholic writers of these texts constantly reiterated the theme of the total moral depravity of the Protestant heretics and their allies, the *politiques*, atheists, witches and doubters. Their tendency to group adversaries as moral degenerates continued well into the seventeenth century, as an attack on *libertinage*.

The perception that the world was especially full of vice was not the monology of the Leaguers, or demonologists. For example, Pierre de l'Estoile's journals are full of descriptions of blasphemers and other debauched people and opinions about the moral shortcomings of the age. In 1599, he tells of "one named Le Mesle, known as La Roquiniere, native of Le Mans and cleric in that town, [who] had his tongue pierced and both his ears cut [off?] for uttering execrable blasphemies against Jesus Christ." In 1607, the son of a tailor was executed: "A true atheist, for the horrible and execrable blasphemies he has vomited against God." In 1606, a young man was executed for murder. "They found on him three cyphers, one for life, one for love and one for money, which are the deities most revered by our courtesans today." In exasperation he stated, "Debaucheries, follies, ballets, duels and other vices and impieties reign more today than ever, as if we wanted to provoke God to anger, rather that to appease him."[54]

This sense of general moral decay pervades the demonological literature. The demonologists almost always attributed the sad condition of their world to the meddling of Satan and his demonic and human helpers, as well as the growth of heresy and atheism. Pierre Dampmartin, *procureur général* to the duke of Anjou, published a very orthodox demonological work in 1585, the year after Anjou's death. The world, he reported, was a "place of tears, sadness and travail, of illness, fears, terrors, ambushes, murders, treasons, adultery and detestable vices, where almost nothing is seen, felt or done except through vanity and lying." For this writer, witchcraft was real and appealed especially to "weak minds, or those of fearful and needy women who are already disposed to receive evil influences." He condemned those who doubted the reality of witches, saying "they have the devil for their guide and as preceptor for all their evil deeds."[55]

Many writers touched on the weakness of human understanding as part of the problem. Antoine de Mory wrote in 1590, "Our fragility is so great that we hold nothing for certain and assured that is taken in by the capacity of our senses, [which are] limited by the extent of our understanding. But faith that surpasses our senses is much more certain and assured. For the senses are often fooled... but understanding that comes from faith can only be certain, even infallible, being founded on the word and promises of our God." The Devil, who drove people to dangerous curiosity, used the weakness of the human senses to trick people into thinking he could perform miracles.[56]

A pro-League lawyer and moral philosopher, Louis Le Caron, published *De la tranquilité de l'esprit* in 1588, as a "consolation for the miseries of our time." He attributed many of these miseries to the opponents of the Catholic League, the Protestants and the *politiques*. He attacked the "epicureans and atheists who arrogantly deny the signs sent by God" and stated that they would, some day, receive their just desserts. "For without faith it is impossible to please God."[57] Attached to this devotional work is a short (forty-page) discourse on a trial for witchcraft. There is no author listed, but the pagination of this discourse is a continuation from the Le Caron text, so it was intended to be part of the entire work. The tract opens with an attack on the opinion that witchcraft is only an illusion. The author stated, "We must not doubt that witches communicate with evil spirits. . . . These unhappy witches who see devils put God out of their minds, abjure their religion, and make detestable oaths against Jesus Christ . . . they are thus idolaters filled with impiety and evil. God commands that they be exterminated from the earth." As it is with so many of these authors, Le Caron attributed the horrible situation of his world to the growth of heresy, stating, "At present, the number of these damnable witches grows as the result of the mistrust, disorder and abuse brought to the Christian religion by these new dogmatists."[58]

The political and moral concerns of these writers merged with a well-established tradition of the literary condemnation of the morals of the nobility, especially at the royal court. The charges of effeminacy and gross sexual misconduct made against Henry III and his courtiers was a potent and effective propaganda weapon much exploited by League writers.[59] These charges continue to colour interpretations of his troubled reign.

Pierre Crespet often bemoaned the particularly evil nature of his own times. Crespet argued that the rise of heresy had provided the opening to the Devil to ruin human morals. Many diverse sects had risen "which try to claim truth and to be true religion. Some are Huguenots, others *politiques*, Machiavellians, atheists and libertines who only recognise that which gives them pleasure, to let them persevere in their comfort."[60] It is typical of these writers to create lists of evildoers that equated Protestants, witches, atheists, libertines, *politiques* and other adversaries, real and imagined of the zealot group, in order to portray them as a single enemy.

A writer named G. de Rebreviettes used vivid images to charge the court of Henry III with immorality and atheism. He called the atheists of his day "these miserable effeminate ones, bearded women who know neither virtue nor courage. They prance down the street, [hair] all curled like hermaphrodites. Their greatest care is to stuff their guts with delicacies."[61]

It was a commonplace among these writers that heresy, atheism and immoral living were all intimately connected. The early anti-Protestant writers attacked what they characterised as Protestant hypocrisy and immorality. The writers of the religious wars added a diabolical element that gave a special urgency to their claims. In the generation after the Edict of Nantes, when co-existence with Protestantism was a forced reality, Catholic zealot writers developed variations on these themes. They found subtler, more acceptable ways to attack their old foes.

This is not the place for a lengthy examination of the issue of libertines and *libertinage* in the early seventeenth century. But there is at least a possibility that the "crisis" of *libertinage* was not the result of a sudden lowering of public morals or a sudden increase in blasphemy, violence and vice. Nor is it necessarily to be found in the isolated, but very dramatic cases of radical free-thinkers like Jules Cesar Vanini or Theophile le Viau. Rather, a likely source of the "crisis" can be found in the well-established tendency of the zealot Catholic writers to charge those not in agreement with their approach to religion and politics with incredulity, atheism, epicureanism and *libertinage*. For the *dévots* of the early seventeenth century, "libertine" was a code label for the range of Gallican Catholics and Protestants who opposed their policies. Since at least the early sixteenth century, "epicurean" and "libertine" were part of the arsenal of pejorative terms used by these writers to discredit their enemies.[62]

A number of writers, mainly literary scholars, have examined this issue in recent years. François Berriot has maintained that there was some degree of atheism present in the sixteenth century. Louise Godard de Donville looks at libertinism as a term of oppobrium based on little reality. She traces the charge back to Calvin and Farel in the 1540s. In the bitter sectarian struggles in France, the term became part of the Catholic arsenal. A similar development occurred in Germany as well.[63]

In France, between 1560 and 1610 or so, writers of this camp relied heavily on the diabolically inspired heretical aspects of their adversaries' crimes. In spite of their arguments, witchcraft was never a major concern of the French elites and huge numbers of witchcraft executions did not occur, any more than the wholesale extermination of heretical Protestants. As emphasis on the Devil waned and witchcraft trials declined sharply in numbers in the early seventeenth century, the dévot polemics shifted to more philosophical approaches.

We can see this in the work of Jean Boucher. In 1622, he published an anti-libertine work that demonstrates the connections between the demonological tradition and the war against *libertinage*. According to Boucher, the main thing that defined libertines was their denial of the immortality of the soul. From this flowed the rest of their evil ways. "Only evil-doing and vice-ridden men deny the immortality of the soul," Boucher wrote, and "they do not apprehend the punishments that are reserved for their crimes in the other world by divine justice.... Unhappy century! in which an error that never found its way into pagan hearts has now lodged in the souls of so many so-called Christians."[64]

Boucher bemoaned the diversity of religions in his day that had caused "great disorder and confusion in the world... a Babel." This diversity had led to people interpreting Scripture as they wished, instead of accepting instruction from qualified authorities. Worst, the libertines, "vain irreligious spirits... want to receive nothing as true and assured except that which they see with their eyes and perceive with their senses. Not only do they destroy all things spiritual and divine which are incomprehensible to the senses but they also ruin nature and all human society and political life."[65]

Thus the libertines denied heaven and hell and the providence of God. So there would be no point to religion or to good conduct in life. In concluding Boucher stated,

> Do not be surprised that, notwithstanding all these evident proofs, an army of libertines fights in this corrupted age. Not only are they the fruit of heresy, that only aims to undermine all religion and service to God; they are brought to this unhappy state by their ignorance of the mysteries of the holy scriptures, by vanity, and the presumptiveness of their minds, by the impunity of their sins and by the love of their desires; they are enemies of the purity of religion.

For Boucher, as for many of these writers, libertines were just a variation on a well-developed theme.[66]

Elite views were shifting in the early seventeenth century, away from the concern with witches and demons that had seemed so important to many people in the second half of the sixteenth century. As already discussed, the *Parlement* of Paris' prosecutions for witchcraft declined sharply after 1610, and by the 1620s hardly anyone was being punished severely for this offence.

However, the continued existence of Protestant communities in France continued to be a problem in French political life. There were rebellions by the Huguenots in 1622 and 1627. The *dévot* Catholics could not reconcile themselves to what they saw as the permanent establishment of treasonous heresy in France, and the willingness of much of the Catholic elite to tolerate it. But the intellectual and political environment had changed considerably. Scientific interest was growing quickly, as many people closely followed the new developments in astronomy and physics. The accession of Cardinal Richelieu to political power in 1624 is significant as well. Richelieu's policies harkened back to those of Henry IV, and he did not tolerate the sort of unfettered, divisive polemical warfare that had flourished earlier. Censorship was tightened and the level of controversy diminished. In this new situation, *dévot* writers, the successors of the Leaguers, had to mute their attacks. They were still offended at the existence of Protestantism. But they had to realize that many, including Cardinal Richelieu, were hostile to their approach.

A good example of a writer of the early seventeenth century who inherited much from his demonologist predecessors is François Garasse (1585-1631). Garasse joined the Jesuits around 1600. All through the 1620s he published a series of attacks on the heretics, libertines and atheists of his day, who he saw as real, numerous, and dangerous. He died in 1631, while helping to tend dying victims of the plague that ravaged France that year.[67]

In his many works, Garasse condemned the atheists and libertines in general, fought against specific enemies, especially Estienne Pasquier and Pierre Charron, and defended the Jesuit order from its many detractors. Pasquier had been dead for seven years when Garasse published his *Les recherches des recherches* (1622) to refute *Le catéchisme des Jésuites*. Garasse stated that Pasquier was a "LIBERTINE, which signifies a Huguenot and a half," who had attacked the Jesuits only because they were the chief opponents of heretics, Lutherans and Calvinists. Pasquier was a typical libertine, according to Garasse, in being soft on heretics and mocking the mysteries and ceremonies of the Catholic church. He also, in condemning the morals of his enemies, stated that the heretics and libertines hated the religious orders because their members lived celibate and continent lives.[68]

In several long works, Garasse attacked, beside Pasquier, a range of writers that he considered dangerous, including Charron and Vanini. These men were at least, he stated, public in their libertine behaviour and writing. Garasse expressed special contempt for the hidden libertines and atheists. He wrote,

> In writing against the atheists, I do not know against whom I write: for there is no one so abandoned that he has enough effrontery to declare himself an atheist by belief.... Come out of your caverns if you have enough courage.... Is it not strange that of an infinite number of

enraged spirits, we see only four or five who, as the advance riders of the Antichrist, have enough impudence to oppose themselves to the light of reason and write in horrible blasphemous words against the truth of our religion.... All the rest of the Libertines, atheists, Epicureans and Deists keep themselves covered in the disorder.[69]

Garasse showed himself to be the successor of the demonologists in his tendency to string together atheists, libertines, heretics and the like in lists that were designed to create guilt by association. He was also a colourful writer, who peppered his work with strong and pithy images. Atheism, which he called an "unhappy gangrene," took up where heresy left off. He called heresy, Mohammedanism and atheism "the three antigraces of Satan."[70] He call the libertines "tavern flies, spirits insensible to piety, who have no other God than their gut, who are enrolled in this evil brotherhood, called the Brotherhood of the Bottle."[71] In his emphasis on the moral depravity and debauchery of his opponents, Garasse harkened back to the early anti-Protestant Catholic writers of the 1530s, 1540s and 1550s.

While Garasse did not concentrate on demons and witches in most of his works, there is, in *La doctrine curieuse des beaux esprits de ce temps*, some discussion of this subject. Generally it is conducted along lines that were, by this time (1623), well established and familiar. Book 7 of the work is a familiar attack on the notion, put forward by epicureans, libertines and heretics, that there are no angels and demons and that the soul of man is not immortal. He stated, "To say there is no devil in the world, is a proposition that has its passport among the Libertines. To say that there are devils in the world is a truth held by all people of good will, who hold them [the devils] for their sworn enemies." Libertines "do not believe in God, in Angels or in Devils."[72]

Garasse also defended the reality of demonic possession, citing Del Rio as one of his supporting sources. He stated that Jules Cesar Vanini, who was executed in 1619 for blasphemy, had been possessed by the Devil.[73] Garasse, as virtually all like-minded writers, condemned as sin the curiosity and incredulity which, as he stated, had led to all the evils of his time. It was necessary, he wrote, that Christians avoid this dangerous curiosity and accept authoritative Catholic teaching about the complex mysteries of religion. "The true liberty of the spirit consists of freely believing what the church proposes to us, without philosophising upon it."[74]

So the themes developed two generations earlier continued to flourish in the writings of this embattled Jesuit. Garasse and other *dévot* critics of the relatively tolerant religious atmosphere of the early seventeenth century were the direct inheritors of the concerns and the rhetoric of the propaganda warriors of the Catholic League. As had been the case during the religious wars, the *dévots* stayed a minority, unable to dominate elite opinion, or to control the government. The situation only became worse for these writers after 1624, as Cardinal Richelieu's policies were, in many ways, a direct continuation of the *politique* tradition.

Six

Three Adversaries of Political Demonology

The complaints of French political demonologists that many people in high places opposed them were not fiction. As has been discussed, the influential high courts did not follow the demonologists' counsel in dealing with witches. The magistrates did not actively seek out witches, and when presented with those accused of witchcraft in court, tended to reduce penalties in a large majority of cases. As a result, France had one of the lowest incidences of executions for witchcraft in all of Europe. While it might be the case that these French judges were motivated primarily by legal conservatism, it might also be possible that they had serious reservations about witchcraft as a crime, especially with the highly politicized demonology put out by the zealot writers.

During the period of most trials for witchcraft in France (1560-1630) no direct attacks on witchcraft beliefs were published. However, several important writers emerged as critics of the intellectual and political systems of the political demonologists. These writers quickly came to be perceived as enemies to the cause of political demonology, and were frequently characterized as such. The three to be

---

Notes to Chapter Six are on pp. 164-66.

discussed here are well-known moderate Catholic writers who backed the Gallican option, placing loyalty to the monarch over the right of the subject to rebel. They deeply regretted their country's descent into chaos and disorder in the religious wars. These three are Michel de Montaigne, Estienne Pasquier and Jean Bodin.

These men had much in common. They were all born around 1530, at the height of enthusiasm for Renaissance humanism in France. As Philippe Desan has pointed out, humanism was always controversial among France's intellectuals. The humanistic universal ideal, based on Latin scholarship, did not suit nationalistic French writers and poets. Furthermore, as religious tensions rose in France, ideals of harmony and universality were increasingly marginal and irrelevant. These three writers' careers mirror these developments. They were educated in Latin classical scholarship and grew to adulthood during the period of the expansion of humanist education.[1] Their early lives were lived at a time when France was led by strong monarchs who sought glory on battlefields against France's enemies, nurtured arts and letters, and who tolerated a certain level of religious controversy and diversity. They were all trained in the law, and had a strong interest in history and philosophy. Their writing is peppered with classical references from a wide range of sources. It was as natural for them to cite classical references to support an argument as to use modern accounts. While their academic formation was in Latin scholarship, they were also immersed in French history, and wrote in lively, expressive French. Their outlooks seem to have distinguished them quite sharply from the polemical demonologist warriors of the religious wars, who correctly saw them as enemies whose works flirted with heresy.

Michel de Montaigne (1533-92) is the best known French writer of the sixteenth century. His *Essays*, popular in his lifetime, have undergone hundreds of editions and translations, and continue to be widely read and studied today.[2] While Montaigne's writing is witty, sometimes ironic, conversational, indirect and full of qualifications, his intentions are quite clear and put him at loggerheads with the Catholic zealot views that underlay French demonology.

Montaigne's writings have been analyzed in great depth by generations of scholars. While many Montaigne specialists are not much interested in the world in which he existed, it seems clear that he was very much shaped by his experiences. Having spent most of his adult life in a land torn by an increasingly ugly and chaotic civil war, his revulsion for violence and his longing for peace was profound. His views on politics, religion and human relationships were shaped by the dreadful reality of everyday life in a world of seemingly endless civil war.

Montaigne continually proclaimed his deep loyalty to the Roman Catholic church and his conviction that the Catholic church was the true church. He repeatedly stated that Catholics must submit to the authority of the church. He upheld official views that opposed making Scriptures available in the vernacular.[3] On his travels to Italy in 1580, he visited twice with Jean Maldonat, for whom he had high regard, submitted his work to papal censors, had an audience with the pope and visited religious shrines.[4] Furthermore, he did not, as did Pasquier, openly attack specific members of the church like the Jesuits.

Montaigne's personal religious views are complex and the subject of considerable scholarly debate. Geralde Nakam points out that conventional aspects of Catholic practice and theology play a very small role in the *Essays*. He states, "Montaigne's faith is not Catholic, or reformed or even Erasmian for it does not have Christ as its vital centre. It is to God alone that he looks, and this God is an impenetrable mystery."[5] And yet, he lived as a normal observant Catholic.

Since Montaigne's personal beliefs seemed to centre on God who cannot be known by humans, he adopted a position of weighing alternatives, constantly withholding judgment. He was very critical of those who were sure that they knew God's intentions and who were willing to fight and kill over what he saw as matters of opinion. He disapproved of France's Protestants, who through pride in their opinions and knowledge embraced a false religion, were willing to rebel against their king, and were tearing the country apart. His famous "Que scay-je?" is set in this context. Humans must, according to Montaigne, recognize their weakness and submit to God. "As a sworn enemy of heresy, he [the author] is free from the vain and irreligious opinion introduced by erroneous sects . . . Human reason goes astray everywhere, but especially when she concerns herself with matters divine."[6] When reason leaves the path of the Catholic church, it gets lost. Over and over, Montaigne pointed to diversity of opinions among philosophers, who could never agree on anything and yet think they have knowledge of Truth. "There is a plague on Man," he argued, "His opinion that he knows something."[7] Humankind's intellectual limitations, unbalanced with profound humility, had led to intellectual and religious chaos and unending violence.

But Montaigne's criticism of religious divisions does not stop here. For much of the time he was writing and adding to the *Essays*, the ultramontane Catholic League, funded by Spain and preaching death to unbelievers, was the party that openly embraced the notion of rebellion against their monarch and was as troublesome or worse than the Protestant heretics. Montaigne had severe criticism for the League, which he saw as tyrannical and dogmatic.[8] For Montaigne, religious disagreements should never have led to the violence of the civil wars. Throughout his work, he appealed to moderation, both through ancient references and his accounts of his own day. He stated, "It is impossible to argue in good faith with a fool . . . the surest proof of animal-stupidity is ardent obstinacy of opinion."[9]

While Montaigne did not oppose the idea of war, and in fact did his share of fighting, he saw the endless civil war that he lived through as a true abomination. In a powerful statement he cried,

> What a monstrosity this war is! [which] destroys us with its own poison. Its nature is so malign and so destructive that it destroys itself along with everything else, tearing itself from limb to limb in its frenzy. . . . It came to cure sedition, yet it is full of it; it seeks to punish disobedience and is an example of it. . . . Ambition, greed, cruelty, revenge do not have enough natural violence of their own, so let us light the match and stir the fire under the glorious pretext of justice and devotion.[10]

Montaigne's opposition to religious war could have led zealots to believe that he did not believe that his Church was worth defending. His statement that his house was safe because he doesn't try to guard it, or that marriages work better if divorce is possible can be read to support this idea. His statement, "I want to win [the religious struggle], but I am not driven mad if we do not. I am firmly attached to the sanest of the parties, but I do not desire to be particularly known as an enemy of the others beyond what is generally reasonable,"[11] could scarcely endear him to the League-allied demonologists.

Toward the end of this enormous work, Montaigne directly addressed the issue of witchcraft. While he touched frequently on popular credulity throughout the *Essays*, this brief discussion in "On the Lame"[12] is quite strong. He revealed his basic scepticism about the supernatural, saying, "To this hour, all such miracles and strange happenings hide away when I am about." He related a story about a recent fiasco in a local village in which some youths had frightened their neighbours by pretending to be ghosts. They were discovered and arrested, after many had been taken in. Montaigne attributed their success and the danger they were in of severe punishment on public gullibility. He stated that "in many similar kinds of cases which surpass our knowledge I consider that we should suspend our judgement, neither believing nor rejecting."[13]

Then, moving into a very famous passage, he stated,

> My local witches go in risk of their lives, depending on the testimony of each new authority who comes and gives substance to their delusions. The Word of God offers us absolutely clear and irrefragable examples of such phenomena, but to adapt and apply them to things happening in our own times because we cannot understand what caused them or how they were done needs a greater intelligence than we possess.

In a direct challenge to the demonological tradition, he argues,

> I am well aware that folks get angry and forbid me to have any doubts about witches on pain of fearful retribution. A new form of persuasion! Thanks be to God my credo is not to be managed by thumps from anyone's fists.... Any man who supports his opinion with challenges and commands demonstrates that his reasons for it are weak.... To kill people, there must be sharp and brilliant clarity; this life of ours is too real, too fundamental, to be used to guarantee these supernatural and imagined events.

In these passages, Montaigne stated that contemporary beliefs of witchcraft are opinions that rest on imagination and delusion.[14]

He continued,

> A few years ago I was passing through the domains of a sovereign prince who, as a courtesy to me and to overcome my disbelief, graciously allowed me to see, in a private place when he was present, ten or a dozen of this kind of prisoner, including one old woman, truly a witch as far as ugliness and misshapenness was concerned, who had long been famous for professing witchcraft. I was shown evidence and voluntary confessions as well as some insensitive spot or other on that wretched old woman. I talked and questioned till I had had enough, bringing to bear the most sane attention that I could—and I am hardly the man to allow my judgements to be muzzled by preconceptions—but in the end, and in all honesty, I would have prescribed not hemlock for them but hellebore. 'Their case seemed to be more a matter of insane minds than of delinquents.' Justice has its own remedies for such maladies.... After all, it is to put a very high value on your surmises to roast a man alive for them.[15]

He concluded this extraordinary discussion, before turning to a consideration of sexual relations with cripples, with an ironic disclaimer:

> I say that, as one who am neither a king's judge nor councillor, and who consider myself far from worthy of being so, I am an ordinary man, born and bred to obey State policy in both word and deed. Anyone who took account of my ravings, to the prejudice of the most wretched law, opinion or custom of his village, would do great wrong to himself and also to me.[16]

It should not be surprising that several demonological writers took issue with Montaigne. The most important critic of Montaigne was Martin Del Rio, related to Montaigne through Montaigne's mother. (As de Lancre points out, she was a Lopez, one of the best known families of "new Christian" Bordeaux merchants.)[17]

Del Rio criticized Montaigne directly several times in his authoritative demonological work, and characterized him as an unbeliever. For instance, in discussing those who described witchcraft as a fantasy of old people which did not deserve punishment, Del Rio pointed out, "Michel de Montaigne has fallen into this error." And when dealing with demonically caused sexual impotence, Del Rio stated, "In all this, Reader, you can understand how audaciously Michel de Montaigne takes this sort of evil deed away from the devil, to attribute it to the force of the imagination." Since Del Rio also stated, "Those who deny that there are demons are impious and heretic," he left his kinsman subject to grave penalties.[18]

Pierre de Lancre, on the other hand, defended Montaigne from these charges. This defence might seem surprising, since de Lancre insisted on the reality of witchcraft and was concerned to the point of obsession with the dangers of unbelief in witchcraft. But de Lancre was related by links of marriage and friendship to Montaigne, and this might account for his rather gentle treatment of the great sceptic.

De Lancre's defence of Montaigne is interesting. He described Del Rio's views at some length and in considerable detail. (We must remember that, for de Lancre, Del Rio was the most authoritative writer on witchcraft). De Lancre wrote, "in speaking of the Sabbats and nocturnal assemblies of witches, he [Del Rio] seems to place sieur de Montaigne with those who follow the heretics. For speaking of the authors who believe that witches attend Sabbats only in their imagination, illusion or fantasy, he says that this opinion is held by the heretics Luther and Melanchton and their followers, followed [he says] by some Catholics, among them M. de Montaigne."[19]

But, in de Lancre's opinion, Montaigne "did not present this proposition as true ... no more than his other opinions ... leaving all things in doubt, where it seemed bold to decide them absolutely." In other words, Montaigne was not really guilty as charged by Del Rio and some other writers, because he did not try to formulate and prove arguments, but merely told stories. De Lancre was, however, concerned lest judges adopt Montaigne's approach and so let witches go unpunished.[20]

Montaigne's oft-stated view that most questions of theology were matters of opinion and that most accounts of the supernatural were probably just misunderstandings caused by gullibility were antithetical to France's political demonologists. The enormous popularity of his writings must have been threatening to them. The *Essays* must have struck a responsive chord in many of his readers and helped them to cast a jaundiced eye on the intense arguments of the demonologists.

Estienne Pasquier (1529-1615) was much more combative than Montaigne. A lawyer, historian and political essayist, Pasquier also reflects the tolerant attitudes of the generation of 1530. He knew many Protestants, and was educated at the College of Presles, under Peter Ramus.[21] He spent a public career spanning fifty years pleading for religious peace. As the religious wars progressed, his writing concentrated on what he saw as the dangerous influence of the Jesuits in France. He was a bitter enemy of the Catholic League in the later phases of the conflict. Pasquier's first major political work was a long pamphlet, published in 1561, appealing to France's government and Church to permit the existence of the Protestant religion in France as a necessary evil. In this remarkable work, Pasquier foretold with astonishing accuracy the disasters waiting to befall his country if an anti-Protestant program were followed.[22] Like Montaigne, Pasquier insisted that he was a good Catholic, stating that only the Catholic religion was true. Also like Montaigne, he suggests that God's intentions are not revealed to humankind, and that warfare over the differences that separated Protestants and Catholics was both unnecessary and undesirable. The best thing, he argued, was for France to permit the existence of two churches. After all, these were both Christian churches, worshipping the same God and united by baptism. Furthermore, in the ancient church, heretics had not been killed. Religious diversity existed in the Ottoman Empire, and in areas controlled by the pope, where Jews lived among Christians with no problems.[23]

Pasquier correctly predicted that a religious civil war would be long and violent. Since the Protestants were well organized and brave, the war would result in great carnage, depopulated countrysides and a badly weakened France. In these circumstances, a Catholic victory would be empty.[24]

While Pasquier was fairly gentle with the Protestant heretics, he was very severe with his fellow Catholics. He laid the blame for the religious crisis on the popes, whose tolerance of abuses had encouraged the development and growth of heresies. He had a special dislike for extremist preachers, especially monks who stirred up violent feelings. He stated that these people needed to be controlled.[25]

Only four years later, with much blood already shed in religious warfare, Pasquier was named the chief attorney of the University of Paris, in its attempt to block the Jesuits' foundation of the College of Clermont. Pasquier argued at great length against the Jesuits in his losing cause, and remained an outspoken enemy of the order for his entire life.

For Pasquier, the Jesuits represented the worst aspects of the Tridentine church. He argued that they were foreigners who were loyal to the Spanish monarch and dedicated to the destruction of the special liberties of the Gallican church, and the very independence of the French nation. Regular clergy were traditionally permitted to teach only theology and canon law, while the Jesuits planned to teach the entire curriculum. Pasquier charged that the Jesuits, a structured order but whose members were not enclosed in monasteries, were regulars who had no business founding a college in Paris. In their response, the Jesuits had to sidestep this charge, denying that they were a traditional regular order while also denying that they were something totally new, since novelty was much opposed in this era.[26]

The lawyer representing the Jesuits was a highly respected orthodox Catholic named Pierre Versoris. He was such a devoted Leaguer in his later days, that he was said to have died of sorrow at the news of the assassination of Duke Henry of Guise in 1588.[27] In his argument, he stuck to the legal aspects of the structure of the university, insisting on the Jesuits' right to teach. He carefully avoided the wider political issues that were the heart of Pasquier's case. These tactics were successful, as the Jesuits were permitted to continue at the university.[28]

By the late 1580s, the political situation had worsened considerably. In 1588 and 1589, Pasquier penned a pair of very interesting pamphlets concerning Henry III's murder of the Duke of Guise and the subsequent assassination of the king. Guise had been regarded as a secular saint by his supporters. Following the murder of the Duke and Cardinal of Guise in December 1588, League presses poured out a stream of invective against the king, calling him a tyrant and inviting any good Catholic to avenge the murders. Pasquier expressed shock at these arguments, stating that subjects had to be obedient to their kings, even if they were tyrants. (Throughout his works he praised Henry, always denying that he was a tyrant.) Pasquier insisted that Guise was a traitor, who had deserved his fate. He even attacked Guise's religious integrity. "As far as the Duke of Guise is concerned," he wrote, "if ambition and tyrannical desire, disguised by a false mask of religion according to the doctrines of Machiavelli should be called religious zeal and affection for the Catholic Church, I grant your proposition. But, on the contrary, if such a thing is called, as it should be, not only hypocrisy, but atheism encumbered with superstition, then who can deny that the Duke of Guise is an atheist, a hypocrite and superstitious." Addressing the Leaguers, he said, "Tell me in good conscience where have you gotten this doctrine, if not from Satan, father and author of calumny, division, sedition and rebellion."[29]

Only a few months later, Jacques Clement murdered Henry III. Pasquier again took up his pen to answer a pamphlet, probably by Jean Boucher, that justified Clement's action and named him a martyr for the faith. Pasquier reiterated his arguments that kings had to be obeyed, and defended Henry III from charges that he was an enemy of the church, an idolater, magician and witch. He charged again that Guise was a traitor, and that he and his brother were "two of the most corrupted men ever seen in the world, monsters of impiety, cruelty, ambition, avarice and all sorts of debauchery." Clement could not have been a martyr, since he had been a servant of the Devil.[30]

Following an attempt on the life of Henry IV, Pasquier returned to the subject of the Jesuits. His arguments cast the Jesuits in the worst possible light. In his *Le catéchisme des Jésuites*, he stated, "When God wants to afflict a kingdom, he uses great and unexpected methods. . . . God has sent us two sects in France, one as dangerous as the other: that of the Ignatians, who call themselves the Company of Jesus and the other the Calvinists, who call themselves the Reformed Religion . . . the sect of Jesuits is a bastard religion of our ancient Catholic Apostolic Religion."[31]

An important aspect of the Gallican point of view, that Pasquier expressed very passionately, was a strong sense of French political, cultural and linguistic nationalism.[32] Pasquier disapproved of the penetration of Italians into French elite society, especially in the court dominated by Catherine de Medici. The great number of Italian bishops in France, the practice of integrating Italian phrases into French and the popular practice of gentlemen finishing their education in Italy were all condemned by Pasquier and his like-minded contemporaries.[33] The Jesuits, represented in France mainly by Italians and Spaniards seemed to exemplify perfectly the problem.

It is impossible to state how typical Pasquier was, in his long opposition to the League, the Jesuits and the spirit of factionalism. Certainly, as a crusader for religious toleration and a member of the high Paris magistrature, he embodied the attitudes that the French demonologists saw necessary to demonize and destroy.

It might seem odd or even perverse to place Jean Bodin with Montaigne and Pasquier, as problems for French demonologists. After all, Bodin was the author of the most famous and widely read demonological work of the sixteenth century. But Bodin had a good deal in common with Montaigne and Pasquier. He was born in 1529 or 1530. His humanist legal training, his methodology and his religious and political outlook place him solidly in their company. His venture into the murky world of demons and witches was highly original, personal and unorthodox, yet was by far the most published and republished French demonology book.

Throughout the religious wars, Bodin maintained that he was a good Catholic. However, he was suspected of heresy by the Leaguers, and there is a likelihood that he was even arrested in the early days of religious strife for suspect opinions. Between 1571 and 1584 he served the duke of Anjou, the younger brother of Henry III, around whom a number of *politique* writers congregated.[34] After the duke's death at twenty-nine years old in 1584, the civil war worsened and Bodin became far removed from political power. Bodin was hostile both to Calvinist and Catholic radicalism and rebellion, advocating, like Pasquier, obedience to royal authority. He was an important formulator of *politique* thought.

His most famous work, published in 1576, was *Les six livres de la république*.[35] This work, considered as one of the classics in the history of European political thought, ranges widely over the world of politics and political institutions. Like Pasquier and Montaigne, Bodin condemned the ruinous nature of civil war. He disapproved of religious disputation and agitation, and he supported the notion that more than one religion could exist in a commonwealth.[36] While emphasizing his Catholic *bona fides*, he stated that it was better to tolerate a diversity of religions than for the prince to attempt to force obedience to a single official religion, since this had led to civil violence and could lead the oppressed group to atheism.[37]

Pervading this massive work is a sense of the crucial importance of hierarchy. The relationships between humans and God, subject and ruler, family members and fathers are crucial to the functioning of human and political society. Bodin stressed, over and over again, the absolute obligation of the subject to the master. A son who defied his father, a subject who defied his prince, were both rebels who deserved death.[38] Even if the father, or the king, were a cruel and immoral tyrant it was not the right of their inferiors to oppose them. Bodin even stated that a subject was guilty of high treason for wishing for or even considering killing his king, even if the act is never carried out.[39] This stand, central to the *politique* response to the civil wars, was antithetical to that of both the Huguenots in the early phases of the conflict and the Catholic Leaguers later in the wars, both of which factions used the notion of the just opposition to royal tyranny to justify their taking up arms. This political position is reinforced by an almost total lack of arguments in defence of the faith and attacks on heresy that came naturally to most committed Catholic writers. Bodin even criticized the church for becoming too wealthy which, he said, contributed to the outbreak of the Reformation.[40]

In the late phases of the civil war, Bodin wrote, but never published, the *Heptaplomeres*, translated in English as the *Colloquium of the Seven about Secrets of the Sublime*. This is a fascinating, highly unorthodox analysis of comparative religious philosophies.[41] As mentioned in the previous chapter, in 1589 and 1590, Bodin subscribed to the League. His motives, according to Paul Lawrence Rose were not as inconsistent as they may seem. He acted through an intense disapproval of the actions and conduct of Henry III, and after his death, opposition to the legal claims of Henry of Navarre to the throne. He also came to believe that the Leaguers were actually on God's side. Not surprisingly, the League was never comfortable with Bodin, since he had been identified with the *politique* cause.[42]

The *Six livres* made Bodin a well-known figure who was widely respected by some and intensely disliked by others in his complex and violent world. This work is responsible for his impressive historical reputation as one of the leading writers of the sixteenth century. His appeal to rational political forces to determine the course of events, rather than religious and emotional ones, and his rejection of any standard contemporary Christian approaches have led historians to see him as a modern man, or at least as an eighteenth-century rationalist. This has made the place of the *Démonomanie* in his *oeuvre* a source of some problems to many historians.

Historians have tended to deal with the *Démonomanie* in either of two ways. Most Bodin specialists have, until fairly recently, ignored the work or treated it as a bizarre aberration. In the past decade or so this group has taken more note of the *Démonomanie*. This has resulted in the work being better understood in the context of Bodin's other writings. Many features in common with the *Six livres* have been noted, especially the emphasis on order and the seriousness with which Bodin regarded treason against higher authority.[43] Still, for the majority of Bodin scholars, the *Démonomanie* is of less interest than his "great" works.

The historians who have specialized in the witch hunt in early modern Europe have seen the *Démonomanie* as extremely important and influential. Many of these writers have asserted that this book exercised tremendous influence over the judges who heard witchcraft cases and was the direct cause of a considerable increase in the number of trials and executions for witchcraft following its appearance and wide dissemination.

Robert Mandrou, in his influential study, *Magistrats et sorciers*, stated of the *Démonomanie*, "this vehement appeal to pitiless repression was understood by the magistrates of higher justice who were charged with the repression of all crimes, of which witchcraft constituted a good part." For Mandrou, demonology books, and especially Bodin's, played the central role in the development of the widespread and violent persecutions for witchcraft that he presumed to have taken place. He stated, "The wave [of prosecutions] did not spare, it seems, any region of France: the demoniacal obsession was not unique to this magistrature instructed and nourished by the abundant publications that, each year, recalled them to the duties of their offices."[44] In one of his earlier works, E.W. Monter declared that Bodin's arguments were so powerful that they silenced any criticism of the persecution of witches. "One consequence of this," Monter wrote, "was an enormous increase in witchcraft trials in Western Europe; in the vast majority of regions, the persecutions reached their peak between 1580 and 1640." Echoing these views, Christopher Baxter stated, "The *Démonomanie* ... more than any other work was responsible for the European witch scare of the late sixteenth century." And Brian Easlea reiterated the view that Bodin "was the man who was so largely responsible for putting the European witchcraze firmly back on its vengeful course." Marie-Sylvie Dupont-Bouchat called the *Démonomanie* "the new *Malleus*, the manual of lay judges."[45]

The quandary of many historians was well stated by Hugh Trevor-Roper in his widely published study of the "witch craze." He wrote,

> Bodin the Aristotle, the Montesquieu of the sixteenth century, the prophet of comparative history, of political theory, of the philosophy of law, of the quantitative theory of money and of so much else ... in 1580 wrote the book which, more than any other, reanimated the witch-fires throughout Europe. To turn over the pages of Bodin's *De la démonomanie des sorciers*, to see this great man, the undisputed intellectual master of the later sixteenth century, demanding death at the stake not only for witches, but for all those who do not believe every grotesque detail of the new demonology, is a sobering experience.[46]

This assertion—that the *Démonomanie* was responsible for a sharp increase in witchcraft trials—has come to be generally accepted as fact. Flowing, as it does, from an understandable sense of indignation by modern intellectuals, it points a finger directly at the demonologists, and especially at Bodin, as instigators of the witch hunt. The problem is that this assertion rests on shaky historical assumptions and fails utterly to place Bodin in the context of his own complex time. By studying the *Démonomanie*, by examining its legal arguments in the context of contemporary practice and by looking at the reception of the work by more orthodox Catholic writers, we should be able to arrive at a better understanding of this interesting book and of its place in the demonological tradition of early modern France.

The publication record of Bodin's *Démonomanie* (1580) is truly impressive. It underwent at least twenty-three editions in four languages. Within twenty-two years of its first appearance, it had ten French editions, two Italian, four Latin and four German. There were two more French editions in the early seventeenth century, and then it went into a long hiatus until the 1690s, when more French, Latin and German editions appeared.

The *Démonomanie* is a lengthy and complex discussion of many aspects of magic and witchcraft. Bodin was an impressive and original writer, who presented his arguments in a cogent, coherent fashion, in very concise language. This work is free of the crude partisan emotionalism and repetitiveness found in most of the other demonology treatises of that period.

Bodin's concern was to define and describe witchcraft accurately, and to examine the ways to eliminate it from the world. His argument that witchcraft was divine treason against God is at the centre of his very severe approach. In this, he differed strongly from most other French demonologists, for whom the defence of the Catholic church was the primary goal. For Bodin, all religions could be worthwhile in controlling and instructing people. The universal laws of God, found in the writings of ancient pagan and Hebrew writers as much as in Christian authorities, were Bodin's guide in his condemnation of illicit magic and witchcraft. Bodin relied as well on hearsay from friends and contemporary writers. For Bodin, the basic agreement, among so many sources, that the Devil really existed, that witches were real and that they were dangerous to individuals and to society, and had to be discovered and destroyed, was the best possible proof that his arguments were true.

In this, Bodin differed from Montaigne and Pasquier, who emphasized the unknowability of God's plans and intentions. Bodin was convinced that God's word, as revealed in Scripture and throughout human history was clear—at least on the subject of demons and witches.

An important aspect of Bodin's methodology is his interest in the definition and derivation of words as keys to knowledge. In this he reflects the centrality of philology to Renaissance modes of thinking. The book opens with an extended explication of the word "witch" and continually uses the determination of the correct definition of terms as the best guide to their meaning as well as to their truth and utility.

For Bodin, the universe was full of occult relationships and was peopled by many demons, who could be good or evil. In this, he shared in the interest in mysticism that was prevalent in his day. For Bodin, people could be interested in this aspect of the universe, but the important thing was that curious humans stay within the bounds of permissible or legal behaviour in their study of the world of spirits. Any occult activity that served the Devil's purposes and led to false religion was evil and could lead humans to damnation. All through the first part of the *Démonomanie*, Bodin's concern was to delineate the boundaries that separated legal magic and magical inquiries from those that were illegal and damnable. As a good lawyer, Bodin emphasized intent as the guide to recognizing the line between good and evil in the occult. But he was also very concerned that well-meaning people could be led astray and into criminal activities through ignorance or carelessness.

An interesting passage in the first part of the *Démonomanie* is Bodin's extended description of an unnamed friend's experience with a guardian angel. Some modern scholars hold that this was actually Bodin himself, that he believed himself to be the beneficiary of special guidance from a benevolent spirit.[47] Another discussion that reveals something of how Bodin thought is his discussion of astrology. He believed in astrology, as did most of his contemporaries, but counselled strongly against its misuse. Astrology could be useful, for example, in medical matters, where it could help to inform a physician about the physiological inclinations of a patient. But people went too far when astrology was used to predict hidden things. Even worse was the attribution of characteristics to planets that really belong to God. This led directly to idolatry.

In the middle section of the *Démonomanie*, Bodin concerned himself mainly with establishing the reality and seriousness of many varieties of diabolical dealings in the world. This part of the work is based more on contemporary events than the first section. Bodin examined in lengthy detail such subjects as witches' attendance at sabbats, the reality of werewolves, and the crimes witches committed through the aid of the Devil. The worst aspect of all of this was the witches' act of renunciation and betrayal of God in order to serve the Devil. Bodin was also concerned that, in the fight against witchcraft, good people might resort to diabolical means themselves. People had to be alert to avoid falling into the Devil's traps. They had to constantly remember that it was easy to fall into idolatry.

Book 4 of the *Démonomanie* is an extended treatise on the judicial handling of witches. Bodin intended it to be a guide to judges, and it is this section of the work that has earned its reputation as an instigator of trials and condemnations for witchcraft.

The legal arguments in this book are complex, sometimes difficult to follow to their conclusion and often ambiguous. Bodin was given to making absolute statements, often extreme ones, and then in long technical discussions with many examples, modifying the initial statement practically out of recognition. The writer who quotes Bodin has to be extremely careful that he is conveying Bodin's whole idea, and not just repeating the colourful phrase.

On the eve of publishing the *Démonomanie*, Bodin wrote a long attack on the works of a German Protestant physician, Johann Weyer, which he appended to the larger work. Bodin considered Weyer as extremely dangerous, and labelled him "defender of witches." Weyer considered learned magic evil and its practitioners worthy of death. But when he discussed witches, Weyer's opinions were in sharp disagreement with Bodin's. For Weyer, the problem of witches was one of foolish old women, suffering from an excess of melancholic humour. This physiological imbalance made them easy prey for the Devil, who tricked them into thinking that they did evil deeds. The proper remedy for their delusion was physical healing and correct religious instruction, not corporal or capital punishment. Weyer even stated that the pact with the Devil, a key aspect of Bodin's concept of witchcraft, was a fantasy.

Bodin attacked Weyer for being a bad Christian and a bad physician. He was especially distressed that Weyer's opinions might influence judges to treat accused women as deluded sick people and let them go unpunished. It was especially shocking to Bodin that Weyer revealed "secrets" of magic and witchcraft that could lead his readers astray.

The tone of the *Démonomanie* is harsh, and it is probably fair to say that Bodin's view of law was essentially repressive. But Edward Peters has pointed out that the whole thrust of late medieval and early modern law was toward severity. The Roman law that was revived and adapted in thirteenth-century Italy, spread across and used all over Europe until the late eighteenth century, was far more severe in procedure and penalties than either the law codes of the Middle Ages or the Enlightenment codes we still live with. Witches were handled severely, but so were all categories of criminals. As Peters states, "Many historians of witchcraft prosecutions tend to distort the nature of punishments for witches by focusing on them exclusively, instead of approaching them in the context of general legal history, especially that of criminal law."[48] Fortunately, in the last few years a number of excellent studies on law and the courts in early modern Europe have been published, so it is possible to understand the general legal context.[49]

Bodin wrote this work so that the guilty would be sought out and punished. His real concern was to ensure that real witches not be able to use the legal system to wriggle out of their justly deserved punishments, and to provide judges with a useful, flexible and judicially correct set of rules to deal with them.

Bodin aimed to prove to all the members of the magistrature, but especially the *procureurs du roi*, that witchcraft was real, that it was a serious matter, usually involving murder, and that it posed a grave threat to public order. He understood that ordinary people would not often go to the authorities to make formal complaints of witchcraft, so the crown prosecutors had to be encouraged to be vigilant and to seek out witches and bring them to justice.[50]

Bodin saw witchcraft as the most horrible crime, combining treason against God, heresy, murder, sexual perversion, violation of family obligations and other horrors. He wanted governments and court authorities to devote the necessary time and energy to its extirpation. He did not see the problem in the same way as other French Catholic demonologists. Nowhere in this work does he charge Protestants with being part of the Devil's forces, or place witchcraft in the framework of a defence of Catholic doctrine. In fact, Catholic beliefs and practices are hardly mentioned in this work.

In a way that was conventional to his legal contemporaries, Bodin defined the various types of evidence and classified them into a hierarchy of proofs and presumptions. There were only two solid proofs, and they were the strongest evidence: the testimony of eyewitnesses or the confession by the accused. Presumptions were what we would call circumstantial evidence. In Bodin's time, it was practically impossible to convict on presumptions. The discussion of evidence, mainly contained in Chapters 2 through 4 of Book 4, is complex and must be read with great care. They are probably the most important part of the technical legal argument of the entire work, and are really what makes the *Démonomanie* a legal manual. It is to these three chapters that we must look in order to understand what Bodin was instructing judges to do. If the work was responsible for a major increase in witchcraft prosecutions and executions, those trials would have been conducted in accordance with these instructions.

In opening a case, the judge had to determine that a crime had actually been committed. Bodin stated, "If one produces fifty witnesses who all with one accord testify that Pierre is dead and bewitched by the action of the person who is accused of the murder, and yet he turns up before the judge quite alive, the judge must disregard the witnesses and their testimony . . . such proof is even stronger than voluntary and legal confession of the accused." Bodin's examples of what constitutes solid proof are interesting.

> If one finds the person who is accused of being a witch in possession of toads, hosts, human members, or waxen images pierced with needles, in the prosecution of this crime, these are concrete facts. . . . If someone dis-

covers the witch or suspected witch killing a child . . . one can declare that it is a clear fact in order to convict her of being a witch. . . . If one sees the witch threaten her enemy who is hale and hearty, or she touches him, and instantly he falls dead, or becomes a leper, or suddenly he becomes deformed or crippled . . . it is a clear and concrete fact, if as well it is rumoured that she is a witch." As he sums up, "The clearest and strongest proof is one that brings into view the truth that we seek with tangible items."[51]

These and more examples are presented, each of which might be quite convincing to show that someone was a witch, but which is equally unlikely to happen in real life. A judge proceeding strictly according to the letter of these proofs would have considerable difficulty in handing down very many guilty verdicts.

The next category of clear proof is the testimony of several sound witnesses as to tangible things that the judge himself can observe. Bodin specifically stated that if witnesses see passing occurrences that the judge could not personally corroborate, such as invocations of Satan or acts of necromancy, this does not constitute concrete fact. But if witnesses agree on many aspects of a crime, and then the accused "in the presence of the judge and others makes some invocation to Satan," then this becomes strong proof. He continues with a most interesting discussion, "If suddenly and at the moment that the witch threatened or touched someone, he fell dead, judges are reluctant to condemn the witch if there is no other proof or presumption or confession. Nor would I want to advise the death penalty in such a case, but rather other corporal punishments."[52]

Things begin to get complicated in the discussion of the value of various sorts of testimony. We must remember the two witness rule and the difficulties this must have imposed on judges in cases of witchcraft, which was by definition a hidden crime. Bodin stated unequivocally, "the law of God does not permit the testimony of one witness to be proof for establishing a judgement of guilt." But if, for example, three irreproachable witnesses each saw a witch commit separate crimes, this "with some other presumption" is sufficient for the judge to impose the death penalty. Disreputable characters or women [whose testimony was worth half that of men, because of "the imbecility and fragility of the sex"] could testify as long as there were several witnesses. In this situation, where dependable witnesses [upstanding males] were not available, Bodin cited the exceptional crime tradition stating, "This crime is singular." If defined as an exceptional crime, judges could take the testimony of daughters against mothers, or fathers against sons, inadmissible in normal cases. In this section he stressed, "One must not insist on the ordinary rules for handling, challenging, or admitting witnesses in such a hateful crime as this one. . . . One must not be limited by normal procedures . . . for this crime surpasses all others. Now it is certain in terms of law where there is danger, necessity or any inordinate situation one must not be bound by legal strictures—on the contrary then, this is proceeding soundly according to the law."[53] In other words, dispensing with ordinary procedure and utilising extraordinary procedure was to be regarded as appropriate and proper in witchcraft cases. Bodin's model for the application of exceptional crime methods of proceeding was the crime of treason. Treason had, even in ancient times, been handled in exceptional ways. Bodin argues, throughout this work, that witches have committed divine treason through their renunciation of God and embracing the Devil. Thus for him, the legal context of exceptional proceedings was correct.

In practice, the real point of the exceptional crime provisions was to enable the judge to bring an accused person to the "question," or torture, on a strong assumption of guilt. John Langbein states that normally a judge would assign torture if half the necessary proof or combination of presumptions was present. If torture produced a confession, the proof was solid and a guilty finding could be reached. While Bodin's line on the use of exceptional crime status to witchcraft would seem to expose the accused to much more rigorous handling than under ordinary rules, in his listing of examples for the application of torture, Bodin does not really stray far from the "half proof" criterion that was used in ordinary proceedings.[54]

Without a confession, most of the types of testimony already discussed would not suffice for a finding of guilt. Bodin exerted much effort in trying to work out a clear set of rules to govern the application of torture. He stated, "I shall take the position that the opinion of Alexander [of Hales] and Jean André [Giovanni d'Andrea] be followed and that to apply the question, all that be required is one sound witness, an upright man above reproach or any kind of suspicion, whose testimony is accompanied by reason or sense." But he would also permit torture based on the accusations of less savoury types, or even accomplices, as long as several testified.[55]

Chapter 3 of Book 4 is entirely concerned with witches' confessions. Bodin showed his concern with judicial scepticism and incredulity stating, "Often judges are puzzled by the confessions of witches and are reluctant to base a sentence on them, given the strange things they confess, because some think that they are fables from what they say."[56] This puzzlement could be a serious problem, if it led to witches going unpunished, letting their evil flourish and spread.

Confessions were a tricky subject in the legal environment of the sixteenth century, and Bodin tried to touch on all sorts of possibilities. The central distinction he made was between voluntary and forced confessions. Here again, he was in the mainstream of legal argumentation in his time. Without doubt, the most valuable confession was made voluntarily in court before any interrogation had begun. Any judicial tricks weakened the value of the confession, and Bodin cautioned against putting words in the mouth of the accused. He stressed that there were different values in the confessions of various kinds of people, and in the circumstances of the confession. "This diversity," he wrote, "must be carefully weighed by a wise and expert judge" and he insisted that a confession be accompanied by "other sufficient presumptions" in order for the accused to be condemned. It is very important to note that a confession obtained through the application of torture, or even through the fear of torture was considered less valuable than a freely made confession. For example, if a person, reputed to be a witch (a presumption in itself) and accused of witchcraft, freely confessed to signing a demonic pact and attending sabbats, the judge was justified in finding her guilty and condemning her to death. But if a person confessed only under torture, the confession could be considered "proof" only if the person persisted in the confession following the torture. Otherwise, the confession under torture is only a "presumption."[57]

Presumptions were much weaker than proofs. Bodin's sense of what constitutes presumption sometimes differs widely from our view of admissible evidence. He regarded reputation and common rumour as "violent presumptions," among the strongest types of supporting evidence. A widespread rumour, agreed upon by at least twenty people, should be sufficient, even without eyewitnesses, to bring an accused to torture. "When it is a question of witches," Bodin wrote, "Rumour is almost infallible, especially if there is apparent reason." Other presumptions were self-incriminating statements, lowering of the eyes, inconsistencies in testimony, being the child of witch parents, inability to cry, and threatening of others, especially if the threats precede the death of the one threatened.[58]

Bodin called for severe torture when the presumptions justified it, in order to get a confession from the accused. It must be remembered, though, that the confession had to be repeated freely in order to retain its validity. He stated,

> After exacting the truth from one who has been put to the question, he must be carefully guarded so that the Devil does not speak to him, and then once again twenty-four hours later repeat the confession.... For to extract the necessary proof, one must persist [in the confession] as the order [of Louis XII] stipulates, which has been confirmed by many decrees. On the other hand, if the witch renounces her confession subsequent to the question, one must not base a death sentence on it, or any other corporal punishments, unless there are other presumptions.[59]

When he turned to the penalties deserved by witches, Bodin indeed seems to be unambiguously severe. He saw witchcraft as a despicable, horrible crime, including divine treason, murder, and sexual perversion. "There is no penalty cruel enough to punish the evil of witches," he wrote, 'since all their wickednesses, blasphemies and all their designs rise up against the majesty of God to offend Him in a thousand ways."[60]

Bodin followed this with several pages that catalogued the horrors committed by witches, and arguments for their death. But then he stated, "The difficulty however, very often lies solely with the proof and judges find themselves hampered only by that.... If there are no valid witnesses, or confessions by the accused, or factual evidence, which are the three proofs on which a death penalty can be based, but there are only presumptions, one must distinguish whether the presumptions are weak or strong." If they were weak, the accused was to be released. If the presumptions were strong, he wrote, "I do not recommend that because of strong presumptions one pass sentence of death.... One must be very sure of the truth to impose the death sentence." He repeated several times that witches should be punished, but that beatings, amputations, branding, prison and fines were appropriate punishments for those convicted on strong circumstantial evidence. "This is the rule that we must adhere to, setting aside the death penalty and softening the rigour of the laws when one proceeds on presumptions," he stated.[61] Throughout this discussion, it is clear that when Bodin spoke of punishments, he was dealing with appropriate penalties for people found guilty through legally correct court proceedings.

It seems clear that Bodin's message to his legal readers was not a radical departure from normal contemporary legal conventions. The

Démonomanie was one of the great literary successes of the period, and the most reprinted of all the French demonology books. Its popularity was most likely based on Bodin's reputation as a stimulating author and on the work's brilliance in dealing with a perplexing subject of considerable general interest. The view, so often reiterated, that it caused a dramatic increase in condemnations for witchcraft must be rejected.

There is, actually, little solid evidence to support the notion that there was any sharp increase in trials and executions for witchcraft, at least in France, after 1580. As has been discussed, the French *Parlements*, at least those of Paris and Rouen for which some statistics exist, did not embark on bloody crusades against witches following the appearance of the *Démonomanie*. Throughout the late sixteenth and early seventeenth centuries, the French high courts were circumspect in their handling of accusations for witchcraft, and rank among the milder jurisdictions of Europe in this area of criminal prosecution. During this period they were strengthening the appeal process and reducing penalties in witchcraft cases. The dignified counsellors of these courts doubtlessly found the *Démonomanie* interesting and educational, but their jurisprudence was not totally altered by it.

What of other jurisdictions for which records exist? In Geneva, the courts heard a few more cases of witchcraft (139) in the forty years after 1580 than they heard before 1580 (116), but in fact fewer of the accused were condemned to death after 1580 (21) than before (34). In the Netherlands, executions for witchcraft, which had begun in the 1520s, ceased altogether around 1600.[62] In Franche-Comté, a French-speaking part of the Spanish Empire, records exist only from 1599 on. But those records show that most of the death penalties for witchcraft (35 in all) were imposed between 1605 and 1610, with very little activity before or after.[63] The duchy of Luxembourg saw a terrifying increase of witchcraft trials after 1580 and a veritable reign of terror that went on into the mid-seventeenth century. This situation however, should probably be ascribed to extraordinary local conditions and to the presence of Peter Binsfeld, a renowned demonologist and witch hunter in his own right, who was coadjutor to the archbishop.[64] In some other parts of Europe, witchcraft was very intensely prosecuted. Germany, Lorraine and parts of Switzerland saw very large scale witch hunts, which reached their peaks in the early seventeenth century. Perhaps one-half to two-thirds of all witchcraft prosecutions took place in the German-speaking parts of the Holy Roman Empire. It is possible that judges in these regions were influenced by Bodin, in either the German or Latin versions. But there would have been many other influences as well besides the *Démonomanie*. The Empire was highly decentralized, both politically and judicially. Local authorities had a very high degree of autonomy, and there was no superstructure resembling the French *Parlements* to act as a check on lower court zeal and credulity. This is undoubtedly the primary reason for the extraordinarily high number of trials and executions for witchcraft, as well as their long time span in this region.[65]

It is important to note as well, that Germany as a whole is rather like a microcosm of Europe in the persecution of witches. The bulk of witchcraft executions in Germany were concentrated in several large towns and several south central and southwest regions. Six thousand were executed in only four states: Bamberg, Wurzburg, Cologne and Mainz. Many other areas had relatively low incidences of witchcraft prosecution. Bavaria, the largest single state in early modern Germany, saw only 271 executions. States like the Palatinate, Upper Palatinate, Tyrol, Cleves and Julich had no persecutions at all.[66]

The *Démonomanie* was of great interest to religious writers and controversialists as well as to lawyers. Bodin, the *politique*, tolerant of all religious viewpoints was far outside the mainstream of orthodox Catholic demonology. His fellow French demonologists must have read his work carefully, for many of them discussed it at some length in their own works.

Many of Bodin's positions on the subject of witchcraft were very unorthodox. As already mentioned, for Bodin, the word of God was clear. He was confident that he understood the law of God, which he did not see as a monopoly of any single sect, but as universal and unambiguous. This belief led other writers to strongly disagree with him.

In the account of his friend's guardian spirit, Bodin relates an account of prayer and contemplation in an attempt to gain salvation. The only sources in this passage are to a psalm and to the ancient Jewish writer, Philo. This discussion is very unorthodox. In Book 3, Chapter 6, Bodin discussed the ways to deal with people who are possessed by demons. The reality of demonic possession was, for Bodin, absolutely true. Throughout this discussion, Bodin rejects the widely practiced Catholic practices of exorcising and questioning possessing demons. He held that prayer and music were the only effective means to cure possession. This stand was bitterly opposed by orthodox demonologists.

Bodin also adopted positions that were more extreme and more literal than those taken by even the most zealous orthodox demonologists.

For example, he stated unequivocally that the transport of witches to their sabbats was real, that they were taken there by the Devil in body and soul. He also firmly stated that lycanthropy—the transformation of humans into werewolves—was genuine and not any sort of illusion.[67]

Several of these writers refuted Bodin on these points and attacked him as a dangerous, heretical writer. Pierre Le Loyer, a lawyer from Angers, published a long study of demons and spectres in 1586. While never naming Bodin, he refuted Bodin's views on lycanthropy in some detail. He cited St. Augustine and Aquinas to argue that, if the Devil could really transform a man into a wolf, this would make him a creator. This was a blasphemous stand, since only God could create a new being. The Devil could only use tricks and illusions to trick human senses to make people believe that such a transformation had taken place. This was the orthodox Catholic position on lycanthropy, and on the powers and method of operation of the Devil.[68]

Martin Del Rio, considered by many of his contemporaries as the most authoritative Catholic demonologist, was very severe toward Bodin's opinions. Del Rio stated flatly that lycanthropy was an illusion and that "anathema and the condemnation of the church threaten those who hold otherwise." He clearly regarded Bodin as a heretic, stating, "Has he not filled his *Démonomanie* full of dangerous errors?" And toward the end of his book, Del Rio listed a number of "heretics" who held that the diabolical pact was real including, "Lambert Daneau, Jean Bodin, Thomas Erastus . . . and (Francois) Hotman."[69] All these, except Bodin, were well-known French Protestants. As far as Del Rio was concerned, Bodin was beyond the pale. It was doubtless the intensity of these attacks by good Catholic writers that led to the placement of the *Démonomanie* on the Index of forbidden works in 1594.[70]

Pierre de Lancre mentioned Bodin often in his history of the 1609 Labourd case over which he presided . While he sometimes cites Bodin's work for support, most of the references to the *Démonomanie* are negative. He discussed the problem of lycanthropy at length, specifically refuting Bodin's views. De Lancre wrote that magical transformation was only "diabolical illusion. Since the evil spirit so thickens the air around the bodies of witches, that it fools our senses making them appear as wolves, dogs, cats and other animals. . . . We repeat our maxim that demons cannot do anything that is supernatural." To believe in the reality of this transformation was "a blasphemy against God."[71]

A physician named J. de Nynauld published a direct attack on Bodin's view of lycanthropy in 1615. Nynauld, a firm believer in the Devil and his evil powers, nonetheless totally rejected the notion of the reality of lycanthropy, stating the orthodox view that the Devil could only cause illusions of the change of humans to animals. If people confessed to being transformed into animals, "it is only pure fable and illusion of the devil, who fools the senses of his slaves." So the confessed werewolf was not completely innocent. "Those who believe such things," he went on, "are unworthy of the name of Christian and hold God in contempt." Bodin's opinions were "against law and reason and against theological and philosophical maxims."[72]

Nynauld repeatedly charged that Bodin was blasphemous in his views, and that he had perverted Scriptures. "It is a blasphemy to say and believe that the devil can really change the nature of things against the natural way that the Creator has given them." At another point he reiterated, "We conclude, that it is a blasphemy to hold that God permits or gives such power to the devil, enemy of His word and of humankind, as Bodin maintains."[73]

According to Nynauld, any writers who maintained the erroneous and blasphemous view that the Devil could actually perform supernatural feats like the transformation of a man into a wolf were, "stupid writers who, since they cannot understand the secrets of nature ... are constrained by their brutish ignorance to attribute the causes to demons, not without impiety, for in doing so, they seem to want to establish a second God." He held that Bodin was "as badly instructed in the Christian faith, as in natural philosophy," and that it was necessary to attack Bodin in order "to remove the belief in such detestable and ridiculous things from those who could be seduced by his arguments."[74]

Numerous other demonologists took Bodin to task over this issue. Claude Prieur, a Franciscan, stated that it was foolish to hold that the transformation was real, "Be it thus resolved that Lycanthropy or transformation has no place among Catholics." And Henri Boguet, the well-known witch judge from the Free County of Burgundy, wrote against Bodin as well, even though Boguet listed Bodin among his sources. According to Boguet, while there existed a considerable debate on the question of the reality of the transformation, "I have always believed lycanthropy to be false, and I hold the metamorphosis of man into beast as impossible."[75]

Perhaps the worst insult to Bodin's reputation was delivered by Father Filesac of Bordeaux. When, as we have discussed, the *Parlement* was faced with a charge of lycanthropy in 1603, Filesac was charged with researching the whole issue in order to help the deliberations. He took his assignment seriously, producing a long scholarly thesis on the question, studded with ancient and contemporary references. He never mentioned Bodin.

We are, perhaps, left with a paradox and with questions in place of historical certainties, when we consider the influence of the *Démonomanie*. It was certainly one of the great publishing successes of the late sixteenth century. Because of this commercial success and the work's wide dissemination, the claims that it played a major role in the progress of witchcraft trials, must be seen as, at least, exaggerated. Bodin was a well-known and controversial writer in his own day. The *Démonomanie* is still a fascinating, and well-written book, supported by references from a wide range of ancient and contemporary sources. Bodin used many vivid anecdotes to give colour and life to the work. Dealing with a complex, perplexing aspect of life in the late sixteenth century, in an impressive scholarly fashion, free from sectarian passion, it was bound to attract an unusually wide readership. The *Démonomanie* is an excellent book, capable of stimulating serious thought and discussion. This is where its success and importance are to be found.

The three men considered in this chapter had much in common. While Pasquier did not discuss witchcraft as a subject, he was able to turn the ideas of the political demonologists against them in his arguments. Certainly, while Montaigne and Bodin could not have agreed on the matter of witches, their basic outlooks were similar. Furthermore, Bodin's approach to witches was so foreign to the political demonologists influenced by Maldonat, that they condemned his work even while making use of it when they could.

Seven

Pierre de Lancre

Of all the French high court magistrates who actually participated in trials of witches, only one wrote extensively of his experiences. This was Pierre de Lancre (c. 1550-1630), certainly one of the best known and most discussed of all the French demonologists. De Lancre is unique in French witchcraft jurisprudence, since he presided over the one case in France in which mass executions were carried out. His role in this grisly process has earned him as bad an historical reputation as one can encounter. A recent French writer says of him, "Libidinous and sensual, Pierre de Lancre was narrow-minded, sectarian and stubborn. Given to an incommensurate vanity, he was infatuated with himself and with his importance. Furthermore, he feared the powers of the Devil, and of demons, and was of an infantile credulity, surprising in a man who possessed, as he did, real culture." The same writer calls him "sadistic and cruel," a "born inquisitor" and "a Tartuffe."[1]

Julio Caro Baroja, writing a few years earlier, was only a bit gentler, stating, "my own (view) is that De Lancre was a typical lawyer, obsessed with the desire to uncover criminal activities, who accepted religion as

---

Notes to Chapter Seven are on pp. 166-68.

the basis for the penal code. I feel he had an essentially repressive concept of the law, and, therefore a rather punitive approach to justice."[2] After a discussion of de Lancre's famous case, Baroja concluded,

> De Lancre emerges as one of the most absurd figures of the movement to repress witchcraft, not so much for the astonishing things he says as for the way in which he says them; mixing a kind of Gascon 'bonhomie' with the most blatant superstition. The only difference between his superstitious beliefs and those of his unfortunate victims was that his were hidden under a layer of learning that seemed relatively extensive and profound.[3]

And Hugh Trevor-Roper called him a "bigoted Catholic" and "the gleeful executioner of the Pays de Labourd."[4]

These views, which are representative of historians' opinions of de Lancre, proceed from an understandable sense of indignation over the fate of people convicted for witchcraft. But they are based on very limited information on what actually happened during the famous 1609 case in the Labourd region, and they fail utterly to place de Lancre in a meaningful historical and intellectual context. It is possible to fill in some gaps in this case, and to look at de Lancre as part of his world. When this is done, he becomes less an isolated bizarre character and emerges as a man who was shaped by specific developments and who shared the values of many of his contemporaries.

Pierre de Lancre was born around 1553 in Bordeaux and was destined from an early age to a position in the *Parlement* of that city. As discussed earlier, he attended the College of Clermont in Paris in the early 1570s and probably heard Father Maldonat's famous lectures on demons and the immortality of the soul, and the importance of these notions to good Catholicism. It is clear from his writing that he was devoted to the intense spiritual dynamic Catholicism fostered by the Jesuits in post-Tridentine France. As we have discussed earlier, he was related to many important citizens of Bordeaux, who played important roles in the complex intellectual life of this period.

The *Parlement* of Bordeaux had been through difficult times in the two decades preceding de Lancre's entry around 1583. Through the Wars of Religion the court seemed to strive for a moderate path between the extremes of Protestantism and the League. Bordeaux experienced the same sorts of violence that occurred throughout the kingdom in that period. The Jesuits established a college in Bordeaux in August of 1572. On 29 September of that year, the Jesuit Father Emond Auger preached a violent sermon against the Protestant heresy, and Bordeaux then saw its own local version of the St. Bartholomew's Day massacre, in which around 250 Protestants were killed. Following this massacre, Protestantism declined sharply in Bordeaux. Interestingly, following this the *Parlement* became more hostile to the zealot Catholic groups and to the Jesuits, expelling the order from the city in 1589. The *Parlement* of Bordeaux was the first to rally to Henry IV, although in 1598 it opposed the registration of the Edict of Nantes.[5]

De Lancre received his doctorate of laws in 1579 and joined the *Parlement* of Bordeaux in 1582. He travelled in Italy in 1599 and 1600. In 1609 he served as a member of a two-man commission to investigate and deal with reports of wide-scale witchcraft in the Pays de Labourd, south of Bordeaux. This commission was the source for his best known book, published in 1612. This commission and the resultant book will be discussed at some length below.

After the trial de Lancre returned to Bordeaux, where he had a long and honourable career. He was a state counsellor in Paris from 1612 to 1622, and died in 1630 or 1631.[6] He wrote copiously for his whole adult life. One book preceded his case in the Labourd. Of the four works he published after this famous case, three concentrated on witches. It is difficult to estimate the reception to these lengthy works, and any influence they may have had. De Lancre was an intelligent, well-educated man who was also a gifted writer. His works are among the most readable and enjoyable of all the demonological tracts of the day. But he was not much cited by other writers of demonology works. Furthermore, by the time his publications were appearing, witchcraft persecutions were already dwindling in France. De Lancre's books do not seem to have done anything to slow that process. Finally, anyone who reads the 1612 and 1622 works attentively cannot escape the strong sense that de Lancre was very much on the defensive, and, especially in the latter work, was trying to influence an unconvinced and possibly even hostile judiciary to take a tougher line in dealing with witchcraft accusations.

De Lancre's writing style was lively, colourful and learned. He brought together his skill in storytelling, his unique judicial experience and his profound commitment to Tridentine Catholicism to produce strongly engaging works. He frequently exhorted his reader directly, in rhythmical repetitive passages, much like spoken sermons. In all of this, Pierre de Lancre becomes the personification of Robert Muchembled's picture of the cleric-magistrate acting as a missionary for reformed

Catholicism in the French countryside. It must be remembered though, that de Lancre was anything but a typical French *parlementaire* in this period. In almost every aspect of his career, personality and obsessions, he was always one of a very small minority among his more moderate Gallican colleagues.

De Lancre's first published work, *Tableau de l'inconstance et instabilité de toutes choses*, was published in Paris in 1607. It was a work of considerable erudition, reflecting his recently concluded studies and travels in Italy. It shows de Lancre as a skillful and passionate writer, with a wide range of references, mostly classical, at his disposal. While a good example of florid early seventeenth-century French prose, the work displays little originality and probably would be of little interest to anyone if the author did not go off to the Labourd only two years after its appearance. As he did, it serves as a fascinating study of a person who would soon have the power of life and death over large numbers of people. While some of the arguments contained in this *Tableau* are chilling forerunners of what was to come, others are quite benign and seem to be quite at variance with the de Lancre of 1609.

The theme of inconstancy and the troubles it caused was a popular one in the early seventeenth century. De Lancre used it as the organizing theme for his second book as well. This is a reflection of the importance of the Christianized neo-stoicism propounded by Justus Lipsius (*On Constancy*, 1584) which was very influential for the intellectuals of this age of violence and disorder. Writers as diverse as de Lancre, Montaigne, Bodin and Charron all drew inspiration from Lipsius and others who propounded the stoic view.[7]

The book opens with a statement that inconstancy is a common vice in mankind, and is to blame for the sorry state of the world. Especially inclined to this vice of inconstancy—and to just about every other vice—was woman. Much of the early part of this 1,057-page work is a detailed discussion of the basically evil nature of women.

For de Lancre, women exemplified the lack of constancy that so plagued the world. He stated, "That is why, peradventure, the woman, recognizing herself so imperfect compared to the man, and also recognizing the weakness of her sex, which makes her so flighty and subject to change, seeks out the man and puts herself under his control." These weaknesses led Satan to choose Eve as his tool for the ruin of mankind for "there is no instrument so appropriate to persuade and seduce man, as woman, who draws him to his ruin.... The serpent, knowing the weakness of woman and of her sex, used his temptations on her, rather than Adam, since he knew that Adam was more perfect and more constant."[8]

Women, he wrote, were naturally inclined to sexual misconduct: "among women, an infinite number are too licentious . . . so that points of honour, nor honourable laws cannot cut the roots of mad desire, nor limit their sensual appetites."[9]

It should be pointed out that, in his condemnation of women, de Lancre was in no way unusual in his milieu or in his time. But it is very interesting, in a chilling way, to see these views examined at length by a man who, so shortly after their publication would be conducting France's largest trial for witchcraft, a crime that across Europe, involved four or five times as many women as men.

There is a lengthy discussion in this work of mental disorders, which de Lancre considered an inconstancy of the brain. He stated that melancholics, their brains filled with the black melancholic humour, "search for horror and hidden places where the evil spirit often visits them, taking advantage of their despair." De Lancre carefully distinguished between mental illness and witchcraft, but showed how melancholic despair could lead one into the clutches of the Devil.[10]

Many other themes are touched on in this long book, but the most interesting, in the light of subsequent events, is a discussion of over three hundred pages on the administration of justice and the judge's relationship to his monarch, his society and the legal system. For de Lancre, justice was divine in its importance. He stated, "It is a beautiful thing to be a judge and to be just. To exercise justice justly is a totally divine thing. Thus people believe in their judges more than in any other sort of person." Therefore judges who did not measure up to this ideal were a very serious problem. De Lancre condemned corruption and ignorance among judges. As he stated, "The ignorance of judges is very dangerous, for there is nothing so evil as an ignorant man: He has no eyes to see good . . . or ears to hear the poor and the just . . . or hands to put his hand to honest work, to hold securely the scales of justice which are law and reason."[11]

De Lancre argued that judges must be both flexible and equitable. He criticized the cruelty of some of his colleagues, arguing that the French judicial system was too inclined to severe punishments. These brutal judges, "resorted to excesses of punishment, using overly cruel remedies to correct all evils."[12]

He went on to argue that all too often slanderers and false accusers were not punished by the courts, and as a result, innocent people often suffered long imprisonments and even torture. These innocent people also suffered material deprivation as well, and were deserving of some sort of compensation for their pains at the hands of the law. He appealed, "Oh Magistrates, the moral philosophy of Boethius will provide you a good lesson if only you deign to study! It will show you a great need to be men of good will! since your judgements are always given before that great judge who sees and hears all." De Lancre recognized that judges were only human, stating, "There is Inconstancy in our judgements, as our jurisconsultants and the Emperors who have given us their responses and prescriptions like oracles are themselves subject to frequent changes of opinion."[13]

The prime remedy recommended by de Lancre for all these grave problems of the practice of jurisprudence was for several judges to act together to moderate individual foibles and to prevent abuses. One judge acting alone was inimical to the course of real justice "since this would give too much sovereignty to a man if he could, by himself, judge the life of another man."[14] This was, of course, the standard approach in higher justice in France. Whether or not President d'Espaignet accompanied de Lancre into the Labourd, all the historians who have discussed the enquiry there hold de Lancre responsible for the proceedings, and indeed he always took credit for them. This whole legal discussion, written on the eve of the Labourd witchcraft case is an invaluable insight into how a well-educated, seventeenth-century intellectual saw his world and his profession, and how events could powerfully change things. In fact, de Lancre proved to be remarkably inconstant when, far from the urbane world of one of Europe's greatest ports, he was faced with the strange world of Basque peasant beliefs.

As has already been discussed, the French *Parlements* heard all criminal cases as panels of judges, acting as judges and jury. Generally, this seemed to encourage compromise and moderation rather than extreme positions and cruelty. There can be little doubt that this is one of the crucial factors in the relative mildness of the French legal system's handling of witchcraft cases, especially when compared to the regions bordering France where several independent judges were extraordinarily severe.

De Lancre's famous case opened in late 1608 or early 1609 when two gentlemen from the Labourd region, a Basque-speaking area in the far southwest corner of France, made a formal complaint alleging widespread witchcraft to the court of Henry IV. They also begged the king to establish a royal court of inquiry into the matter. Henry granted their request, ordering President Jean d'Espaignet and Counsellor Pierre de Lancre to proceed to the Labourd, about one hundred fifty kilometres south of Bordeaux, to investigate the witchcraft allegations, and to take whatever action they deemed necessary to deal with the problem. The *Parlement* protested, declaring that two judges, operating on their own, should not be able to apply torture in their questioning of suspects and should not have the authority to apply the death penalty to those found guilty. Henry rejected this appeal and ordered the court to register the original edict that established the mission. This the *Parlement* did on 5 June 1609. We should not assume that the court's opposition to the royal decree had anything to do with the personalities or reputations of de Lancre or d'Espaignet. Most likely it reflected the *Parlements*'s tradition of large boards of judges hearing cases and reaching judgments. In any case, the two men left Bordeaux around 28 June and headed south. Most writers have assumed that d'Espaignet did not stay with de Lancre, and thus that de Lancre proceeded into the Labourd and carried out the ensuing trials alone. But Gustav Henningsen, the most reliable historian who has dealt with this case, states that this is highly unlikely, and that the two judges probably stayed together well into the fall. The proceedings were concluded by the beginning of November.[15]

For almost three centuries, historians have accepted as fact that Pierre de Lancre sentenced six hundred people to death. This is, of course, an enormous number, considering that the whole commission lasted only four months. Henningsen argues that this figure "cannot possibly be correct and probably derives from a misinterpretation of some figures given in the preface to his book." While the exact number of de Lancre's victims cannot be determined, Henningsen points out that "(Father) Salazar (a Spanish Jesuit Inquisitor) who was well-informed regarding the witch persecution in the Pays de Labourd, states, in 1612, that the French judges managed to burn over eighty persons as witches during the course of the commission, and this is undoubtedly as close to the truth as we shall ever get."[16] In her recent edition of de Lancre's 1612 book, Nicole Jacques-Chaquin states, "It seems, without being absolutely certain, that around fifty accused were burnt."[17]

The story of this four-month commission has been told many times. But the accepted version of what happened is based largely on what seems to be a superficial reading of what de Lancre wrote about his experience. There are no records of the case in the Bordeaux archives, since they were destroyed in a fire in 1710.[18] However, a fuller version can be provided.

In his outstanding work *The Witches' Advocate*, Gustav Henningsen presents a detailed account of the hunt for witches in the Spanish-controlled Basque region, just across the border from where de Lancre's commission operated. The Spanish Inquisition kept meticulous records, many of which still exist and provide very important information. We can see the mirror image of the de Lancre case, in which commissioners from the Inquisition investigated the same kinds of reports with which their French counterparts were dealing. In 1609, the Inquisitors operated from similar intellectual positions as did de Lancre, and arrived at similar results. Furthermore, the Spanish officials followed developments across the border in France very closely and, in their correspondence between 1609 and 1612 supply valuable information on the French situation. The other main source for a fuller understanding of this important case is de Lancre's own work. In *Tableau de l'inconstance des mauvais anges et demons*, de Lancre tells a lot about this case. This work deserves to be read with care.

In the standard account of this case, which has been repeated in many works, de Lancre was the primary agent for a brutal suppression of witchcraft in the Labourd. He is held to have worked at a feverish pace, hearing the testimony of hundreds of witnesses and relying on a liberal use of torture in order to extract confessions from those accused of this imaginary crime. For example, Margaret McGowan stated that d'Espaignet did not stay in the region. "Pierre de Lancre continued his investigation of the 30,000 inhabitants alone. He heard the evidence of over 500 witnesses; and, in the space of four months, he burned and had tortured some 600 souls."[19] Most other authors also emphasize his use of torture.[20] In this scenario, de Lancre is seen as a sexually obsessed bigot who, driven by his own peculiar obsessions, submitted many innocent victims to torture and death. He is often depicted as enjoying his cruel role in this affair. Since the appearance of Henningsen's work, historians have adopted the figure of eighty executions rather than the traditional six hundred used by McGowan, but otherwise their views have not changed.

Let us re-examine the small bits of evidence on this case. The origins of the witch panic in the Basque region straddling the Franco-

Spanish border are obscure, but the fear of a diabolical sect seems to have been very intense. Henningsen emphasizes that the panic and demands for investigation and repression came from the bottom up. The local villagers demanded help from the Inquisition authorities.[21] The testimony concerning the existence of countless witches who gathered at huge Sabbaths closely matches what de Lancre reported hearing. Moreover, at these stages of investigation, the Spanish Inquisition did not apply torture.[22] The Inquisitors focused on the idea of an infernal sect as the result of the testimony they heard, even though they had, at the outset of their investigation, been explicitly ordered to search out physical evidence of spell-casting and maleficia.

De Lancre and d'Espaignet spent four months in the Labourd. De Lancre stated that, during their commission, they visited all twenty-seven parishes of the region. The region is small. St. Pee is only 15 kilometres from the capital, Bayonne, and Hendaye is barely twice that. However, the country is mountainous and the roads must have been winding and difficult. The travelling must have been time-consuming and fatiguing. There is no direct evidence as to the pace to which the commissioners worked. Spanish Inquisitors normally heard evidence and interrogated witnesses or the accused for around six hours a day. At this pace, they could deal with two individuals a day. This process was slow and laborious due in part to the ponderous caution with which the Inquisitors worked, but also because everything had to be translated from Spanish to Basque and back to Spanish again.[23] De Lancre discussed at length the difficulties imposed by the Basque language. It was not easy to find interpreters who were fully competent in both languages. He was keenly aware of the need for accurate understanding, so that people would not be tortured or punished who did not deserve it.[24]

Notwithstanding these difficulties, the French *parlementaires* seemed to work more briskly than the Spanish Inquisitors. Late in August of 1609 a Spanish judge in the area near the French border wrote his superiors,

> In many places on the other side of the border witches have been discovered, and the authorities are prosecuting them severely. They are burning one after another and conducting the cases very quickly. But I am assured (by Frey León) that the judge, who is a president of the Parliament at Bordeaux (Jean d'Espaignet) is conducting the cases very efficiently. The villages in which the wicked sect is to be found have themselves requested the investigation. The judges' commission runs for four months, as the whole area is infested with witches.[25]

Even if they worked much more intensely than their Spanish counterparts, it is difficult to imagine that, given the administrative difficulties, travelling and organization time, holidays and the like, that d'Espaignet and de Lancre really could have heard five hundred witnesses, distinguished between mere attenders at sabbats and heretical witches who renounced Christianity and adored the Devil, and conducted trials that resulted in fifty to eighty death sentences, all in only four months.

On the Spanish side of the border, the Inquisition at Longroño dealt with the accused witches, carrying out sentences on 7 November 1610, over a year after the investigation began. They had thirty-one accused witches in their prisons. They condemned only those who refused to confess, even under torture, eleven in all. Since five had died in prison, six witches were actually burned at the great Auto-de-Fe.[26]

De Lancre's commission actually worked in a very similar way. Many suspected witches were transferred to Bordeaux to be investigated and tried. In fact, de Lancre reported that so many were sent to Bordeaux that the prison could not house them all, so that a local ruined château had to be pressed into service as an auxiliary prison.[27] In the capital, their cases were dealt with by the criminal chamber of the *Parlement*, in accordance with their regular procedures.

There is no firm information on the *Parlement*'s disposition of these cases, or even of how many there were. A member of the *Parlement*, Armand de Gourges, attended the Auto-de-Fe at Longroño as an observer. According to the report of the Longroño tribunal, he "expressed his admiration for the clemency which was shown by the tribunal." Furthermore, in early 1611, a report to the Tribunal stated that, "The judges from the Parliament at Bordeaux who have been appointed to deal with witchcraft cases this year have gone to the other extreme from the judges of the previous year. If no facts or external evidence are available, they will neither institute proceedings nor receive evidence. They have gone so far as to release many of those who have been imprisoned. This will greatly damage the Pays de Labourd."[28]

It appears then, that the *Parlement*, when it took up de Lancre's cases, acted with its customary care, and was not very interested in the notion of a demonic sect that obsessed both de Lancre and the Spanish Inquisitors of 1609 and 1610. This statement also gives us a major clue as to why de Lancre wrote *L'inconstance des mauvais anges et demons*, and why it is so concerned with the witches' sabbath.

Most historians have agreed that the popular views of witchcraft in the early modern period centred on evil deeds, or *maleficia*. The idea of a sect of witches who renounced God and the church and who gathered at horrible assemblies called sabbats was a later idea, developed by learned demonologists like Bodin and de Lancre. This notion is seen as being divorced from popular folkloric culture.

In his discussion of the Spanish Basque witch hunt of 1609-12, Gustav Henningsen repeatedly insists that the pressure on the authorities to address the perceived cult of witches came from the populace. It is clear that the common people believed in the witches' sabbath. Hundreds confessed to having attended these diabolical assemblies and they implicated a few dozen as the ringleaders of the sect. The testimony heard by the Inquisitors closely matches what de Lancre reported about the frequency of sabbats and what happened at them. The Spanish Inquisitors, though specifically ordered to search out crimes (*maleficia*) committed by witches and physical evidence of their activities, quickly became entirely concerned with the sabbat and the demonic sect. Detailed accounts from hundreds of witnesses, gained without torture and agreeing in most details made these judges convinced of the reality of the sect.

In his provocative recent work, Carlo Ginzburg argues that the idea of the witches' sect and the sabbats that were crucial to the sect had a long and complex history. The notion of the Sabbath emerged as early as the fourteenth century in western Europe. It seems to have been partly the result of religious and political paranoia on the part of the elites but also was shaped by very widespread popular ideas which centred on ancient shamanistic religion and cults of fertility and the dead.[29] The more the elites learned of these beliefs in the later Middle Ages the more the notion of a secret sect of witches who gathered in huge demonic nocturnal assemblies was solidified. In turn, this notion seems to have been passed back to the people through preaching, Inquisitions and missionary activities. It fit well into their folkloric structure of beliefs.

Hearing hundreds of self-proclaimed eyewitnesses of sabbats, de Lancre, student of Maldonat and admirer of Del Rio, became totally convinced that the real problem in the Labourd was a sect of heretical witches which held ghastly immoral gatherings on a frequent basis. These witnesses did not have to be pressured to tell their stories. De Lancre stated, "I can say of the women and girls of the Labourd who have gone to sabbats, that instead of being quiet about this damnable coupling [with demons at sabbats], or of blushing and crying about it, they tell the dirtiest and most immodest circumstances with such freedom and gaiety that they glory in it and take a great pleasure in telling about it."[30] One witness even proclaimed that "the sabbat was the real Paradise, where there was more pleasure than could be expressed."[31]

For those who said that the whole thing was a matter of illusions or dreams, de Lancre argued, "If they were dreams, how could they all have the same dreams? How is it possible that these things happened in the same way, in the same place, in the same time, the same day, the same hours? ... Did they dream the same thing, little ones and big ones, old people and young people, men and women, billious and phlegmatic, sanguine and melancholic?"[32] When the *Parlement* of Bordeaux, relying on its conventional jurisprudence, insisted in most cases on proof of "facts or external evidence" and refused to convict based solely on testimony of witnesses, de Lancre must have felt the need to defend his record and to try to present a convincing argument for the existence of a dangerous and widespread demonic sect.

This was, after all, the whole point of de Lancre's argument. Convinced, as the Spanish Inquisitors had been, by a mountain of peasant testimony about sabbats, de Lancre was obsessed with the sect of witches. He seems to have convinced his colleagues of this and the court was, for a time, willing to apply the death penalty to those accused of being leaders at sabbats even if no *maleficia* could be proved. He mentioned at least four such executions in the aftermath of his commission.[33]

Pierre De Lancre must have started work on his second book very soon after his return to Bordeaux from the Labourd. This work, his best known—some would say his most notorious—is entitled *L'inconstance des mauvais anges et demons* and was published in Paris in 1612.

De Lancre's experiences in the Labourd only confirmed the reality and dangers of witchcraft. He went out of his way to attack unbelief in witchcraft, a theme to which he returned at length in his later work. He believed that his accounts

> should fully convince the hardest, stupidest, blindest and most stubborn that there is now no way to cast doubt on [the reality of] witchcraft and that the Devil actually and bodily transports witches to sabbats. ... I can state that sixty or eighty certain witches and five hundred witnesses marked with the character of the Devil—which marvellously confirms

their disposition—have stated that Satan has done this.... Demons have a thousand ways to seduce men and induce them to temptation. Where the finesse of the serpent cannot win, he uses the power of the lion and the subtlety of the ape.

He continued, in a drawn-out mixed baroque metaphor,

> The world is a theatre where the Devil plays an infinity of diverse and varied roles. It is the globe that this bloodthirsty beast turns, always in search of victims with whom he can fill this Hell, who never says, "that is enough," tending always to its centre, where he finally discharges his prey, who he wins, some by ruse, some by violence, knowing very well how to sew the skin of the fox to that of the lion.[34]

Unfortunately, de Lancre's own *Parlement* of Bordeaux had a reputation for mildness and lack of intensity in dealing with witchcraft cases. He stated,

> Demons are the most powerful enemies, not only of man, but of God himself... we must confess, to our great regret, that this *Parlement* of Guyenne has seen examples [of witchcraft] so extraordinary, so clear and in such great number that their novelty and their multiplicity have strongly deterred our judges, so that instead of leading them to punishment, they have often been led to pardon.... [In the Labourd] the number of witches there was so great that Satan had become absolute master.... The officers of Justice found themselves very weak in that place, before an enemy so subtle and tricky who often mixes with the very relatives of Judges.... And the evil has moved so far forward that we must fear that it will come to dominate all sorts of Judges, like the ancient philosophers, who treated this abomination lightly, trying to pass off the strangeness of the crimes and evil deeds of witches as impossible.[35]

The dangers of judicial scepticism in the pursuit of witches was tremendous for de Lancre, and he returned to it again and again.

De Lancre presented an extraordinary sociological study of the Labourd region to justify his severe repression of popular witchcraft there—and incidentally, of the long book that was to follow.[36] This discussion is interestingly modelled on his earlier study of inconstancy and the evils it perpetuates in the world. De Lancre's views speak mostly about his own moral and social values and the complex conflict between an upper-class, well-educated Catholic, part of the heartland of an old French civilization and Basque-speaking, illiterate, superficially Christianized peasants and fishermen. De Lancre's mission is a pointed example of a linguistic and intellectual imperialist who could have little understanding or trust of a people, so foreign and primitive, who lived almost in his own backyard.

To begin his analysis of the area, de Lancre pointed out that it was dangerous that French, Spanish and Basque were all spoken in the region,

> For all these diversities give Satan marvellous ease to hold assemblies and sabbats in this place, since it is a seacoast that makes people rustic, rude and badly ordered, among whom a flighty spirit is like their fortune attached to lines and banners moving like the wind, which have no other field than the mountains and the sea.... In short, their country is so infertile that they are constrained to throw themselves into that unquiet element, the sea... not undertaking the constant labour and culture of the earth.

For de Lancre, obviously a landlubber, the sea was trackless and changeable and was far inferior as a place of occupation than was Guyenne, with its steady agricultural life. Since the natives of the Labourd nearly all went to sea, "their fields are in the greatest part uncultivated and poverty is widespread and these are the two qualities that the Devil most desires in his subjects."[37]

For de Lancre, what he saw as normal family and community life was impossible with the men being off at sea for so much of the time. "The men do not love their homeland, nor their wives and children," he wrote. "The absence and long voyages they make on sea cause their lack of love and engenders hatred in some and tepidness or coldness in others. So there are only children and old people who keep the household, people without conduct and without judgement who for their feebleness the Devil manipulates as he pleases."[38]

Another grave result of this wild seafaring way of life was a very poor quality of Christian life. Even the priesthood had been infiltrated by the Devil. De Lancre stated, "These people are not nourished in the fear of God. Pastors, priests and curés are set up by the devil in all the better-known parishes, to such an extent that Satan begins to possess not only these priests, but even some churches have been polluted and profaned."[39]

Many subjects are examined at considerable length in this long work. One such is the sabbat—the witches' nocturnal assemblies—that was so crucial to local popular beliefs. De Lancre described, in strong and colourful prose, the horrifying, perverted actions of witches and demons at their meetings. His descriptions were based on the well-established image of the sabbat then current, but were confirmed and enriched by the testimony of the accused, including children, that he heard during the trials. De Lancre's acceptance of these views has caused historians to cast him in a very negative light. As Margaret McGowan stated, "Two hundred pages fill in the detail of this picture, almost gloatingly presented by de Lancre. There are many times when his fevered imagination gets the better of him, and one marvels at the ease with which an experienced lawyer, in his fifties, gives credence to the undisciplined imaginings of frustrated children and adolescents."[40]

In this book there is an interesting discussion of the problem of how witches were transported to the sabbats which sheds a lot of light on de Lancre's approach to his subject. As is evident in many places, de Lancre's main intellectual influence is Martin Del Rio. De Lancre states often that Del Rio was the principal authority, "For his reasons are so strong that the beliefs of the Church being universal one cannot be of any other opinion."[41] For de Lancre, all Christians had to believe in the real transportation of witches to the sabbats, which sometimes was done by the soul only, but could also be done in both body and soul. In the latter case, a simulated body of the witch would be left in the place of the sabbat-goer. Witches could travel to the sabbat in their thoughts only, by walking or being flown by Satan. "We add that the apostolic Roman Catholic Church, which cannot err, punishes them by death; for it would be greatly in error to treat them so severely if they were only criminals and witches in their dreams. We must thus necessarily infer that whoever believes that these transports [of witches to sabbats] are only tricks, dreams and illusions, sins against the Church which does not punish uncertain occult and non-manifest crimes and only punishes as heretics those who are [heretics] truly and not in dreams and illusions." Furthermore, "this is the opinion of Remy, of Boguet and Del Rio, the three I rely on primarily because the first two as sovereign judges have seen an infinite number of examples, and the last has spoken more Christianly and according to the faith than anyone else."[42] So we can see that de Lancre based his views on a combination of likeminded demonological writers, a loosely defined idea of religious orthodoxy and his own personal experiences of hearing witches' confessions.

Through hearing confessions in the Labourd, he was able to refute strongly Bodin's view that the Devil could not make a pact with prepubescent children. He stated, "We have seen a hundred depositions to the contrary by many children who, from the age of six to twelve or older have made a pact with him, renounced God and received the insensitive [diabolical] mark as his slaves." The Devil's mark was a key element in the detection of witches. De Lancre argued, "I confess that what Del Rio says is very true—that Satan marks them [his witches] hides the marks and sometimes does not mark them at all, according to what he thinks is most advantageous; but if the mark is found, it serves as an index and violent presumption of guilt and there can be no doubt at all." De Lancre's colleagues seemed to recognize his expertise and defer to it. He reported, "On 3 September 1610 they called me to see if I recognised the mark in the eye of a seventeen-year-old girl: I saw it as soon as I entered the room . . . the girl confessed that her mother had taken her to the Sabbat."[43]

De Lancre believed that severe penalties were necessary for those who had joined the Devil in his evil work. Those witches "have fallen into heresy and apostasy, having abjured the true God, being dedicated to the service of Satan." Witchcraft was the most dangerous of all heresies:

> For heresy manifests and reveals itself, which does not happen with witchcraft, which only seeks darkness and shadows. The enemy hidden in ambush is more dangerous. . . . Heresy only does evil to heretics. . . . on the other hand witchcraft does not only damn the witches and those who are infected with their venom, but also kills good people by poison or by charms, engenders plagues by the infection of the air, kills livestock, destroys the fruit of the earth by hailstorms, and tempests that it creates through enchantments and by all these means it troubles the public welfare of men, animals and all nature. . . . the abominable and execrable hugeness and horror of this crime makes us now see that it cannot be treated as a common crime.[44]

De Lancre, at this point agreeing with Bodin, argued that witches deserved death even if they had not actually done any evil deeds, for the great crime of renouncing God. He argued, again with Bodin, that if judges did not do their duty toward witches, the people would take justice into their own hands. Lynchings of witches were "a lesson to Judges, of the just judgement of God, who testifies clearly to them on this point, that often they treat them [witches] too softly, so that God who is the sovereign judge, puts then His hand into the world against them and often punishes and chastises the pernicious curiosity of judges and their mildness."[45]

As already indicated, many historians have described de Lancre as a ridiculous obsessed fanatic. Terms like "gleeful," "gloating," "infantile," "sadistic" and "bigoted" have all been applied to him. But in his writing, de Lancre constantly emphasized the distastefulness of the task in which he was engaged. Certainly, he believed totally the testimony that he heard, sentenced people to death based on that testimony, and worked to convince his colleagues to follow his lead. But there is little evidence in his work to support the picture that has so often been drawn. Describing his term in the Labourd, he stated, "Toward the end of our commission which had already lasted almost four months, we were harassed by great pain and by a disagreeable buzzing in our ears that were so constantly battered by such horrible discourse of the Evil Spirit, of sabbats, carrying off of children, and other execrable deeds so that we had an extreme desire to get away from this commission as from a hell."[46]

It is very difficult to determine what effect this book may have had on its readers in its own time. It might be that de Lancre's book has been more important for historians than it was for its contemporaries. Certainly the trend in the sovereign courts to diminish witchcraft prosecutions and to curb the discretionary powers the lower courts in witchcraft cases seemed to continue unabated. Few new works that supported the arguments of the demonologists appeared after 1612, and those that did were often the products of the generation of the religious wars who continued to publish well into their old age, like de Lancre himself, or Jean Boucher.

In 1617, de Lancre published a moral political treatise called *Le livre des princes*. This work, nominally written to warn the young king, Louis XIII, against flatterers, actually seems to be an attack on the hated royal favourite, Louis Concini. Concini was assassinated by the king's order on 24 April, only a few weeks after the book's appearance on 1 March. It is a long-winded (807 pages) work that picks up on many of the themes in the 1607 *L'inconstance et instabilité*. It is interesting though in revealing some aspects of early seventeenth-century Catholic puritanism, a subject that has not been much explored. For de Lancre, as for Garasse and others, the royal court was licentious, luxurious and hypocritical. He stated," The court is the forge for all sorts of illicit pleasures—it is the place where the vices are out in great number." De Lancre expressed his disapproval of passionate love, dancing and luxurious clothing. As he said, "There is no doubt that under the luxury and dissoluteness in clothing and in the attraction of them, Satan is accustomed to making open war on good morals and primarily on the chastity of ladies."[47] Flattery, luxury and curiosity, combined with unmanly morals had led to a grave situation, according to de Lancre, and made it an easy task for Satan to pervert morals and lead humans astray. Magic, witchcraft and immorality all flowed from the lax morals of the court, and the easy going attitude of the young king in the policing of these morals set a bad example for the whole kingdom. This combination of Catholic piety, moral uprightness and obsessive concern with the Devil was a potent combination in early seventeenth-century France and was not unique to Pierre de Lancre.

De Lancre returned to the subject of witchcraft in 1622, with another long book, this time concerned solely with the serious problem of unbelief in demons and witches. In his dedication (to the king) he stated that he had again taken pen in hand "to dislodge whatever incredulity that the Sovereign Companies [the *Parlements*], all judges and other important people might have, and to convince them of the error and blindness of those who are more interested in the darkness of eclipses than in the pure and clear rays of the Sun. New academicians who sustain that there is no truth in what is said of witches and witchcraft, but that all of it is only an illusion." De Lancre hoped "to inspire your majesty, to put him ardently in the desire to banish and exterminate from your court and from this august and holy kingdom magicians, witches, diviners, casters of horoscopes, Jews, Apostates, Atheists and all other enemies of God."[48]

This work has a strongly defensive tone, and was clearly inspired by the author's perception that there was widespread scepticism concerning the reality and dangers of demons and witches. If, as so many modern authors have stated, the social elites believed in witchcraft, and were committed to using the justice system to wipe them out as part of an effort to reform peasant culture, there would have been little point for de Lancre to write this long book. He wrote, "I know that doubt of magic and witchcraft, whether there are magicians or witches, is so great that there has grown a greater [doubt], that is that there are no demons.... Many have sustained that there are no demons, so that it is foolish to believe all the evil and evil deeds that are imputed to them."[49]

He appealed to these allegedly numerous unbelievers,

> Unbeliever, I beg you to quit the error of those who have thought there are neither good or bad angels ... do you want to leave the belief of the Universal Church who prays every day to deliver you from them? ... We must not doubt that there are demons ... and that demons have such

power in this world that God himself calls them Princes of the world.... And since there are demons, there also exists a certain demonic magic, practiced by magicians and witches, enrolled under the banner of Satan.... All Europe being touched by this sickness, is it possible that everyone is dreaming? And if they are dreaming, how could it be that people so distant and dissimilar from each other have the same dreams and the same grotesque images... having the Devil appear in the same form."[50]

De Lancre continually drew on his own judicial experience in the Labourd, where "many people were afflicted by witches, many infected by this abomination and abused by the Devil, who called them to the Sabbat almost every night.... At Biarritz almost all the witches in our time were marked in the eye in the form of a cat or toad paw. Is this an illusion?" He also cited recent cases in Bordeaux, such as "the witch Stevenote de Audebert who was burned by order of the *Parlement* in January 1619, who showed us an oath, containing a pact she had made with the devil, who had seduced her, written in menstrual blood and so horrible we were in horror to look at it."[51]

In this work, de Lancre reiterated his strong views on the evil inclinations of women. He wrote, "Women are more likely to be witches, and in greater numbers than men. It is a fragile sex, which takes demonic suggestions as divine. Secondly, they forge many dreams which they believe to be true... further they abound in vehement passions."[52]

An unusual aspect of this work is an extended attack on Jews, towards whom de Lancre uses the strongest terms. Most of Book 8 is directed against Jews, who de Lancre calls "our most ancient enemies." He condemned "their blasphemies against the Christian Church, their impieties and absurdities... their besotted beliefs and the cruelty they have always used toward Christians." Their blasphemies, he wrote "are so horrible, and such an enraged and diabolical invention that it would be better to suppress them... than to publicize them in an age as evil and perverse as this one." He admired the severity of the Spanish Inquisition toward the Jews, but regretted that this had caused many Jews to emigrate to France, where they pretended to be Christians. He proclaimed, "it would be better to spread plague among us, and put serpents to our breast than to tolerate this vermin."[53]

This extraordinary diatribe of de Lancre's has no parallel in the demonological literature of the age. Jews were rarely mentioned by other writers, and when they were, they were usually a sort of abstraction, rather than a real aspect of the contemporary world.

But Jews were a reality of de Lancre's world, and he clearly hated them. Bordeaux was one of the few places in France that had a Jewish community. Beginning in the early sixteenth century, Spanish and then Portuguese *conversos*, or New Christians, moved into Bordeaux, fleeing the Spanish Inquisition's campaign for *limpieza del sangre*. Since the Jews of medieval France had been expelled in 1394, there was no legal existence of Judaism until the Revolution granted full rights of citizenship in 1789. While the Jews of Bordeaux, who were officially called "The Portuguese," observed all the external aspects and signs of Christianity, they were suspected by many of secretly maintaining their Jewish religion and practices. Among the fifty or so "Portuguese" families in Bordeaux in de Lancre's time, were several wealthy merchant families, like the Lopes and the Govea, who married into the local nobility and gentry, and served in high offices in the courts, the civil administration and even the church in the city. It was undoubtedly their success that earned them the hatred of some of Bordeaux's Catholic inhabitants.[54] In de Lancre's case, we are probably seeing genuine hatred, based on a sincere belief that Jews were evil, and were practitioners of the diabolical arts.

These sentiments were also probably nurtured by de Lancre's lifelong close relationship with the Jesuit order, the most Spanish of the religious orders in France. In 1593, at their general congregation, the Jesuits excluded all those of Jewish origins from membership in the order, even though some of Loyola's early close associates had Jewish backgrounds.[55]

De Lancre concludes the book with a long appeal to judges to lay aside their unbelief, which de Lancre terms ignorance, and to open their eyes to the reality, prevalence and dangers of witchcraft. The doubts that so worried him came from the Devil himself. "He supports doubt in religion and faith to those who cannot simply hold the beliefs of the true Church." But he was confident that the scoffers and doubters would eventually receive their just desserts, "they will learn, at their expense, that there are executioners in Hell. . . . Oh miserable witches, whose pleasures and abominable curiosity are sufficient crimes! Blind judges! Unbelief is the daughter of ignorance; it is the smoke of Hell that the Devil introduces into the Palace [of Justice], to take from you the means of discerning and judging sanely the abominations of witches!"[56]

It would be a mistake to assume that, because de Lancre wrote long books, packed with erudition and colourful language, that he exercised a good deal of influence on the judicial practices in matters relating to witchcraft in his time. De Lancre's judicial career spanned the period of the growth of witchcraft trials in France and then their sharp decline in the early seventeenth century. His writing career, though, corresponds only to the latter period, when there is a drop in the frequency of trials and the use of capital punishment to penalize witches. As a convinced believer in witchcraft and a proponent of active witch hunting and severe treatment of witches, he was increasingly isolated intellectually and judicially as time went on. This is clearly reflected in the stridently defensive tone of his works. Only the *L'inconstance des mauvais anges et demons* of 1612 was republished, and it only received one additional edition in 1613.

It would also be a mistake, though, to dismiss de Lancre as a crank, a bizarre or ridiculous figure. He was an earnest advocate of a worldview that was not insignificant in his time. He took seriously his instruction from respectable orthodox scholars, and did not waver from them for his long life. He was part of the generation of 1550, shaped by the religious wars, who sought, unsuccessfully, to reshape French society into their mould.

Conclusion

Although to us he is one of the best-known French judges of the early seventeenth century, Pierre de Lancre was not a typical French high court magistrate. His work as a demonologist author and judge is unique in France. While he fits Muchembled's picture of the Catholic Reformation man, he cannot serve as an exemplar for elite society.

Accusations for witchcraft occurred fairly frequently in the late sixteenth and early seventeenth centuries. In general, while the local courts could be quite severe with accused witches, relatively few of their sentences were actually carried out. The *Parlements*, acting as appeals courts, did not torture the accused very often, regularly overturned guilty verdicts, and rarely imposed the death penalty for this crime.

The *Parlements* of Old Regime France were prestigious bodies, staffed by members of the social and educational elite of the age. They examined evidence and delivered their judgments as panels. They seemed to work diligently in criminal cases, taking time to examine the often puzzling testimony that came to them. This judicial approach, together with their efforts to regularize appeals of lower court verdicts

---

Notes to the Conclusion are on p. 168.

meant that very few people were executed for witchcraft in France. While many *parlementaires* seemed to believe in witchcraft as a phenomenon, this belief did not lead them to suspend their normal caution in order to condemn many people to death for witchcraft.

In their practice of criminal law, the *Parlements* were almost entirely independent of the royal government. They proceeded according to the well-defined principles of Roman law, as was the case almost everywhere in Europe. They seem to have been careful about the broad discretionary powers they possessed, especially their ability to commit the accused to torture in order to extract a confession.[1]

This moderation of the French courts occurred in spite of a substantial corpus of demonological writings, published by reputable Catholic authorities, which appeared with a fair degree of regularity between 1565 or so and the 1620s. These works all regarded witchcraft as real, as a dangerous act of treason against God, and as closely related to the diabolically inspired Protestant heresy. Their authors were unanimous in counselling judges to believe in witchcraft, to take it seriously and to work with dedication to eradicate it from the earth. Even Bodin, not an orthodox Catholic writer, argued much of this case.

It seems clear that the courts, at least the *Parlements*, did not follow this advice and integrate demonology into their legal practice. If they had, the prosecution of witches in France would have resembled that in places like Lorraine, where 90 percent of those accused were executed,[2] and many thousands would have died in France.

There are several reasons for this relative moderation. For one thing, the *Parlements* seemed clearly to be quite conservative in their legal work. They insisted on proper procedure and close examination of the evidence. As we have discussed, even Bodin was very cautious in his procedural advice. If the judges had followed his legal advice, the persecution of witches in France would not have been very different from what it was. The role of the *Parlements* as appeal courts was of capital importance in the overall moderation of the French legal system in the business of witchcraft.

Just as important, and much less closely examined to date, is the crucial area of the profound divisions in elite opinion. While the relationship between elites and the popular masses has been discussed by many historians, the differences of opinion among the upper classes and their influence in witchcraft trials has not been sufficiently scrutinized. Far from representing universal or even majority elite opinion, the orthodox demonologists seem to have been on the fringe of political society. Many of them were Jesuits, or students and supporters of the Jesuits or at least of the Holy League in the religious wars. As such they had clear objectives that were well known and perceived by their contemporaries to be a political program. Though they claimed to be the party of God, they were regarded with deep hostility by many influential French Catholics. As propaganda, issued by one religious-political faction among several, French demonology could only have limited appeal.

So the demonologists' message was blunted. From their beginning in the 1560s they ran directly into the hostility of the Gallican tradition's hostility to the Roman-dominated ostentatious religion of the post-Tridentine era. The courts had long played an active role in the introduction and maintenance of Gallican Catholicism in France. It is not at all surprising that they resisted the blandishments of the enemies of Gallicanism. The failure to place demonology in its contemporary Christian and political context has led historians to generalize and to arrive at erroneous conclusions. It is in the bitter divisions of elite Catholic society that the failure of demonology in France is to be found.

The refusal of the royal and legal establishment to strike out at heretics and witches in a sufficiently violent way to destroy them was seen by the zealots as a sign of the alliance of this establishment with the Devil. As time went on and the Gallican-*politique*-Protestant forces headed toward victory in the civil war, the zealots became more desperate. But the more shrill they became, the more marginal was their message. The French accepted and came to idolize a Protestant who converted twice to Catholicism. For many people, the settlement of the Wars of Religion represented a major compromise, one that was necessary for the restoration of order to France. Political, religious and judicial moderation triumphed over extremism. Though the demonologists demanded death for witches, the high courts acquitted them. Demonology did not carry the day in France.

Notes

Introduction

1 This point of view can be seen in Julio Caro Baroja, *The World of the Witches*, translated by O.N.V. Glendenning (Chicago: University of Chicago Press, 1965); Hugh Trevor-Roper, "The European Witch-Craze of the Sixteenth and Seventeenth Centuries," in *The European Witch-craze of the Sixteenth and Seventeenth Centuries and Other Essays* (New York: Harper & Row, 1969); and Sydney Anglo, ed., *The Damned Art: Essays in the Literature of Witchcraft* (London: Routledge, 1977).
2 John Bossy, "Unrethinking the Sixteenth-Century Wars of Religion," in Thomas Kselman, ed., *Belief in History* (Notre Dame: University of Notre Dame Press, 1991), and Denis Crouzet, *Les guerriers de dieu: la violence au temps des troubles de religion*, 2 vols. (Seyssel: Champ Vallon, 1990), vol. 1, p. 75.
3 See Mack P. Holt, *The French Wars of Religion, 1562-1629* (Cambridge: Cambridge University Press, 1995), and R.J. Knecht, *The Rise and Fall of Renaissance France* (London: n.p., 1996).
4 See, for example, H.C.E. Midelfort, *Witch Hunting in Southwestern Germany 1562-1684* (Stanford, CA: Stanford University Press, 1972), p. 68.
5 Jacques Ellul, *Propaganda*, translated by Konrad Kellen and Jean Lerner (New York: Knopf, 1968).

Chapter One

1 Debates among historians on the causes and meaning of European witchcraft continue. Recent publications in which these issues are discussed include Lyndal Roper, *Oedipus and the Devil: Witchcraft, Sexuality and Religion in Early Modern Europe* (London: Routledge, 1994); Robin Briggs, *Witches and Neighbours: The*

Social and Cultural Concept of European Witchcraft (London: HarperCollins, 1996); and Jonathan Barry, Marianne Hester and Gareth Roberts, eds., *Witchcraft in Early Modern Europe: Studies in Culture and Belief* (Cambridge: Cambridge University Press, 1996), which is dedicated to a discussion of the theoretical and methodological problems in the history of witchcraft, centring on the now classic work of Keith Thomas, *Religion and the Decline of Magic* (London: Penguin, 1971).

2 See Sophie Houdard, *Quatre démonologues* (Paris: n.p., 1992), and Gerhild Scholz Williams, *Defining Dominion: The Discourses of Magic and Witchcraft in Early Modern France and Germany* (Ann Arbor: University of Michigan Press, 1995).

3 Stuart Clark, "Inversion, Misrule and the Meaning of Witchcraft," *Past and Present* (1980), and Stuart Clark, "The Rational Witchfinder: Conscience, Demonological Naturalism and Popular Superstitions," in Stephen Pumfrey, Paolo Rossi and Maurice Slawinski, eds., *Science, Culture and Popular Belief in Renaissance Europe* (Manchester: Manchester University Press, 1991).

4 See, for example, Brian Levack, *The Witch-Hunt in Early Modern Europe* (London: Longman, 1987, 1994), p. 108.

5 Trevor-Roper, "The European Witch-Craze of the Sixteenth and Seventeenth Centuries," pp. 96-97.

6 Robert Mandrou, *Magistrats et sorciers en France au XVIIe siècle: essai de psychologie sociale* (Paris: Plon, 1968).

7 Soon after its publication, E. William Monter wrote, "The product of nearly fifteen years of research, this book provides historians with the first truly thorough investigation of the decline of witchcraft persecution. Mandrou has established the basic chronology of French persecution.... Mandrou's account of this evolution ... is a full and rich narrative" (E. William Monter, "Law, Medicine, and the Acceptance of Witchcraft," in E. William Monter, *European Witchcraft* [New York: Wiley, 1969], p. 127).

8 Mandrou, *Magistrats et sorciers en France*, pp. 92-103.

9 Jean Delumeau, *La peur en occident* (Paris: Fayard, 1978), p. 376.

10 Ibid., p. 884.

11 Ibid., p. 376.

12 Robert Muchembled, *La culture populaire et la culture des élites* (Paris: Flammarion, 1978), p. 300.

13 Robert Muchembled, "Lay Judges and Acculturation," in Kaspar von Greyerz, ed., *Religion and Society in Early Modern Europe, 1500-1800* (London: Allen and Unwin, 1984), pp. 58, 60, 64-65.

14 Joseph Klaits, *Servants of Satan: The Age of the Witch Hunts* (Bloomington: Indiana University Press, 1985), pp. 3, 5, 85.

15 Levack, *The Witch-hunt in Early Modern Europe*, pp. 17, 25, 52.

16 Jean Wirth, "Against the Acculturation Thesis," in von Greyerz, ed., *Religion and Society in Early Modern Europe*, p. 67.

17 Peter Burke, "A Question of Acculturation," in *Scienze, credenze occulte, livelli di cultura* (Florence: Olschki, 1982).

18 Robin Briggs, *Communities of Belief: Cultural and Social Tensions in Early Modern France* (Oxford: Oxford University Press, 1989).

19 Briggs, *Witches and Neighbours*.

20 Ibid., p. 400.

21 Alfred Soman, *Sorcellerie et justice criminelle* (Hampshire: n.p., 1992). This volume brings together twenty of Soman's articles, published since 1977. The pagination is as in the original articles.
22 Ibid., I, p. 790.
23 Ibid., XIV, p. 30.
24 Ibid., XV, p. 15.
25 Ibid., VI, p. 25.
26 Ibid., VI, p. 128.
27 Ibid., XV, p. 6.
28 Ibid., XIII, p. 43; XV, p. 5.
29 Ibid., VII, p. 38; XII, p. 189; XII, fig. 2; VII, pp. 19, 33, 40; Corrigenda, p. 2.
30 Soman has provided crucial statistical data on witchcraft prosecution in France, and his work has been part of a significant revision of historical approaches to witchcraft trials. In the larger picture, though, Soman's work remains incomplete. Figures vary from article to article. He discusses the "decriminalization" of witchcraft in France when one could argue that it never was a major concern of the criminal justice system.
31 Ibid., XII, p. 194.
32 Jonathan Dewald, *The Formation of a Provincial Nobility* (Princeton: Princeton University Press, 1980), pp. 318-19.
33 Mandrou, *Magistrats et sorciers en France*, p. 450.
34 Robert Muchembled, *Le roi et la sorcière* (Paris: Desclée, 1994).
35 Robert Muchembled, "Terres de Contrastes: France, Pays-Bas, Provinces-Unies," in Robert Muchembled, ed., *Magie et sorcellerie en Europe du Moyen Âge à nos jours* (Paris: Armand Colin, 1994), p. 120.
36 Ibid., p. 98.
37 Robert Muchembled, *Société, cultures et mentalités dans la France moderne: XVIe-XVIIIe siècles* (Paris: SEDES, 1994), p. 128. In closely examining this one issue, I do not wish to imply a negative view of Muchembled's impressive *oeuvre*. His works, especially since 1988, are very complex and wide ranging. He poses big questions about the nature and evolution of societies that are challenging and significant.
38 See Gustav Henningsen, *The Witches' Advocate: Baroque Witchcraft and the Spanish Inquisition (1609-1614)* (Reno: University of Nevada Press, 1980); Wolfgang Behringer, "Allemagne, 'Mère du tant de sorcières,' Au coeur des persécutions," in Muchembled, ed., *Magie et sorcellerie en Europe*, p. 82; and Briggs, *Witches and Neighbours*, pp. 263, 339, 398.
39 Muchembled, *Le roi et la sorcière*, 69-70.
40 Ibid., p. 98.
41 Bernadette Paton, "'To the Fire, To the Fire. Let Us Burn a Little Incense to God': Bernardino, Preaching Friars and *Maleficio* in Late Medieval Siena," in Charles Zika, ed., *No Gods Except Me: Orthodoxy and Religious Practice in Europe, 1200-1600* (Melbourne: Melbourne University Press, 1991).
42 See A. Lynn Martin, *Henry III and the Jesuit Politicians* (Geneva: Droz, 1973).
43 Paul Lawrence Rose, "The *Politique* and the Prophet: Bodin and the Catholic League 1589-1594," *The Historical Journal* (1978), pp. 783-808.
44 Mario Turchetti, "Religious Concord and Political Tolerance in Sixteenth- and Seventeenth-Century France," *Sixteenth Century Journal* (1991), p. 17, and Knecht, *The Rise and Fall of Renaissance France*, pp. 347-49, 378.

Chapter Two

1 Robert Scribner, *Popular Culture and Popular Movements in Reformation Germany* (London: Hambledon Press, 1987), p. 13. Also, the Devil appears on stage as a comic figure in many English moral and cycle plays.
2 John Bossy, "Moral Arithmetic: Seven Sins into Ten Commandments," in Edmund Leites, ed., *Conscience and Casuistry in Early Modern Europe* (Cambridge: Cambridge University Press, 1988).
3 Ibid., pp. 215, 217, 230.
4 See, among others, Norman Cohn, *Europe's Inner Demons* (London: Chatto/Heinemann, 1975); Richard Keickhefer, *European Witch Trials: Their Foundation in Popular and Learned Culture, 1300-1500* (London: Routledge and Kegan Paul, 1976); Klaits, *Servants of Satan*; Edward Peters, *The Magician, the Witch, and the Law* (Philadelphia: University of Pennsylvania Press, 1978); and Julio Caro Baroja, "Witchcraft and Catholic Theology," in Bengt Ankarloo and Gustav Henningsen, eds., *Early Modern European Witchcraft* (Oxford: Oxford University Press, 1990).
5 See Holt, *The French Wars of Religion*; J.H.M. Salmon, *Society in Crisis: France in the Sixteenth Century* (London: Ernest Benn, 1975); and Mark Greengrass, *France in the Age of Henry IV* (London: Longman, 1984), for good, recent accounts of the wars of religion. They also have excellent bibliographies for the reader who wants to go further. Henry Heller, *Iron and Blood* (Montreal: McGill-Queen's University Press, 1991), is excellent, and N.M. Sutherland, *The Massacre of St. Bartholomew and the European Conflict 1559-1572* (New York: Barnes and Noble, 1973), is useful as well, though, like many works, their focus is almost exclusively political.
6 See Heller, *Iron and Blood*.
7 Holt, *The French Wars of Religion*, p. 47.
8 Crouzet, *Les guerriers de dieu*, vol. 1, pp. 109ff.
9 Frederic J. Baumgartner, *Henry II, King of France* (Durham, NC: Duke University Press, 1988).
10 Nancy Lyman Roelker, *One King, One Faith: The Parlement of Paris in the Religious Reformation of the Sixteenth Century* (Berkeley: University of California Press, 1996), pp. 88-93.
11 There are many discussions of the Council of Trent. For a good discussion of the Council from a French perspective, see Jean Delumeau, *Catholicism between Luther and Voltaire*, translated by Jeremy Moiser (London: Burns & Oates, 1977), especially pp. 4-42, 175-202.
12 Baumgartner, *Henry II, King of France*, pp. 117-18.
13 Delumeau, *Catholicism between Luther and Voltaire*, p. 7.
14 Roelker, *One King, One Faith*, p. 328. Also see Christopher Bettinson, "The Politiques and the Politique Party: A Reappraisal," in Keith Cameron, ed., *From Valois to Bourbon: Dynasty, State and Society in Early Modern France* (Exeter: University of Exeter Press, 1989).
15 See among others, Henry Kamen, *Inquisition and Society in Spain in the Sixteenth and Seventeenth Centuries* (Bloomington: Indiana University Press, 1985); Edward Peters, *Inquisition* (Philadelphia: University of Pennsylvania Press, 1988); and E. William Monter, *Ritual, Myth, and Magic in Early Modern Europe* (Athens: Ohio University Press, 1984).
16 Baumgartner, *Henry II, King of France*, pp. 231-33.

17 G. Wylie Sypher, "'Faisant ce qu'il leur vient a plaisir': The Image of Protestantism in French Catholic Polemic on the Eve of the Religious Wars," *Sixteenth Century Journal* (Summer 1980), pp. 78-79, and David Nicholls, "The Theatre of Martyrdom in the French Reformation," *Past and Present* (November 1988), pp. 50-52.
18 This is a central point in the work of Klaits (*Servants of Satan*) and Barstow (*Witchcraze*).
19 John H. Langbein, *Prosecuting Crime in the Renaissance* (Cambridge, MA: Harvard University Press, 1974), pp. 243ff.
20 A good discussion of how cases were handled in French courts is to be found in Malcolm Greenshields, *An Economy of Violence in Early Modern France: Crime and Justice in the Haute Auvergne, 1587-1664* (University Park: Pennsylvania State University Press, 1994).
21 Ibid., and Julius R. Ruff, *Crime, Justice and Public Order in Old Regime France* (London: Croom Helm, 1984), pp. 45-48.
22 Ibid., pp. 55-57.
23 Edward Peters, *Torture* (New York: Basil Blackwell, 1985), pp. 44, 46.
24 John H. Langbein, *Torture and the Law of Proof* (Chicago: University of Chicago Press, 1974), pp. 3, 12ff.
25 Christina Larner, "Crimen Exeptum? The Crime of Witchcraft in Europe," in Victor Gatrell, ed., *Crime and the Law* (London: Europa Publications, 1980).
26 Bernard de la Roche Flavin, *Treize livres des parlemens de France* (Geneva, 1621), pp. 2, 5.
27 Ibid., pp. 603, 749, 759, 645.
28 Ibid., p. 1135.
29 Briggs, *Communities of Belief*, p. 46.
30 J. de Nynauld, *De la lycanthropie* (Paris, 1615).
31 Sieur de Beauvois de Chauvincourt, *Discours de la lycanthropie* (Paris, 1599), p. 19.
32 Ibid., pp. 21, 30.
33 Pierre de L'Estoile, *Journal inédit du règne de Henri IV 1598-1602* (Paris, 1862), p. 50.
34 Robert Mandrou, "Jean Grenier, pretendue lycanthrope (Bordeaux, 1603)," in Robert Mandrou, ed., *Possession et sorcellerie au XVIIe siècle* (Paris: Fayard, 1979), pp. 45-46. There is a detailed narrative of this case in Caroline Oates, "The Trial of a Teenage Werewolf, Bordeaux, 1603," *Criminal Justice History* 9 (1988).
35 Mandrou, "Jean Grenier," p. 47.
36 Ibid., pp. 48, 59.
37 Ibid., p. 59.
38 Oates, "The Trial of a Teenage Werewolf," p. 25.
39 Mandrou, "Jean Grenier," pp. 67-69.
40 Ibid., p. 90.
41 Ibid., pp. 94-95.
42 Ibid., pp. 105, 109.
43 Ibid., p. 60.
44 Mandrou, "Jean Grenier," pp. 39-41.
45 Oates, "The Trial of a Teenage Werewolf," pp. 20-21.

Chapter Three

1. E. William Monter, *Witchcraft in France and Switzerland* (Ithaca, NY: Cornell University Press, 1976), p. 10, and Mandrou, *Magistrats et sorciers en France*.
2. D.P. Walker, *Unclean Spirits: Possession and Exorcism in France and England in the Late Sixteenth and Early Seventeenth Centuries* (London: Scholar Press, 1981); H.C.E. Midelfort, "The Devil and the German People: Reflections on the Popularity of Demon Possession in Sixteenth Century Germany," in Steven Ozment, ed., *Religion and Culture in the Renaissance and Reformation* (Kirksville, MO: Sixteenth Century Journal Publishers, 1989); Philip M. Soergel, *Wondrous in His Saints: Counter-Reformation Propaganda in Bavaria* (Berkeley: University of California Press, 1993); and Roper, *Oedipus and the Devil*.
3. Mandrou, *Magistrats et sorciers en France*, p. 126.
4. Monter, *Witchraft in France and Switzerland*, and Walker, *Unclean Spirits*, have already been cited. Henri Weber, "L'Exorcisme à la fin du XVIe siècle, instrument de la contre réforme et spectacle baroque," *Nouvelle revue du seizième siècle* 1 (1983), pp. 79-101.
5. Ibid., p. 82.
6. Florimond de Raemond, *Histoire de la naissance progrez et décadence de l'hérésie de ce siècle* (Paris, 1605), p. 140v.
7. Jehan Boulaese, *Le trésor et entière histoire de la triomphante victoire du corps de Dieu sur l'esprit maling Beelzebub, obtenue à Laon l'an mil cinq cens soixante six* (Paris, 1578), pp. 11, 103ff., 139, 174.
8. See Delumeau, *La peur en occident*, chap. 9.
9. Boulaese, *Le trésor et entière histoire de la triomphante victoire du corps de Dieu*, introduction (n.p.); pp. 34v., 152.
10. Florimond de Raemond, *L'Anti-Christ* (Lyon, 1597), p. 417.
11. Raemond, *Histoire de la naissance progrez et décadence*, p. 140v.
12. Boulaese, *Le trésor et entière histoire de la triomphante victoire du corps de Dieu*, pp. 192, 194.
13. Ibid., introduction (n.p.); pp. 11, 21v.
14. Charles Blendec, *Cinq histoires admirables* (Paris, 1582), introduction (n.p.); pp. 29v., 32.
15. Louis Richeome, *Trois discours pour la religion catholique et miracles et images* (Bordeaux, 1598), pp. 193, 199, 211-12. The account of Luther's failed attempt at exorcism was published in Germany by the Bavarian preacher Johann Jakob Rabus in 1571 (Soergel, *Wondrous in His Saints*, p. 141).
16. Greengrass, *France in the Age of Henry IV*, p. 80, and Roelker, *One King, One Faith*, pp. 444-49.
17. L'Estoile, *Journal inédit du règne de Henri IV*, pp. 56, 65, 75.
18. For a detailed narrative of the Brossier case, see Sarah Ferber, "The Demonic Possession of Marthe Brossier, France, 1598-1600," in Charles Zika, ed., *No Gods Except Me: Orthodoxy and Religious Practice in Europe, 1200-1600* (Melbourne: University of Melbourne Press, 1991).
19. Mandrou, *Magistrats et sorciers en France*, pp. 164-67.
20. Michel Marescot, *Discours véritable sur le faict de Marthe Brossier de Romorantin, prétendue démoniaque* (Paris, 1599), pp. 2-4.
21. Ibid., pp. 6, 15.
22. Ibid., pp. 9-25, 30.

23. Ibid., p. 48.
24. See Jean Dagens, *Berulle et les origines de la restauration catholique* (Bruges: Desclée, 1952).
25. Leon d'Alexis, *Traicté des energumens* (Troyes,1599), pp. 3v, 18v, 21v, 25r, 33r.
26. See Mandrou, *Magistrats et sorciers en France*, for a good narrative of all these cases.
27. Jonathan Pearl, "Peiresc and the Search for Criteria of Scientific Knowledge in Seventeenth Century France," *Proceedings of the Western Society for French History* (1977), and Jonathan Pearl, "The Role of Personal Correspondence in the Exchange of Scientific Information in the Early Seventeenth Century," *Renaissance and Reformation* (May 1984).
28. Alfred Soman, "Les procès de sorcellerie au Parlement de Paris (1565-1640)," *Annales* (July 1977); Alfred Soman, "La decriminalisation de la sorcellerie en France," *Histoire, economie et société* 2 (1985); and Dewald, *The Formation of a Provincial Nobility*.
29. Mandrou, *Magistrats et Sorciers*; Klaits, *Servants of Satan*; and Walker, *Unclean Spirits*.
30. Marc Venard, *Réforme protestante, réforme catholique dans la province d'Avignon au XVIe siècle* (Paris: Cerf, 1993), pp. 795-97.
31. Jacques Fontaine, *Discours des marques des sorciers et de la réele possession que le Diable prend sur le corps des hommes* (Paris, 1611), pp. 4-13.
32. Mandrou, *Magistrats et sorciers en France*, p. 203.
33. Weber, "L'Exorcisme à la fin du XVIe siècle, p. 96.
34. Jean Bodin, *De la démonomanie des sorciers* (Paris, 1580).
35. Thomas, *Religion and the Decline of Magic*, pp. 570ff.
36. Jonathan Pearl, "La rôle enigmatique de la *Démonomanie* dans la chasse aux sorciers," in *Jean Bodin: Actes du Colloque interdisciplinaire d'Angers, 1984* (Angers: Presses de l'Université d'Angers, 1985), pp. 407-408.
37. Jean Benedicti, *La triomphante victoire de la vierge Marie, sur sept malins esprits* (Lyon, 1611), pp. 64-74.
38. Sanson Birette, *Refutation de l'erreur du vulgaire, touchant les responses des diables exorcez* (Rouen, 1618), dedication (n.p.).
39. Ibid., dedication (n.p.); pp. 84, 103.
40. Claude Pithoys, *La déscouverture des faux possedez* (Chalons, 1621), p. 7. This work is reproduced in its entirety in P.J.S. Whitmore, ed., *A Seventeenth Century Exposure of Superstition: Select Texts of Claude Pithoys* (The Hague: Nijhoff, 1972).
41. Pithoys, *La déscouverture des faux possedez*, pp. 8, 13-14.
42. Ibid., p. 16.
43. Ibid., pp. 24-25, 27.
44. Ibid., pp. 31-32, 48.
45. Remy Picard, *Admirable vertu des saincts exorcismes sur les princes d'enfer* (Nancy, 1622), pp. 155, 251, 276, 399.
46. Ibid., p. 213.

Chapter Four

1. Henri Fouqueray, *Histoire de la companie de Jesus en France des origines à la suppression (1528-1762)*, 5 vols. (Paris: Picard, 1910-25), and J.M. Prat, *Maldonat et l'université de Paris au XVIe siècle* (Paris, 1856), are especially helpful.
2. See, for example, Paul Schmitt, *La réforme catholique, le combat de Maldonat, 1534-1583* (Paris: Beauchesne, 1985); Martin, *Henry III and the Jesuit Politicians*;

A. Lynn Martin, *The Jesuit Mind* (Ithaca, NY: Cornell University Press, 1988); and Claude Sutto, "Introduction to Estienne Pasquier," in Claude Sutto, ed., *Le catéchisme des Jésuites* (Sherbrooke, QC: Éditions de l'Université de Sherbrooke, 1982).
3. Prat, *Maldonat et l'université de Paris au XVIe siècle*, pp. 25-34.
4. Fouqueray, *Histoire de la companie de Jesus en France*, pp. 250ff.
5. Prat, *Maldonat et l'université de Paris au XVIe siècle*, p. 77.
6. Schmitt, *La réforme catholique, le combat de Maldonat*, p. 252, and Walter J. Ong, *Ramus: Method and the Decay of Dialogue* (Cambridge, MA: Harvard University Press, 1958), pp. 18-29.
7. Martin, *The Jesuit Mind*, p. 19.
8. Roger Chartier, Marie-Madeleine Compere and Dominique Julia, *L'éducation en France du XVIe au XVIIIe siècle* (Paris: Société d'édition d'enseignement, 1976), p. 163.
9. Martin, *The Jesuit Mind*, pp. 67-75.
10. Chartier et al., *L'éducation en France du XVIe*, p. 165.
11. Schmitt, *La réforme catholique, le combat de Maldonat*, pp. 138, 285.
12. Ibid., p. 310.
13. Prat, *Maldonat et l'université de Paris au XVIe siècle*, pp. 187-88.
14. Estienne Pasquier, *Lettres historiques pour les années 1556-1594*, edited by D. Thickett (Geneva: Droz, 1966), p. 155.
15. Fouqueray, *Histoire de la companie de Jesus en France*, pp. 417-22, and Schmitt, *La réforme catholique, le combat de Maldonat*, pp. 260-63.
16. Ibid.
17. Ibid., pp. 296ff.
18. Pierre Miquel, *Les guerres de religion* (Paris: Fayard, 1980), pp. 267-76.
19. Janine Estebe Garrisson, *La Saint-Barthelemy* (Brussels: Complexe, 1987), pp. 32-39.
20. Jacqueline Boucher, *La cour de Henri III* (Rennes: Ouest-France, 1986), pp. 175-76, and Martin, *Henry III and the Jesuit Politicians*, pp. 31-43.
21. Georges Bordonove, *Histoire du Poitou* (Paris: Hachette, 1973), pp. 200-208.
22. Ibid., pp. 208-11.
23. Ibid., p. 211.
24. Prat, *Maldonat et l'université de Paris au XVIe siècle*, p. 235, and Schmitt, *La réforme catholique, le combat de Maldonat*, pp. 336ff.
25. Ibid., pp. 347-48.
26. Prat, *Maldonat et l'université de Paris au XVIe siècle*, p. 248.
27. Ibid.
28. Schmitt, *La réforme catholique, le combat de Maldonat*, p. 357.
29. Salmon, *Society in Crisis*, p. 170.
30. Holt, *The French Wars of Religion*, p. 70.
31. Sutherland, *The Massacre of St. Bartholomew and the European Conflict*, pp. 118-21.
32. Janine Estebe Garrisson, "The Rites of Violence: A Comment," *Past and Present* (May 1975), p. 128.
33. Barbara Diefendorf, *Beneath the Cross: Catholics and Huguenots in Sixteenth-Century Paris* (Oxford: Oxford University Press, 1991), pp. 84-92.
34. Prat, *Maldonat et l'université de Paris au XVIe siècle*, p. 264.
35. Le R.P. Maldonat, *Traicté des anges et demons, mis en français par Maistre François de la Borie* (Paris, 1605).

36 Prat, *Maldonat et l'université de Paris au XVIᵉ siècle*, p. 512.
37 Martin Del Rio, *Les controverses et recherches magiques* (Paris, 1611).
38 Maldonat, *Traicté des anges et demons*, p. 152.
39 Ibid., pp. 156-59v.
40 Ibid., p. 177v.
41 Ibid., pp. 6, 182r.
42 Ibid., p. 179r.
43 Ibid., p. 211v.
44 Ibid., pp. 213r-14r.
45 Ibid., pp. 215r, 230r.
46 Delumeau, *La peur en occident*, conclusion.
47 Garrisson, "The Rites of Violence," p. 128.
48 Natalie Z. Davis, "The Rites of Violence: Religious Riot in Sixteenth Century France," *Past and Present* (May 1973); Garrisson, *La Saint-Barthelemy*; and Garrisson, "The Rites of Violence."
49 Janine Estebe Garrisson, *Tocsin pour un massacre* (Paris: Le Centurion, 1968), pp. 191- 94.
50 See Diefendorf, *Beneath the Cross*.
51 Garrisson, *La Saint-Barthelemy*, p. 74.
52 Schmitt, *La réforme catholique, le combat de Maldonat*, p. 384.
53 Martin, *The Jesuit Mind*, p. 102.
54 Ong, *Ramus: Method and the Decay of Dialogue*, p. 29.
55 Garrisson, *Tocsin pour un massacre*, p. 151.
56 Levack, *The Witch-hunt in Early Modern Europe*, p. 51.
57 Del Rio, *Les controverses et recherches magiques*, pp. 8-9.
58 Ibid., pp. 2, 5-9.
59 Ibid., pp. 143-46, 157, 383.
60 Ibid., pp. 717, 751, 761.
61 Ibid., pp. 1020ff.
62 Pasquier, *Le catechisme des Jesuites*, introduction, pp. 67, 73, and Robert Boutruche, *Bordeaux de 1453 à 1715* (Bordeaux: Fédération historique du Sud-Ouest, 1966), p. 388.
63 Prat, *Maldonat et l'université de Paris au XVIᵉ siècle*, p. 334, and Martin, *Henry III and the Jesuit Politicians*, p. 260.
64 Louis Richeome, *L'immortalité de l'âme, declarée avec raisons naturelles tesmoignages humains et divins pour la foy catholique contre les athées et libertins* (Paris, 1621), introduction (n.p.).
65 Ibid., pp. 2-4.
66 Ibid., p. 6.
67 Ibid., pp. 76, 182-83, 354, 375, 396.
68 Ibid., pp. 181ff.
69 Alan N. Boase, "Montaigne et la sorcellerie," *Humanisme et renaissance* 2 (1935), pp. 402, 406; Schmitt, *La réforme catholique, le combat de Maldonat*, pp. 498, 501; and Alan N. Boase, *The Fortunes of Montaigne* (London: Methuen, 1935), p. 41.
70 Boutruche, *Bordeaux de 1453 à 1715*, pp. 251, 388; on Boucher, see Elie Barnavi, *Le parti de dieu, étude sociale et politique des chefs de la ligue parisienne 1585-1594* (Louvain: Editions Nauwelaerts, 1980).

71 Lambert Daneau, *Les sorciers: dialogue très-utile et nécessaire pour ce temps* (Paris, 1574), p. 10.
72 Ibid., p. 31.

Chapter Five

1 See Fredric J. Baumgartner, *Radical Revolutionaries: The Political Thought of the French Catholic League* (Geneva: Droz, 1975), for a full discussion of the evolution of League political thought.
2 Myriam Yardeni, *La conscience nationale en France pendant les guerres de religion (1559-1598)* (Louvain: Editions Naewelaerts, 1971), pp. 100-104.
3 Elie Barnavi, "Hérésie et politique dans les pamphlets ligueurs," in M. Yardeni, ed., *Modernité et non-conformisme en France à travers les âges* (Leiden: Brill, 1983), p. 55. Louis D'Orleans was a leaguer member of the Parlement of Paris and an active pamphleteer (Baumgartner, *Radical Revolutionaries*, p. 67).
4 Crouzet, *Les guerriers de dieu*.
5 Philip Benedict, *Rouen during the Wars of Religion* (New York: Cambridge University Press, 1980), p. 191.
6 Sypher, "'Faisant ce qu'il leur vient a plaisir': The Image of Protestantism," and Benedict, *Rouen*, pp. 66-67.
7 Charles Labitte, *De la démocratie chez les predicateurs de la ligue* (Paris, 1841), and Benedict, *Rouen*, pp. 66-67.
8 Ibid., pp. 65-66. There are several more couplets to this little work, which I have not quoted.
9 Pierre Nodé, *Déclamation contre l'erreur execrable des maleficiers* (Paris, 1578), p. 4.
10 Ibid., p. 32.
11 Ibid., p. 33.
12 Ibid., pp. 46, 54-55.
13 Denis Pallier, *Recherches sur l'imprimerie à Paris pendant la ligue (1585-1594)* (Geneva: Droz, 1975), pp. 55, 170.
14 Ibid., pp. 170, 295, 392. David A. Bell, "Unmasking a King: The Political Uses of Popular Literature Under the French Catholic League, 1588-89," *Sixteenth Century Journal* (1989), p. 37.
15 Labitte, *De la démocratie chez les predicateurs de la ligue*, p. 72.
16 Pierre Crespet, *Deux livres de la Hayne de Sathan et Malins esprits contre l'homme* (Paris, 1590), pp. 14v, 42v.
17 Ibid., pp. 64r, 66r.
18 Ibid., pp. 194r, 230r-31r, 287v.
19 Ibid., p. 200v.
20 Ibid., pp. 83v, 115r.
21 Ibid., pp. 311r, 372v, 389vff.
22 See Barbara Sher Tinsley, *History and Polemics in the French Reformation: Florimond de Raemond, Defender of the Church* (Selingrove: Susquehanna University Press, 1992).
23 Raemond, *L'Anti-Christ*, p. 9.
24 Ibid., p. 96.
25 Ibid., p. 98.
26 Ibid., p. 103.
27 Raemond, *Histoire de la naissance progrez et décadence*, introduction (n.p.); dedication (n.p.).

28 Ibid., pp. 4, 372v, 376r.
29 Ibid., p. 350r.
30 Richeome, *Trois discours pour la religion catholique*, pp. 22, 245-46.
31 Sutto, "Introduction to Estienne Pasquier," pp. 76-77.
32 Louis Richeome, *Plainte apologétique au Roy Très-Chrestien de France & de Navarre pour la compagnie de Jesus* (Toulouse, 1603), pp. 9, 15.
33 Richeome, *L'immortalité de l'âme*, p. 234.
34 Barnavi, *Le parti de dieu*, pp. 21, 30-31; Baumgartner *Radical Revolutionaries*, p. 96; and Labitte, *De la démocratie chez les predicateurs de la ligue*.
35 Elie Barnavi, "Le cahier de doleances de la ville de Paris aux états generaux de 1588," *Annuaire-bulletin de la Société de l'histoire de France* (1976-77), pp. 88, 100-101.
36 Greengrass, *France in the Age of Henry IV*, pp. 43, 53.
37 In Roelker, *One King, One Faith*, pp. 389, 396.
38 Labitte, *De la démocratie chez les predicateurs de la ligue*, pp. 142-47, 187-88, 199.
39 Barnavi, *Le parti de dieu*, p. 244.
40 Baumgartner, *Radical Revolutionaries*, pp. 123ff.
41 Michael Wolfe, "The Conversion of Henri IV and the Origin of Bourbon Absolutism," *Historical Reflections* (1987), pp. 294-95.
42 Jean Boucher, *Sermons de la simulée conversion, et nullité de la prétendue absolution de Henry de Bourbon* (Paris, 1594), pp. 5, 39-40, 90-91, 480, 563-64.
43 Jean Boucher, *Apologie pour Jean Chastel, parisien, executé à mort, et pour les pères et escolliers de la Société de Jesus, bannis du royaume de France* (1595), pp. 33, 75, 94, 104.
44 Ibid., pp. 178, 222.
45 Jean Boucher, *La mystère d'infidelité* (Chalons, 1614), pp. 70-71.
46 Ibid., pp. 79, 137.
47 Jean Boucher, *Coronne mystique ou armes de piété contre tout sorte d'impiété, hérésie, athéisme, schisme, magie et mahometisme* (Tournai, 1624), pp. 423, 534.
48 Ibid., pp. 536, 582ff., 812.
49 Noel Taillepied, *Histoire des vies, meurs, actes doctrines, et mort des trois principales hérétiques de nostre temps* (Douay, 1616), pp. 18r, 26r; on Bolsec's biography of Calvin, see François Wendel, *Calvin*, translated by Philip Mairet (London: Collins, 1963), p. 91.
50 Taillepied, *Histoire des vies, meurs, actes doctrines*, pp. 30v, 32r, 122v.
51 Roper, *Oedipus and the Devil*, pp. 145ff.
52 See Martin, *The Jesuit Mind*, chap. 4.
53 Venard, *Réforme protestante, réforme catholique*, pp. 839ff.
54 Pierre de L'Estoile, *Journal de L'Estoile* (Paris, 1906), pp. 227, 273, 267, 269.
55 Pierre Dampmartin, *De la conoissance et merveilles du monde et de l'homme* (Paris, 1585), pp. 26v, 123r, 124r.
56 Antoine de Mory, *Discours d'un miracle* (Paris, 1598), pp. 8, 83.
57 Louis Le Caron, *De la tranquilité de l'esprit* (Paris, 1588), pp. 4, 19, 50, 55, 65.
58 Ibid., pp. 160-64. On other works of Le Caron, see Pauline M. Smith, *The Anti-Courtier Trend in Sixteenth Century French Literature* (Geneva: Droz, 1966).
59 Ibid., pp. 188ff.
60 Crespet, *Deux livres de la Hayne de Sathan et Malins esprits contre l'homme*, p. 83v.
61 G. de Rebreviettes, *L'impiété combatue par des infidèles* (Paris, 1612), p. 29.

62 Jean Delumeau, ed., *Croyants et sceptiques au XVIe siècle. ACTES du Colloque à Strasbourg*, 9-10 Juin 1978 (Strasbourg, 1981).
63 François Berriot, *Athéismes et athéistes au XVIe siècle en France* (Lille: Atelier national de reproduction des thèses, 1976); Louise Godard de Donville, *Le libertin des origines à 1665: un produit des apologetes* (Paris: Papers on French Seventeenth-Century Literature, 1989); and Williams, *Defining Dominion*.
64 Jean Boucher, *Mariage de la vertu avec la religion* (Paris, 1622), introduction (n.p.).
65 Ibid., pp. 215, 352, 355.
66 Ibid., pp. 381, 411.
67 Joseph Lecler, "Le P. François Garasse (1585-1631): un adversaire des libertins au debut du XVIIe siècle," *Études* (1931), p. 55.
68 François Garasse, *Les recherches des recherches* (Paris, 1622), pp. 123, 126, 683-86, 704.
69 François Garasse, *La somme théologique des vérités capitales de la religion chrétienne* (Paris, 1625), p. 15.
70 Ibid., pp. 11, 20.
71 François Garasse, *La doctrine curieuse des beaux esprits de ce temps* (Paris, 1623), p. 37.
72 Ibid., pp. 793, 843, 847.
73 Ibid., pp. 850, 853.
74 Garasse, *La somme théologique des vérités capitales*, p. 210.

Chapter Six

1 Philippe Desan, ed., *Humanism in Crisis* (Ann Arbor: University of Michigan Press, 1991), pp. 4-16.
2 Michel de Montaigne, *The Essays of Michel de Montaigne*, translated and edited by M.A. Screech (London, 1991).
3 Ibid., I, pp. 56, 355, 359.
4 See Michel de Montaigne, *Journal de voyage de Michele de Montaigne* (Paris: Presses Universitaires de France, 1992).
5 Géralde Nakam, *Les essais de Montaigne, miroir et procès de leur temps* (Paris: Nizet/Publications de la Sorbonne, 1984), p. 110.
6 Montaigne, *The Essays of Michel de Montaigne*, I, pp. 12, 543, 564, 581, 591.
7 Ibid.
8 Nakam, *Les essais de Montaigne*, pp. 178ff.
9 Montaigne, *The Essays of Michel de Montaigne*, III, pp. 8, 1048, 1063.
10 Ibid., pp. 12, 1178, 1181.
11 Ibid., II, pp. 15, 700; III, pp. 10, 1145.
12 Ibid., III, p. 11.
13 Ibid., pp. 1164-56.
14 Ibid., pp. 1166-67.
15 Ibid., pp. 1168-69.
16 Ibid., p. 1169.
17 Ibid., p. 540.
18 Del Rio, *Les controverses et recherches magiques*, pp. 109, 419, 852.
19 Pierre de Lancre, *L'incredulité et mescreance du sortilege plainement convaincue* (Paris, 1622), p. 339.
20 Ibid., pp. 340, 353.
21 D. Thickett, *Estienne Pasquier (1529-1615): The Versatile Barrister of 16th Century France* (London: Regency Press, 1979), p. 18.

Notes to pages 107-11 165

22 Estienne Pasquier, *Exhortation aux princes et seigneurs du conseil privé du roi* (1561), in Pasquier, *Lettres historiques pour les années 1556-1594*. There is some controversy regarding the attribution of this anonymous work to Pasquier. In his recent work, Mack Holt states that the *Exhortation* is not Pasquier's work, because Vittorio de Caprariis "convincingly demonstrated ... that Pasquier could not have written this work and that his other writings completely contradicted it" (Holt, *The French Wars of Religion*, p. 169). Caprariis did argue strongly that the *Exhortation* was not typical of Pasquier's thought (Vittorio de Caprariis, *Propaganda e pensiero politico en Francia durante la guerre di religione* [Naples: Edizione scientifiche italiene, 1959], pp. 153-58). But Dorothy Thickett argued just as strongly that it was Pasquier's. She points out that contemporaries regarded it as Pasquier's and it was attributed to him when it was placed on the Index in 1609 (Pasquier, *Écrits politiques*, p. 24). Claude Sutto, who edited Pasquier's *Le catéchisme des Jésuites*, discusses the *Exhortation* as Pasquier's work, and indicates (pp. 33-37, 85-89) that he regards it as consistent with the body of Pasquier's work.

A comparison of the *Exhortation* with Pasquier's letters written in the early 1560s is interesting. This is not the place for a full analysis of this work. While all of the sentiments and formulations of the *Exhortation* are not duplicated in Pasquier's letters, there are many opinions and points of view that match this pamphlet. The writing styles seem very similar as well. At this point, while scholars are divided on the issue, a good case could be made to attribute this work to Pasquier.

23 Pasquier, *Exhortation*, pp. 40, 46-47, 54, 62, 65, 85.
24 Ibid., pp. 50-57.
25 Ibid., pp. 58, 70-74.
26 Sutto, "Introduction to Estienne Pasquier," p. 56.
27 Fouqueray, *Histoire de la companie de Jesus en France*, vol. 1, p. 391.
28 Ibid., p. 393.
29 Estienne Pasquier, *Remonstrance aux François sur leur sédition et rebellion*, in Estienne Pasquier, *Écrits politiques*, edited by D. Thickett (Geneva: Droz, 1966), pp. 148, 154, 164.
30 Estienne Pasquier, *L'antimartyre de Frère Jacques Clement*, in ibid., pp. 195, 235.
31 Pasquier, *Le catéchisme des Jésuites*, pp. 21v-22r, 602.
32 Claude Sutto, "Tradition et innovation, réalisme et utopie: l'idée Gallicane à la fin du XVIe et au début du XVIIe siècles," *Renaissance and Reformation* (November 1989), p. 284.
33 Jacqueline Boucher, *La cour de Henri III*, pp. 98-105.
34 See Holt, *The French Wars of Religion*.
35 Jean Bodin, *Les six livres de la république*, 6 vols. (Paris, 1576); reprints, 10th ed. (Lyon, 1593; Paris, 1986).
36 Ibid., vol. 6, chap. 4, p. 176; vol. 5, chap. 5, p. 131; vol. 2, chap. 5, p. 75; vol. 4, chap. 7, pp. 204-209.
37 Ibid., vol. 4, chap. 7, p. 207.
38 Ibid., vol. 2, chap. 5, p. 80.
39 Ibid., vol. 2, chap. 5, p. 75.
40 Ibid., vol. 5, chap. 2, pp. 71-74.
41 Jean Bodin, *Colloquium of the Seven about Secrets of the Sublime*, translated by Marion Leathers Daniels Kuntz (Princeton: Princeton University Press, 1975).

42 Rose, "The *Politique* and the Prophet."
43 See Pierre Mesnard, "La *Démonomanie* de Jean Bodin," in *L'Opera e il pensiero di Giovanni Pico Della Mirandola* (Florence: n.p., 1965); E. William Monter, "Inflation and Witchcraft: The Case of Jean Bodin," in J. Rabb and E. Siegel, eds., *Action and Conviction in Early Modern Europe* (Princeton: Princeton University Press, 1969); and Maxime Preaud, "La *Démonomanie des Sorciers*, Fille de la *République*," in *Jean Bodin: Actes du Colloque interdisciplinaire d'Angers, 1984* (Angers: Presses de l'Université d'Angers, 1985), vol. 2.
44 Mandrou, *Magistrats et sorciers en France*, pp. 133, 136.
45 Monter, "Law, Medicine, and the Acceptance of Witchcraft," p. 69; Christopher Baxter, "Bodin's Daemon and His Conversion to Judaism," in *Jean Bodin: Proceedings of the International Conference on Bodin in Munich* (Munich: Beck, 1973), p. 18; Brian Easlea, *Witch Hunting, Magic and the New Philosophy: An Introduction to the Debates of the Scientific Revolution, 1450-1750* (Sussex: Harvester Press, 1980); and Marie-Sylvie Dupont-Bouchat, "La répression de le sorcellerie dans le duché de Luxembourg aux XVIe et XVIIe siècles," in *Prophètes et sorciers dans le Pays-Bas XVIe-XVIIe siècle* (Paris: Hachette, 1978), p. 78.
46 Trevor-Roper, "The European Witch-Craze of the Sixteenth and Seventeenth Centuries," p. 122.
47 Baxter, "Bodin's Daemon and His Conversion to Judaism."
48 Peters, *The Magician, the Witch, and the Law*, p. 154.
49 See, among others, Langbein, *Prosecuting Crime in the Renaissance*; Langbein, *Torture and the Law of Proof*; Peters, *Torture*; and Ruff, *Crime, Justice and Public Order in Old Regime France*, as well as the articles by Alfred Soman already cited.
50 Jean Bodin, *On the Demon-Mania of Witches 1580*, edited, abridged and translated by Jonathan Pearl and Randy Scott (Toronto: Centre for Reformation and Renaissance Studies, 1995), p. 175.
51 Ibid., pp. 181-82.
52 Ibid., p. 183.
53 Ibid., pp. 185-87.
54 Langbein, *Torture and the Law of Proof*, p. 14.
55 Bodin, *On the Demon-Mania of Witches*, pp. 185-86. Alexander of Hales and Giovanni d'Andrea were important medieval canonists.
56 Ibid., p. 190.
57 Ibid., pp. 191-95.
58 Ibid., pp. 198-200.
59 Ibid., p. 201.
60 Ibid., p. 204.
61 Ibid., p. 208.
62 Marijke Gijswijt-Hofstra, "Six Centuries of Witchcraft in the Netherland," in Marijke Gijswijt-Hofstra and Willem Frijhoff, eds., *Witchcraft in the Netherlands from the Fourteenth to the Twentieth Century* (Rotterdam: Universitaire Pers, 1991), pp. 25-27.
63 Monter, *Witchcraft in France and Switzerland*, pp. 208-16.
64 Dupont-Bouchat, "La répression de le sorcellerie," pp. 79-80, 127.
65 Levack, *The Witch-hunt in Early Modern Europe*, pp. 176-79.
66 Muchembled, *Le roi et la sorcière*, p. 74, and Behringer, "Allemagne, 'Mère du tant de sorcières,'" pp. 72-73.

Notes to pages 124-35

67 Bodin, *On the Demon-Mania of Witches*, pp. 87ff.
68 Pierre Le Loyer, *IIII livres des spectres* (Angers, 1586).
69 Del Rio, *Les controverses et recherches magiques*, pp. 24, 812.
70 Caro Baroja, "Witchcraft and Catholic Theology," p. 34. Bodin's other major published works were also placed on the Index, but this does not seem to have affected their publication or distribution.
71 De Lancre, *L'incredulité et mescreance*, pp. 244-91.
72 Nynauld, *De la lycanthropie*, p. 18
73 Ibid., pp. 18, 85.
74 Ibid., 73, 84.
75 Claude Prieur, *Dialogue de la lycanthropie* (Louvain, 1596), p. 44, and Henri Boguet, *Discours exécrable des sorciers* (Paris, 1603), pp. 112, 115.

Chapter Seven

1 Josanne Charpentier, *La sorcellerie en Pays Basque* (Paris: Librairie Guénégaud, 1977), p. 34.
2 Caro Baroja, *The World of the Witches*, p. 157.
3 Ibid., p. 169.
4 Trevor-Roper, "The European Witch-Craze of the Sixteenth and Seventeenth Centuries," pp. 112, 139.
5 Boutruche, *Bordeaux de 1453 à 1715*, pp. 240-50.
6 Caro Baroja, *The World of the Witches*, p. 157. Baroja states that de Lancre died in 1630, while Charpentier, *La sorcellerie en Pays Basque*, opts for 1631 (p. 143).
7 See Quentin Skinner, *The Foundations of Modern Political Thought* (Cambridge: Cambridge University Press, 1978), vol. 1, pp. 277ff.; Nanerl Keohane, *Philosophy of the State in France* (Princeton: Princeton University Press, 1980), pp. 130-40; and Houdard, *Quatre démonologues*, p. 165.
8 Pierre de Lancre, *Tableau de l'inconstance et instabilité de toutes choses* (Paris, 1607), pp. 56, 59, 73.
9 Ibid., p. 170.
10 Ibid., p. 417.
11 Ibid., pp. 793, 795.
12 Ibid., pp. 782-83.
13 Ibid., pp. 787, 810, 813-14.
14 Ibid., p. 789.
15 Henningsen, *The Witches' Advocate*, pp. 24-25; see also Caro Baroja, *The World of the Witches*, and Charpentier, *La sorcellerie en Pays Basque*.
16 Henningsen, *The Witches' Advocate*, p. 25.
17 Pierre de Lancre, *L'inconstance des mauvais anges et demons*, abridged and edited by Nicole Jacques-Chaquin (Paris: Aubier-Montagne, 1980), p. 11.
18 Henningsen, *The Witches' Advocate*, p. 24.
19 Margaret McGowan, "The Sabbat Sensationalised: Pierre de Lancre's Tableau," in Sidney Anglo, ed., *The Damned Art: Essays in the Literature of Witchcraft* (London: Routledge, 1977), p. 183.
20 Klaits, *Servants of Satan*, p. 136, and de Lancre, *L'inconstance des mauvais anges et demons*, p. 12.
21 Henningsen, *The Witches' Advocate*, p. 18.
22 Ibid., pp. 44, 54, 125.

23 Ibid., p. 242.
24 De Lancre, *L'inconstance des mauvais anges et demons*, p. 278.
25 Henningsen, *The Witches' Advocate*, p. 109. The brackets are Henningsen's.
26 Ibid., pp. 150-89.
27 De Lancre, *L'inconstance des mauvais anges et demons*, p. 361.
28 Henningsen, *The Witches' Advocate*, p. 497.
29 See Carlo Ginzburg, *Ecstasies: Deciphering the Witches' Sabbat* (New York: Pantheon Books, 1991).
30 De Lancre, *L'inconstance des mauvais anges et demons*, p. 197.
31 Ibid., p. 142.
32 Ibid., p. 344.
33 De Lancre, *L'inconstance des mauvais anges et demons*, pp. 127-55, 361-62.
34 Pierre de Lancre, *Tableau de l'inconstance des mauvais anges et demons* (Paris, 1612), pp. 2, 13.
35 Ibid., introduction (n.p.).
36 There is a good discussion of de Lancre's depiction of the society of the Labourd in Chapter 5 of Gerhild Scholz Williams' *Defining Dominion*.
37 Ibid., pp. 32, 36.
38 Ibid., pp. 37, 38.
39 Ibid., p. 39.
40 McGowan, "The Sabbat Sensationalised," p. 192.
41 De Lancre, *Tableau de l'inconstance des mauvais anges et demons* p. 81.
42 Ibid., pp. 79-80, 88, 104, 109.
43 Ibid., pp. 179, 188-89.
44 Ibid., p. 517.
45 Ibid., pp. 542, 585.
46 De Lancre, *L'inconstance des mauvais anges et demons*, p. 319.
47 Pierre de Lancre, *Le livre des princes* (Paris, 1617), pp. 56, 184-85, 188, 453.
48 De Lancre, *L'incredulité et mescreance*, pp. 4, 6.
49 Ibid., p. 7.
50 Ibid., pp. 10, 34, 37.
51 Ibid., pp. 35-38.
52 Ibid., p. 627.
53 Ibid., pp. 447-48, 491, 498.
54 Théophile Malvezin, *Histoire des juifs à Bordeaux* (Marseilles: Lafitte, 1976), pp. 49, 91-118.
55 Delumeau, *La peur en occident*, p. 302.
56 De Lancre, *L'incredulité et mescreance*, pp. 608, 636.

Conclusion

1 For a vivid example of a court system that did not have such a careful attitude about the law, and was not free from political interference, see Michael Kunze, *Highroad to the Stake*, translated by William E. Yuill (Chicago: University of Chicago Press, 1987).
2 In Lorraine, with a population of only some 400,000, around 2,700 witches were executed (Briggs, *Communities of Belief*, p. 67).

Bibliography

Primary Sources

Alexis, Leon de. *Traicté des energumens*. Troyes, 1599.

Beauvois de Chauvincourt, Sieur de. *Discours de la lycanthropie*. Paris, 1599.

Benedicti, Jean. *La triomphante victoire de la vierge Marie, sur sept malins esprits*. Lyon, 1611.

Birette, Sanson. *Refutation de l'erreur du vulgaire, touchant les responses des diables exorcez*. Rouen, 1618.

Blendec, Charles. *Cinq histoires admirables*. Paris, 1582.

Bodin, Jean. *De la démonomanie des sorciers*. Paris, 1580.

―――――. *On the Demon-Mania of Witches 1580*. Edited, abridged and translated by Jonathan Pearl and Randy Scott. Toronto: Centre for Reformation and Renaissance Studies, 1995.

―――――. *Les six livres de la république*. 6 vols. Paris, 1576. Reprints, 10th ed.: Lyon, 1593. Paris, 1986.

―――――. *The Six Books of a Commonwealth*. Edited with an Introduction by Kenneth McRae. Cambridge, MA: Harvard University Press, 1962.

―――――. *Colloquium of the Seven about Secrets of the Sublime*. Translated by Marion Leathers Daniels Kuntz. Princeton: Princeton University Press, 1975.

Boguet, Henri. *Discours exécrable des sorciers*. Paris, 1603.

Boucher, Jean. *Sermons de la simulée conversion, et nullité de la prétendue absolution de Henry de Bourbon*. Paris, 1594.

———. *Apologie pour Jean Chastel, parisien, executé à mort, et pour les pères et escolliers de la Société de Jesus, bannis du royaume de France*. 1595.

———. *La mystère d'infidelité*. Chalons, 1614.

———. *Mariage de la vertu avec la religion*. Paris, 1622.

———. *Coronne mystique ou armes de piété contre tout sorte d'impiété, hérésie, athéisme, schisme, magie et mahometisme*. Tournai, 1624.

Boulaese, Jehan. *Le trésor et entière histoire de la triomphante victoire du corps de Dieu sur l'esprit maling Beelzebub, obtenue à Laon l'an mil cinq cents soixante six*. Paris, 1578.

Crespet, Pierre. *Deux livres de la Hayne de Sathan et Malins esprits contre l' homme*. Paris, 1590.

Dampmartin, Pierre. *De la conoissance et merveilles du monde et de l'homme*. Paris, 1585.

Daneau, Lambert. *Les sorciers: dialogue très-utile et nécessaire pour ce temps*. Paris, 1574.

Del Rio, Martin. *Les controverses et recherches magiques*. Paris, 1611.

du Pont, Rene. *La philosophie des esprits*. Paris, 1602.

Fontaine, Jacques. *Discours des marques des sorciers et de la réele possession que le Diable prend sur le corps des hommes*. Paris, 1611.

Garasse, François. *Les recherches des recherches*. Paris, 1622.

———. *La somme théologique des vérités capitales de la religion chrétienne*. Paris, 1625.

———. *La doctrine curieuse des beaux esprits de ce temps*. Paris, 1623.

Lancre, Pierre de. *Tableau de l'inconstance et instabilité de toutes choses*. Paris, 1607.

———. *Tableau de l'inconstance des mauvais anges et demons*. Paris, 1612.

———. *Le livre des princes*. Paris, 1617.

———. *L'incredulité et mescreance du sortilege plainement convaincue*. Paris, 1622.

———. *L'inconstance des mauvais anges et demons*. Abridged and edited by Nicole Jacques-Chaquin. Paris: Aubier-Montagne, 1980.

Le Caron, Louis. *De la tranquilité de l'esprit*. Paris, 1588.

La Roche Flavin, Bernard de. *Treize livres des parlemens de France*. Geneva, 1621.

Le Loyer, Pierre. *IIII livres des spectres*. Angers, 1586.

L'Estoile, Pierre de. *Journal inédit du règne de Henri IV 1598-1602*. Paris, 1862.

———. *Journal de L'Estoile*. Paris, 1906.

Maldonat, Le R.P. *Traicté des anges et demons, mis en français par Maistre François de la Borie*. Paris, 1605.

Mandrou, Robert, ed. "Jean Grenier, pretendue lycanthrope (Bordeaux 1603)." In *Possession et sorcellerie*. Paris: Fayard, 1979.

Marescot, Michel. *Discours véritable sur le faict de Marthe Brossier de Romorantin, prétendue démoniaque*. Paris, 1599.

Montaigne, Michel de. *The Essays of Michel de Montaigne*. Translated and edited by M.A. Screech. London: Penguin, 1991.

———. *Journal de voyage de Michel de Montaigne*. Edited by François Rigolet. Paris: Presses Universitaires de France, 1992.

Mory, Antoine de, *Discours d'un miracle*. Paris, 1598.

Nodé, Pierre. *Déclamation contre l'erreur execrable des maleficiers*. Paris, 1578.

Nynauld, J. de. *De la lycanthropie*. Paris, 1615.

Pasquier, Estienne. *Écrits politiques*. Edited by D. Thickett. Geneva: Droz, 1966.

———. *Exhortation aux princes et seigneurs du conseil privé du roi*. 1561. In Estienne Pasquier, *Lettres historiques pour les années 1556-1594*. Edited by D. Thickett. Geneva: Droz, 1966.

———. *L'antimartyre de Frère Jacques Clement*. in Estienne Pasquier, *Écrits politiques*. Edited by D. Thickett. Geneva: Droz, 1966.

———. *Lettres historiques pour les années 1556-1594*. Edited by D. Thickett. Geneva: Droz, 1966.

———. *Remonstrance aux François sur leur sédition et rebellion*. In Estienne Pasquier, *Écrits politiques*. Edited by D. Thickett. Geneva: Droz, 1966.

———. *Le catéchisme des Jésuites*. Edited by Claude Sutto. Sherbrooke, QC: Éditions de l'Université de Sherbrooke, 1982.

Picard, Remy. *Admirable vertu des saincts exorcismes sur les princes d'enfer*. Nancy, 1622.

Pithoys, Claude. *La déscouverture des faux possedez*. Chalons, 1621.

Prieur, Claude. *Dialogue de la lycanthropie*. Louvain, 1596.

Raemond, Florimond de, *L'Anti-Christ*. Lyon, 1597.

———. *Histoire de la naissance progrez et décadence de l'hérésie de ce siècle*. Paris, 1605.

Rebreviettes, G. de. *L'impiété combatue par des infidèles*. Paris, 1612.

Richeome, Louis. *Trois discours pour la religion catholique et miracles et images*. Bordeaux, 1598.

———. *Plainte apologétique au Roy Très-Chrestien de France & de Navarre pour la compagnie de Jesus*. Toulouse, 1603.

———. *L'immortalité de l'âme, déclarée avec raisons naturelles tesmoignages humains et divins pour la foy catholique contre les athées et libertins*. Paris, 1621.

Taillepied, Noel. *Histoire des vies, meurs, actes doctrines, et mort des trois principales hérétiques de nostre temps*. Douay, 1616.

Valderama, R.P. *Histoire générale du monde*. Paris, 1619.

Secondary Sources

Anglo, Sydney, ed. *The Damned Art: Essays in the Literature of Witchcraft*. London: Routledge, 1977.

Barnavi, Elie. "Le cahier de doleances de la ville de Paris aux états generaux de 1588." *Annuaire-bulletin de la Société de l'histoire de France* (1976-77).

———. *Le parti de dieu, étude sociale et politique des chefs de la ligue parisienne 1585-1594*. Louvain: Editions Nauwelaerts, 1980.

———. "Hérésie et politique dans les pamphlets ligueurs." In M. Yardeni, ed., *Modernité et non-conformité en France à travers les âges*. Leiden: Brill, 1983.

Barry, Jonathan, Marianne Hester and Gareth Roberts, eds. *Witchcraft in Early Modern Europe: Studies in Culture and Belief*. Cambridge: Cambridge University Press, 1996.

Barstow, Anne Llewellyn. *Witchcraze: A New History of the European Witch Hunts*. San Francisco: Pandora, 1994.

Baumgartner, Frederic J. *Henry II, King of France, 1547-1559*. Durham, NC: Duke University Press, 1988.

———. *Radical Revolutionaries: The Political Thought of the French Catholic League*. Geneva: Droz, 1975.

Baxter, Christopher. "Bodin's Daemon and His Conversion to Judaism." In *Jean Bodin: Proceedings of the International Conference on Bodin in Munich*. Munich: Beck, 1973.

Behringer, Wolfgang. "Allemagne, 'Mère du tant de sorcières,' Au coeur des persécutions." In Robert Muchembled, ed., *Magie et sorcellerie en Europe du Moyen Âge à nos jours*. Paris: Armand Colin, 1994.

Bell, David A. "Unmasking a King: The Political Uses of Popular Literature Under the French Catholic League, 1588-89." *Sixteenth Century Journal* (1989).

Benedict, Philip. *Rouen during the Wars of Religion*. New York: Cambridge University Press, 1980.

Berriot, François. *Athéismes et athéistes au XVIe siècle en France*. Lille: Atelier national de reproduction des thèses, 1976.

Bettinson, Christopher. "The Politiques and the Politique Party: A Reappraisal." In Keith Cameron, ed., *From Valois to Bourbon: Dynasty, State and Society in Early Modern France*. Exeter: University of Exeter Press, 1989.

Blendec, Charles. *Cinq histoires admirables*. Paris, 1582.

Boase, Alan N. *The Fortunes of Montaigne*. London: Methuen, 1935.

⸻. "Montaigne et la sorcellerie." *Humanisme et renaissance* (1935).

Bordonove, Georges. *Histoire du Poitou*. Paris: Hachette, 1973.

Bossy, John. "Moral Arithmetic: Seven Sins into Ten Commandments." In Edmund Leites, ed., *Conscience and Casuistry in Early Modern Europe*. Cambridge: Cambridge University Press, 1988.

⸻. "Unrethinking the Sixteenth-Century Wars of Religion." In Thomas Kselman, ed., *Belief in History*. Notre Dame: University of Notre Dame Press, 1991.

Boucher, Jacqueline. *La cour de Henri III*. Rennes: Ouest-France, 1986.

Boutruche, Robert. *Bordeaux de 1453 à 1715*. Bordeaux: Fédération historique du Sud-Ouest, 1966.

Briggs, Robin. *Communities of Belief: Cultural and Social Tensions in Early Modern France*. Oxford: Oxford University Press, 1989.

⸻. *Witches and Neighbours: The Social and Cultural Concept of European Witchcraft*. London: HarperCollins, 1996.

Burke, Peter. "A Question of Acculturation." In *Scienze, credenze occulte, livelli di cultura*. Florence: Olschki, 1982.

Cameron, Keith, ed. *From Valois to Bourbon: Dynasty, State and Society in Early Modern France*. Exeter: University of Exeter Press, 1989.

Caprariis, Vittorio de. *Propaganda e pensiero politico in Francia durante le guerre di religione*. Naples: Edizione scientifiche italiene, 1959.

Caro Baroja, Julio, *The World of the Witches*. Translated by O.N.V. Glendenning. Chicago: University of Chicago Press, 1965.

⸻. "Witchcraft and Catholic Theology." In Bengt Ankarloo and Gustav Henningsen, eds., *Early Modern European Witchcraft*. Oxford: Oxford University Press, 1990.

Charpentier, Josanne. *La sorcellerie en Pays Basque*. Paris: Librairie Guénégaud, 1977.

Chartier, Roger, Marie-Madeleine Compere and Dominique Julia. *L'éducation en France du XVIe au XVIIIe siècle*. Paris: Société d'édition d'enseignement, 1976.

Chatellier, Louis. *The Europe of the Devout: The Catholic Reformation and the Foundation of a New Society*. Translated by Jean Birrell. Cambridge: Cambridge University Press, 1989.

Clark, Stuart. "King James's *Daemonologie*: Witchcraft and Kingship." In S. Anglo, ed., *The Damned Art*. London: Routledge, 1977.

———. "Inversion, Misrule and the Meaning of Witchcraft." *Past and Present* (1980).

———. "Protestant Demonology: Sin, Superstition and Society, c. 1520-c. 1630." In Bengt Ankarloo and Gustav Henningsen, eds., *Early Modern Witchcraft*. London: Clarendon Press, 1990.

———. "The 'Gendering' of Witchcraft in French Demonology: Misogyny or Polarity?" *French History* (1991).

———. "The Rational Witchfinder: Conscience, Demonological Naturalism and Popular Superstitions." In Steven Pumfrey, Paolo Rossi and Maurice Slawinski, eds., *Science, Culture and Popular Belief in Renaissance Europe*. Manchester: Manchester University Press, 1991.

Cohn, Norman. *Europe's Inner Demons*. London: Chatto/Heinemann, 1975.

Crouzet, Denis. *Les guerriers de dieu: la violence au temps des troubles de religion*. 2 vols. Seysell: Champ Vallon, 1990.

Dagens, Jean. *Berulle et les origines de la restauration catholique*. Bruges: Desclée, 1952.

Davis, Natalie Z. "The Rites of Violence: Religious Riot in Sixteenth Century France." *Past and Present* (May 1973).

Delcambre, Étienne. "The Psychology of Judges in Lorraine." In E. William Monter, ed., *European Witchcraft*. New York: Wiley, 1969.

Delumeau, Jean. *Catholicism between Luther and Voltaire*. Translated by Jeremy Moiser. London: Burns & Oates, 1977.

———. *La peur en occident*. Paris: Fayard, 1978.

———, ed. *Croyants et sceptiques XVIe siècle: ACTES du Colloque à Strasbourg, 9-10 Juin 1978*. Strasbourg, 1981.

Desan, Philippe, ed. *Humanism in Crisis*. Ann Arbor: University of Michigan Press, 1991.

Dewald, Jonathan. *The Formation of a Provincial Nobility*. Princeton: Princeton University Press, 1980.

Diefendorf, Barbara. "Simon Vigor: Radical Preacher in Sixteenth-Century Paris." *Sixteenth Century Journal* (1987).

———. *Beneath the Cross: Catholics and Huguenots in Sixteenth-Century Paris*. Oxford: Oxford University Press, 1991.

Dupont-Bouchat, Marie-Sylvie. "La répression de la sorcellerie dans le duché de Luxembourg aux XVIe et XVIIe siècles." In *Prophètes et sorciers dans le Pays-Bas XVIe-XVIIe siècle*. Paris: Hachette, 1978.

Easlea, Brian. *Witch Hunting, Magic and the New Philosophy: An Introduction to the Debates of the Scientific Revolution, 1450-1750*. Sussex: Harvester, 1980.

Ellul, Jacques. *Propaganda*. Translated by Konrad Kellen and Jean Lerner. New York: Knopf, 1968.

Ferber, Sarah. "The Demonic Possession of Marthe Brossier, France, 1598-1600." In Charles Zika, ed., *No Gods Except Me: Orthodoxy and Religious*

Practice in Europe, 1200-1600. Melbourne: University of Melbourne Press, 1991.

Fouqueray, Henri. *Histoire de la companie de Jesus en France des origines à la suppression (1528-1762)*. Paris: Picard, 1910-25.

Garrisson, Janine Estebe. *Tocsin pour un massacre*. Paris: Le Centurian, 1968.

———. "The Rites of Violence: A Comment." *Past and Present* (May 1975).

———. *La Saint-Barthelemy*. Brussels: Complexe, 1987.

Gauna, Max. *The Dissident Montaigne*. New York: Lang, 1989.

Gijswijt-Hofstra, Marijke. "Six Centuries of Witchcraft in the Netherland." In Marijke Gijswijt-Hofstra and Willem Frijhoff, eds., *Witchcraft in the Netherlands from the Fourteenth to the Twentieth Century*. Rotterdam: Universitaire Pers, 1991.

Ginzburg, Carlo. *Ecstasies: Deciphering the Witches' Sabbat*. New York: Pantheon Books, 1991.

Godard de Donville, Louise. *Le libertin des origines à 1665: un produit des apologetes*. Paris: Papers on French Seventeenth-Century Literature, 1989.

Greengrass, Mark. *France in the Age of Henry IV*. London: Longman, 1984.

Greenshields, Malcolm. *An Economy of Violence in Early Modern France: Crime and Justice in the Haute Auvergne, 1587-1664*. University Park: Pennsylvania State University Press, 1994.

Heller, Henry. *Iron and Blood*. Montreal: McGill-Queen's University Press, 1991.

Henningsen, Gustav. *The Witches' Advocate: Baroque Witchcraft and the Spanish Inquisition (1609-1614)*. Reno: University of Nevada Press, 1980.

Holt, Mack P. *The French Wars of Religion, 1562-1629*. Cambridge: Cambridge University Press, 1995.

Houdard, Sophie. *Quatre démonologues*. Paris: n.p., 1992.

Jones, Martin. *The Counter-Reformation: Religion and Society in Early Modern Europe*. Cambridge: Cambridge University Press, 1995.

Kamen, Henry. *Inquisition and Society in Spain in the Sixteenth and Seventeenth Centuries*. Bloomington: Indiana University Press, 1985.

Keickhefer, Richard. *European Witch Trials: Their Foundation in Popular and Learned Culture, 1300-1500*. London: Routledge & Kegan Paul, 1976.

Keohane, Nanerl. *Philosophy of the State in France*. Princeton: Princeton University Press, 1980.

Klaits, Joseph. *Servants of Satan: The Age of the Witch Hunts*. Bloomington: Indiana University Press, 1985.

Knecht, R.J. *The Rise and Fall of Renaissance France*. London: n.p., 1996.

Kunze, Michael. *Highroad to the Stake*. Translated by William E. Yuill. Chicago: University of Chicago Press, 1987.

Labitte, Charles. *De la démocratie chez les predicateurs de la ligue*. Paris, 1841.

Langbein, John H. *Prosecuting Crime in the Renaissance*. Cambridge, MA: Harvard University Press, 1974.

———. *Torture and the Law of Proof*. Chicago: University of Chicago Press, 1974.

Larner, Christina. "Crimen Exeptum? The Crime of Witchcraft in Europe." In Victor Gatrell, ed., *Crime and the Law*. London: Europa Publications, 1980.

Lecler, Joseph. "Le P. François Garasse (1585-1631): un adversaire des libertins au debut du XVIIe siècle." *Études* (1931).

Levack, Brian. *The Witch-hunt in Early Modern Europe*. London: Longman, 1987, 1994.

Malvezin, Théophile. *Histoire des juifs à Bordeaux*. Marseilles: Lafitte, 1976.

Mandrou, Robert. *Magistrats et sorciers en France au XVIIe siècle: essai de psychologie sociale*. Paris: Plon, 1968.

———. "Jean Grenier, pretendue lycanthrope (Bordeaux, 1603)." In Robert Mandrou, ed., *Possession et sorcellerie au XVIIe siècle*. Paris: Fayard, 1979.

———, ed. *Possession et sorcellerie au XVIIe siècle*. Paris: Fayard, 1979.

Martin, A. Lynn. *Henry III and the Jesuit Politicians*. Geneva: Droz, 1973.

———. *The Jesuit Mind*. Ithaca, NY: Cornell University Press, 1988.

McGowan, Margaret. "The Sabbat Sensationalised: Pierre de Lancre's Tableau." In Sidney Anglo, ed., *The Damned Art: Essays in the Literature of Witchcraft*. London: Routledge, 1977.

Mesnard, Pierre. "La *Démonomanie* de Jean Bodin." In *L'Opera e il pensiero di Giovanni Pico Della Mirandola*. Florence: n.p., 1965.

Midelfort, H.C.E. *Witch Hunting in Southwestern Germany 1562-1684*. Stanford, CA: Stanford University Press, 1972.

———. "The Devil and the German People: Reflections on the Popularity of Demon Possession in Sixteenth Century Germany." In Steven Ozment, ed., *Religion and Culture in the Renaissance and Reformation*. Kirksville, MO: Sixteenth Century Journal Publishers, 1989.

Miquel, Pierre. *Les guerres de religion*. Paris: Fayard, 1980.

Monter, E. William. "Inflation and Witchcraft: The Case of Jean Bodin." In J. Rabb and E. Siegel, eds., *Action and Conviction in Early Modern Europe*. Princeton: Princeton University Press, 1969.

———. "Law, Medicine, and the Acceptance of Witchcraft." In E. William Monter, ed., *European Witchcraft*. New York: Wiley, 1969.

———. *Witchcraft in France and Switzerland*. Ithaca, NY: Cornell University Press, 1976.

———. *Ritual, Myth, and Magic in Early Modern Europe*. Athens: Ohio University Press, 1984.

Muchembled, Robert. *La culture populaire et la culture des élites*. Paris: Flammarion, 1978.

———. "Lay Judges and Acculturation." In Kaspar von Greyerz, ed., *Religion and Society in Early Modern Europe 1500-1800*. London: Allen and Unwin, 1984.

———. *L'invention de l'homme moderne: sensibilités, moeurs et comportements collectifs sous l'ancien régime*. Paris: Fayard, 1988.

———. *Société, cultures et mentalités dans la France moderne: XVIe-XVIIIe siècles*. Paris: SEDES, 1994.

———. *Le roi et la sorcière*. Paris: Desclée, 1994.

———, ed. *Magie et sorcellerie en Europe du Moyen Âge à nos jours*. Paris: Armand Colin, 1994.

Nakam, Géralde. *Les essais de Montaigne, miroir et procès de leur temps*. Paris: Nizet/Publications de la Sorbonne, 1984.

Nicholls, David. "The Theatre of Martyrdom in the French Reformation." *Past and Present* (November 1988).

Oates, Caroline. "The Trial of a Teenage Werewolf, Bordeaux, 1603." *Criminal Justice History* 9 (1988).

Ong, Walter J. *Ramus: Method and the Decay of Dialogue*. Cambridge, MA: Harvard University Press, 1958.

Pallier, Denis. *Recherches sur l'imprimerie à Paris pendant la ligue (1585-1594)*. Geneva: Droz, 1975.

Paton, Bernadette. "'To the Fire, To the Fire. Let Us Burn a Little Incense to God': Bernardino, Preaching Friars and *Maleficio* in Late Medieval Siena." In Charles Zika, ed., *No Gods Except Me: Orthodoxy and Religious Practice in Europe, 1200-1600*. Melbourne: Melbourne University Press, 1991.

Pearl, Jonathan. "Peiresc and the Search for Criteria of Scientific Knowledge in Seventeenth Century France." In *Proceedings of the Western Society for French History* (1977).

⎯⎯⎯. "French Catholic Demonologists and Their Enemies in the Late Sixteenth and Early Seventeenth Centuries." *Church History* (1983).

⎯⎯⎯. "The Role of Personal Correspondence in the Exchange of Scientific Information in the Early Seventeenth Century." *Renaissance and Reformation* (May 1984).

⎯⎯⎯. "La rôle enigmatique de la *Démonomanie* dans la chasse aux sorciers." In *Jean Bodin: Actes du Colloque interdisciplinaire d'Angers, 1984*. Angers: Presses de l'Université d'Angers, 1985.

⎯⎯⎯. "Demons and Politics in France, 1560-1630." *Historical Reflections* (1985).

⎯⎯⎯. "'School for the Rebel Soul': Politics and Demonic Possession in France" *Historical Reflections* (1989).

Peters, Edward. *The Magician, the Witch, and the Law*. Philadelphia: University of Pennsylvania Press, 1978.

⎯⎯⎯. *Inquisition*. Philadelphia: University of Pennsylvania Press, 1988.

⎯⎯⎯. *Torture*. New York: Basil Blackwell, 1985.

Prat, J.M. *Maldonat et l'université de Paris au XVIe siècle*. Paris, 1856.

Preaud, Maxime. "La *Démonomanie des Sorciers*, Fille de la *République*." In *Jean Bodin: Actes du Colloque interdisciplinaire d'Angers, 1984*. Angers: Presses de l'Université d'Angers, 1985.

Roelker, Nancy Lyman. *One King, One Faith: The Parlement of Paris in the Religious Reformation of the Sixteenth Century*. Berkeley: University of California Press, 1996.

Roper, Lyndal. *Oedipus and the Devil: Witchcraft, Sexuality and Religion in Early Modern Europe*. London: Routledge, 1994.

Rose, Paul Lawrence, "The *Politique* and the Prophet: Bodin and the Catholic League 1589-1594." *The Historical Journal* (1978).

Ruff, Julius R. *Crime, Justice and Public Order in Old Regime France*. London: Croom Helm, 1984.

Salmon, J.H.M. *Society in Crisis: France in the Sixteenth Century*. London: Ernest Benn, 1975.

Schmitt, Paul. *La réforme catholique, le combat de Maldonat, 1534-1583*. Paris: Beauchesne, 1985.

Scribner, Robert. *Popular Culture and Popular Movements in Reformation Germany*. London: Hambledon Press, 1987.

Skinner, Quentin. *The Foundations of Modern Political Thought*. Cambridge: Cambridge University Press, 1978.

Smith, Pauline M. *The Anti-Courtier Trend in Sixteenth Century French Literature*. Geneva: Droz, 1966.

Soergel, Philip M. *Wondrous in His Saints: Counter-Reformation Propaganda in Bavaria*. Berkeley: University of California Press, 1993.

Soman, Alfred. "Les procès de sorcellerie au Parlement de Paris (1565-1640)." *Annales* (July 1977).

—————. "La decriminalisation de la sorcellerie en France." *Histoire, economie et société* 2 (1985).

—————. *Sorcellerie et justice criminelle*. Hampshire: n.p., 1992.

Sutherland, N.M. *The Massacre of St. Bartholomew and the European Conflict 1559-1572*. New York: Barnes & Noble, 1973.

Sutto, Claude. "Introduction to Estienne Pasquier." In Claude Sutto, ed., *Le catéchisme des Jésuites*. Sherbrooke, QC: Éditions de l'Université de Sherbrooke, 1982.

—————. "Tradition et innovation, réalisme et utopie: l'idée Gallicane à la fin du XVIe et au debut du XVIIe siècles." *Renaissance and Reformation* (November 1989).

Sypher, G. Wylie. " 'Faisant ce qu'il leur vient a plaisir': The Image of Protestantism in French Catholic Polemic on the Eve of the Religious Wars." *Sixteenth Century Journal* (Summer 1980).

Thickett, D. *Estienne Pasquier (1529-1615): The Versatile Barrister of 16th Century France*. London: Regency Press, 1979.

Thomas, Keith. *Religion and the Decline of Magic*. London: Penguin, 1971.

Tinsley, Barbara Sher. *History and Polemics in the French Reformation: Florimond de Raemond, Defender of the Church*. Selingrove: Susquehanna University Press, 1992.

Trevor-Roper, Hugh. "The European Witch-Craze of the Sixteenth and Seventeenth Centuries." In *The European Witch-craze of the Sixteenth and Seventeenth Centuries and Other Essays*. New York: Harper & Row, 1969.

Turchetti, Mario. "Religious Concord and Political Tolerance in Sixteenth- and Seventeenth-Century France." *Sixteenth Century Journal* (1991).

Venard, Marc. *Réforme protestante, réforme catholique dans la province d'Avignon au XVIe siècle*. Paris: Cerf, 1993.

—————, ed. *Le temps des confessions, 1530-1620/30*. Paris: Desclée, 1992.

Walker, D.P. *Unclean Spirits: Possession and Exorcism in France and England in the Late Sixteenth and Early Seventeenth Centuries*. London: Scholar Press, 1981.

Weber, Henri. "L'exorcisme à la fin du XVIe siècle, instrument de la contre réforme et spectacle baroque." *Nouvelle revue du seizième siècle* 1 (1983).

Wendel, François. *Calvin*. Translated by Philip Mairet. London: Collins, 1963.

Whitmore, P.J.S., ed. *A Seventeenth Century Exposure of Superstition: Select Texts of Claude Pithoys*. The Hague: Nijhoff, 1972.

Williams, Gerhild Scholz. *Defining Dominion: The Discourses of Magic and Witchcraft in Early Modern France and Germany*. Ann Arbor: University of Michigan Press, 1995.

Wirth, Jean. "Against the Acculturation Thesis." In Caspar von Greyerz, ed., *Religion and Society in Early Modern Europe*. London: Allen and Unwin, 1984.

Wolfe, Michael. "The Conversion of Henri IV and the Origin of Bourbon Absolutism." *Historical Reflections* (1987).

Yardeni, Myriam. *La conscience nationale en France pendant les guerres de religion (1559-1598)*. Louvain: Editions Nauwelaerts, 1971.

――――, ed. *Modernité et non-conformisme en France*. Leiden: Brill, 1983.

Index

Aubrey, Nicole, 43-45, 48, 59, 66, 80
Auger, Emond, 21, 70

Barnavi, Elie, 78
Baxter, Christopher, 113
Benedict, Philip, 79
Benedicti, Jean, 54
Berriot, François, 96
Berulle, Pierre, 50, 53, 54
Birette, Sanson, 54-55
Blendec, Charles, 45-46
Bodin, Jean, 3, 6, 8, 16, 21, 33, 35, 41, 53, 102, 110-26, 129, 141
Boguet, Henri, 125
Borie, François de la, 66
Bossy, John, 5, 24
Boucher, Jean, 74, 87-92, 96, 143
Boulaese, Jehan, 45
Briggs, Robin, 14, 35
Brossier, Marthe, 48-50, 55, 56
Burke, Peter, 13

Calvin, Jean, 91, 92, 96
Caro Baroja, Julio, 127

Charles IX, 2
Charron, Pierre, 98
Chastel, Jacques, 86, 90-91
Clark, Stuart, 8
Clement, Jacques, 109
Coligny, Gaspard de, 64-65
College of Clermont, 59-69, 74, 108-109
Condé, Prince of, 44, 64
Corgordan, Ponce, 69
Council of Trent, 27, 30
Crespet, Pierre, 82, 84, 95
Crouzet, Denis, 5, 27, 78

Dampmartin, Pierre, 94
Daneau, Lambert, 6, 74-75
Davis, Natalie, 68
de Lancre, Pierre, 3, 70, 73,74, 78, 84, 93, 106-107, 124, 127-49
de Mory, Antoine, 94
de Rebreviettes, Guy, 95
Del Rio, Martin, 66, 70-71, 74-75, 84, 99, 106, 124, 137, 141-42
Delumea, Jean, 11, 68
demonic possession, 41ff., 50

Desan, Philippe, 102
Dewald, Jonathan, 17-18

Edict of Nantes, 47, 50, 95
Ellul, Jacques, 6
Espaignet, Jean, 133, 134, 135
exorcism, 41-46, 48, 52, 54, 55, 123

Filesac, Jean, 37-39, 126
Formicarius, 25
Francis I, 26, 27
Francis II, 26, 41, 60

Gallicanism, 27-28, 31, 110, 148-51
Garasse, François, 98, 143
Garrisson, Janine Estebe, 68, 69
Gaufridy, Louis, 51, 52, 57
Ginzburg, Carlo, 137
Godard de Donville, Louise, 96
Grandier, Urbain, 57
Grenier, Jean, 36-39
Guise, Cardinal of, 21, 64
Guise, Dukes of, 29
Guise, François de, 21, 26, 27
Guise, Henri de, 47, 64, 65, 82, 108, 109

Henningsen, Gustav, 133-34, 137
Henry II, 26, 27, 30, 60
Henry III, 26, 29, 63, 79, 82, 87, 95, 109, 111
Henry IV, 28, 47, 57, 69, 86, 87, 89, 111
Holt, Mack, 5
Holy League, 6, 77, 88, 104

Jacques-Chaquin, Nicole, 133
Jesuits, 6, 9, 53, 59ff., 79, 86, 87, 108, 109, 127
Jews, 146-47

Knecht, R.J., 5

La Roche Flavin, Bernard de, 34-35
Langbein, John, 33

Larner, Christina, 33
Le Caron, Louis, 94
Le Loyer, Pierre, 31, 124
L'Estoile, Pierre, 36, 48, 88, 93
Levack, Brian, 13
Luther, Martin, 85, 91
lycanthropy, 35, 40, 124-26

Maldonat, Jean, 61-75, 80, 93, 103, 137
Malleus Maleficarum, 3, 25, 68
Mandrou, Robert, 9, 10, 14, 36, 39, 42, 52, 57, 111
Marescot, Michel, 48-50, 53
Martin, A. Lynn, 21, 72
Mayenne, Charles de, 87, 89
McGowan, Mary, 134, 141
Medici, Catherine de, 26, 27, 30, 79, 110
Michaelis, Sebastien, 52
Midelfort, Erik, 42
Montaigne, Michel de, 34, 84, 102-107, 110, 114, 126, 129
Monter, William, 42, 43, 112
Muchembled, Robert, 9, 11, 14, 18-20, 129, 149

Nakam, Geralde, 103
Nantes, Edict of, 47, 50, 95
Nodé, Pierre, 81
Nynauld, J., 125

Oates, Caroline, 40

Parlement of Aix, 51-52
Parlement of Bordeaux, 37, 74, 128, 129, 133, 136, 139
Parlement of Paris, 10, 14, 15, 16, 19, 28, 30, 47, 60, 61, 91, 97
Parlement of Rouen, 17-18
parlements, 11, 15, 20, 27, 28, 30, 34, 35, 140-41
Pasquier, Estienne, 62, 98, 102, 107-10, 114, 126
Paton, Bernadette, 20-21
Peters, Edward, 116
Picard, Remy, 56

Pithoys, Claude, 55-57
possession, 41-56
Prat, J.M., 66
Prieur, Claude, 125

Raemond, Florimond de, 45, 74, 84-86
Ramus, Peter, 62, 69, 107
Richeome, Louis, 46, 70-73, 74, 75, 86-87, 93
Roper, Lyndal, 42
Rose, Paul L., 111

Schmitt, Paul, 69
Scribner, Robert, 24
Soergel, Philip, 42
Soman, Alfred, 6, 14-17
Spanish Inquisition, 85, 133-34, 136
St. Bartholomew's Day Massacre, 29, 48, 68-70

Taillepied, Noel, 92
torture, 33
Trevor-Roper, Hugh, 9, 113, 128

Vanini, Jules Cesar, 96, 98, 99
Vassy, massacre at, 27, 63-65

Walker, D.P., 42-43
Wars of Religion, 5, 25, 27, 63-65
Weber, Henri, 42
Weyer, Johann, 115-16
Wirth, Jean, 13
Wolfe, Michael, 89

Yardeni, Myriam, 77